FUTURE PRIMITIVE REVISITED

BY JOHN ZERZAN

FERAL HOUSE

10 9 8 7 6 5 4 3 2 1

Design by Sean Tejaratchi

Other titles by John Zerzan available from Feral House
Against Civilization
Running on Emptiness
Twilight of the Machines

Feral House
1240 W. Sims Way Ste. 124
Port Townsend, WA 98368
Send S.A.S.E. for free catalogue of publications

info@feralhouse.com
www.feralhouse.com

TABLE OF
CONTENTS

INTRODUCTION
BY MICHAEL BECKER

AS I WRITE THIS INTRODUCTION to John Zerzan's latest collection of essays, three of the six reactors at the Fukushima Daiichi nuclear complex in northeastern Japan are in varying states of collapse. Radiation is cascading into the atmosphere, and the frontline workers trying to fix the problem are the first of millions, human and non-human, who will suffer fatal radiation sickness as a result.

The deadly particles irradiating my body as I write these words, and yours, as you read them, only exist through the ingenious work of civilized human hands. Civilization creates complexity and pits it against nature. The more civilized a culture, the more complexity it entails; the more complexity, the greater the danger. In the end, civilization always loses because civilizations run up against natural limits, and "nature bats last." We can say that civilizations have have life spans, and various indicators suggest that modern Western civilization (now global in scope) may be reaching its senescence. Efforts to save civilization become increasingly desperate and far-fetched (consider the Zeitgeist movies" Venus Project or Stewart Brand's *Whole Earth Discipline*). An entire social movement to escape seemingly inevitable collapse masquerades as "environmentalism." On shopping bags and light bulb packages we are exhorted to "save the Earth." A raft of texts on the ecological crisis similarly speak of saving nature or preserving ecosystems. Really these texts are about saving civilization. Ecosystems, like individual species, have only instrumental value for the "greater good."

But is civilization worth saving? In saving civilization do we sacrifice ourselves in the same way we have sacrificed Earth, nature, ecosystems, and species? Such questions are, obviously, non-sensical to anyone who is already fully committed to the project of civilization. Unfortunately, this comprises nearly all academics in the social and natural sciences, the academy, especially in its current corporatized form, being the epitome of civilization. Thus they continue to neglect Zerzan's writings and the emerging body of work that has come to be known as anarcho-primitivism.

This they do at their peril. In this new collection of essays, Zerzan once again reminds us that we are the ones who must be saved by the Earth. Humans living in civilization have already lost their health, their freedom, their natural sense of social solidarity and, most of all, a primordial kinship and identification with the natural world. In evolutionary terms it has been demonstrated time and again that civilization is a mistake. Civilization is inherently unsustainable. Only primitive cultures are sustainable over the long term. Today, in its most advanced form, civilization is precipitating the Earth's sixth great extinction crisis. Ultimately our species is also in the balance. But civilization has already, for the most part, eradicated our essence as natural beings thriving in a natural lifeworld. Were this civilization to survive in its current form and direction, humans would be further transformed into automatons entirely integrated within an exclusively artifactual environment. Whether by catastrophe or design, what is needed instead is a "future primitive" that restores the nature of humans and the nature of the lifeworld simultaneously. Anarcho-primitivism and Zerzan in particular steadfastly assert that only a return to primitive culture can restore authentic human dignity.

My background is in political theory, and what I would like to try to do in this introduction is read some basic motifs of Western political thought against Zerzan's anarcho-primitivism. This is by way of homage to Zerzan's impressive body of work and influence in the development of green anarchy. But it is also as an attempt to show his place in social theory, a matter that I think has been woefully neglected.

We think of civilization as a type of society emerging some five thousand years ago and consisting of a number of interconnected features: domestication of plants and animals and increasingly large-scale agriculture; food surplus and population growth; writing, specifically the development of records concerning measured space (agricultural fields), measured time (the calendar and official history), and economic output (accounting); continually intensifying division of labor and specialization and an emerging class structure; increasingly sophisticated technical means of production; urbanization and a demand for luxuries, especially among the wealthy, powerful classes; complex trade and the expansion of territory; a professional military; and centralized political and religious authority which oversees an administrative bureaucracy, directs the military, and controls the population. Civilizations collapse under their own weight within a relatively short period of time due to population "overshoot" and exhaustion of resources, climate change, the disruption of increasing sophisticated trade and alliance networks, and social disorder from within.

One important factor missing from an "objective" definition of civilization is any sense of the influence of ideas. The particular practices of any civilization are informed by the way people living in those civilizations make sense of their lives, especially in regards to religion, politics, philosophy, and a more or less mythical account of their origins. My contention, via Zerzan's significant influence, is that founding, fundamental ideas in various stages of Western civilization have involved a basic, distorted tension or dialectic between the city and nature. In this false dialectic, the depiction of primitive peoples has always been imbued with what are actually tendencies of civilization. The latter, in turn, has always been presented as a fulfillment or completion of the allegedly primitive characteristics and elevated above the primitive. The very retention of the idea of nature, especially in various stories of a lost "golden age," is not actually so much about what has been lost. Rather, especially because these stories have always distorted the nature of the primitive and thus provided a kind of fun-house mirror to civilization, they provide a psychologically powerful reinforcement of what civilization has allegedly gained by compensation. Still, these stories served to restrain certain practices and provided (even in their tendentious form) an intellectual and spiritual lifeline for citizens to retain a sense of belonging to the primordial world of creation.[1]

It is not surprising, then, that the nature of the relationship between that which humans create and that which is natural has always been a central theme in social theory. Philosophers have been particularly concerned with the tension between social conventions—norms, mores, laws, and institutions, what the Greeks called *nomos*—and that which comes about independently of human action, nature or phusis. The paradox is that humans are a part of nature; the distinction between nomos and *physis* would thus seem irrelevant or even impossible. As natural creatures, anything humans do must, ipso facto, be natural. Yet so much of convention seems designed to restrain what is natural in humans, to redirect natural desire and postpone satisfaction in the pursuit of an objective which the mass of humans have had no say in determining as ends-worthy. "Man is born free," as Rousseau so eloquently put it, "and everywhere is in chains."

Yet, like nearly all Western social theorists, Rousseau makes the move back toward civilization by raising two important claims. The first is that a return to primitive existence is impossible. The long development of civilization, especially in the way property has corrupted innate self-concern, has allegedly so altered the nature of man that the option of a return to simplicity is off the table. Second, Rousseau claims that rational man can invent social institutions (the General Will) that reclaim and surpass the original, unconscious freedom and social solidarity of savages. There is no going back, and who would want to? These are the two basic catechisms of life under the Law; they show up almost without exception in the history of political ideas.

Rousseau's false dialectic between civilization and nature is typical. An authentic dialectic can exist only where two contradictory possibilities are each instances of reality. But Rousseau and other leading Western social theorists implant in their conception of the primitive, natural man certain conventions which are actually facets of civilization. They falsify the natural side of the dialectic. In Rousseau's case, he posits two allegedly innate traits that are, in fact, paradigmatic of modern civilization: "a faculty of improvement" and an isolated, egoistic conception of the individual. In the formation of the General Will, each participant must express his own views in an entirely direct and unmitigated fashion and then accept without question the determinations of the public vote. The primitive is allegedly surmounted, then, by raising up and completing a trait—atomistic individualism—that is not primitive at all. Plato does this in his Republic by asserting that division of labor and complex, monetized trade relations are part and parcel of every social group, including the simplest precursor of the modern city. They are not. The schemes Plato develops for locking individuals into immutable social classes do not refine and lift up original, unconscious harmony among separate classes. Class division is instead integral to the extreme social stratification in civilized society. In The Second Treatise, Locke does this by insisting that the labor theory of property acquisition is natural. It is not. The conception of one's body as owned by oneself and the idea that intermingling one's own labor with nature creates an exclusive, individual entitlement to private property are quite at odds with primitive communalism. It is, instead, a necessary facet of a labor commodity market under capitalism.

The falsehood of the dialectic between civilization and nature in Western political theory is reinforced by sanctifying the move to civilization. Thus, the other side of the dialectic is similarly distorted. In cases like those of Plato, Locke, and Rousseau, there is a contrived sense of a fall from primitive grace. In Book II of *The Republic*, in discussing the formation of communities, Glaucon chastises Socrates for his depiction of humans in primitive villages, communities "fit for pigs." They lack luxuries; civilized people are "accustomed to lie on sofas, dine off tables, and they should have sweets and sauces in the modern style." "Yes," says Socrates,

> now I understand: the question you would have me consider is, not only how a State, but how a luxurious State is created; and possibly there is no harm in this, for in such a State we shall be more likely to see how justice and injustice originate. In my opinion the true and healthy condition of the State is the one which I have described. But if you wish also to see a State at fever-heat, I have no objection. For I suspect that many will not be satisfied with the simpler way of Life [emphasis added].[2]

It is Plato's "opinion" that the primitive village is the "true and healthy" community. His use of the word *doxa* here cannot be accidental when the entire purpose of his dialectic is to move from the uncertain ground of opinion to absolute knowledge. It is only through civilization that the possibility of coming to know the form of Justice and the ultimate Form of the Good can be realized. Since coming to know the Form of the Good is the pinnacle of human existence, civilization must be a natural prerequisite. It seems obvious that Plato cannot regret that which he depicts in a priori terms. Besides, Plato makes the demand for luxury into a sort of secondary, inevitable cause of the transition to civilization, that which spurs along those "naturally" devoid of sufficient reason.

Perhaps Plato's mock-tragic sense of civilization as a fall from grace is for those benighted enough to believe that the primitive is actually preferable to civilization. This would almost certainly be targeted at the anarcho-primitivists of his own day, the Cynics (especially Diogenes who allegedly tramped muddy footprints across Plato's carpets). But humans are not designed by nature to fit a preordained system of division of labor; the shift to civilization is not inevitable; and Plato's theory of forms, not to mention his theory of Justice and the ideal state, does not even remotely recuperate the inherent social solidarity of the original, "true and healthy" community.

The dialectical tension between the civitas and nature is deepened and strengthened though the depiction of a fall from natural grace. That the depiction of primitive human life in the rendering of this dialectic is false serves to privilege civilized humans" alleged transcendence of the primitive. In Locke this occurs in his account of property in *The Second Treatise*. Locke's analysis, like that of his predecessor, Hobbes, proceeds from an allegedly original, primitive state of nature, one devoid of social and political institutions. Private property—the mixing of one's self-owned labor with nature—is only limited by the degree of labor one can perform, the spoilage of that which is removed from nature, and the sufficiency of land and natural resources for others. The invention of money, Locke contends, is rational and natural inasmuch as it facilitates trade and thus access to the conveniences of life. Yet, inasmuch as it allows for the acquisition of unlimited amounts of property, money is simultaneously depicted by Locke in Biblical terms of original sin. "This is certain, that in the beginning, before the desire of having more than one needed had altered the intrinsic value of things, which depends only on their usefulness to the life of man...each one of himself [had] as much of the things of nature as he could use [with] the same plenty...left to those who would use the same industry."[3] Life in a state of nature is initially marked by "peace, good will, mutual assistance and preservation." With money, greed and property inequality create conflict and the need for a state to adjudicate property disputes.

As with Plato, though, remorse at the fall amounts to crocodile tears. The achievements of civilization more than make up for the loss of primitive innocence. In Locke's case the fall is compensated for by the superabundance which investment of money in land allows. Money does not spoil, allows for wage contracts to purchase others" labor, and increases productivity indefinitely. Whereas primitive life entails a zero-sum game, moneyed capitalism enables a constantly expanding array of luxuries. References to a transcendent Law of Nature help to cover the gap between the primitive and those rights still retained under the state. Moreover, they are useful in combating the primitivists of his time, the radical Levellers and Diggers of the English revolution who proclaimed the retaking of private landholdings as their natural birthright. But in reality Locke's political thought is straightforwardly materialistic: for those who work hard, "the rational and industrious," the abundance and variety of material pleasures in civilization more than make up for the loss of primitive equality and freedom. The world is theirs by legal right, founded in social contract among property holders; state coercion and disqualification from political participation exist for the "covetous and quarrelsome."

While Rousseau sees Locke's social contract as morally bankrupt, he does not propose a return to the primitive. The healthy self-love of the savage is irrevocably lost. Vainglorious self-love, amour propre, develops in tandem with civilization and especially with property. But Rousseau too sanctifies civilization by arguing that reason is sufficient to "find a form of association which may defend and protect with the whole force of the community the person and property of every associate and by means of which each, coalescing with all, may nevertheless obey only himself, and remain as free as before."[4] Rousseau's revised social contract allegedly achieves this self-conscious act of redemption. Traditional anarchism has always insisted on the plausibility of such a social arrangement, without considering that it is the very socioeconomic and political practices of civilization along with the fake dialectics supporting them that seem to make such an arrangement impossible.

In spite of their portrayal of the transition to civilization in terms of loss, each of the theorists mentioned actually presents a definite continuity between nature and the city. Civilization compensates for loss by refining and perfecting tendencies allegedly at the heart of primitive humankind. In reality there is a radical rupture or break between primitive and civilized life. In known historical instances, the shift from one to the other involved violent conquest, not consent. The move resulted from coercion on pain of death, dislocation and cultural destruction, not the inevitable working out of allegedly intrinsic human characteristics. Archeological evidence makes clear that the precursors of civilization emerged over a long period, certainly not through the consent of any particular group. But there is an unmistakable disjuncture between the earliest megamachines of the Tigris-Euphrates river valley and the gatherer-hunter and horticulturalist communities that preceded civilization for a hundred millennia.

With few, partial exceptions, Paul Shepard among them, social theorists have returned to the false dialectics of the tradition rather than look this rupture square in the face.[5] Even in the emerging academic field of environmental political theory, where sustainability is a leading theme, theorists consistently fail to make more than passing mention of the only cultures that are sustainable for extended periods—primitive cultures. Where primitive lifeways receive any notice, a variety of caveats are always included: the author is in no way suggesting that a return to stone-age technologies is either possible or desirable; similarly, that no one would prefer such a life to modernity; and that, at any rate, these previous cultures also damaged their environments.[6] In Devall and Sessions" groundbreaking work *Deep Ecology*, a full two pages is devoted to primitive peoples, concluding with the statement that "Supporters of deep ecology do not advocate 'going back to the stone age," but seek inspiration from primal traditions."[7] Most notable in this regard, perhaps, is Joel Kovel's *The Enemy of Nature*. An otherwise excellent critique of the disastrous impact of capitalism on the natural environment, Kovel, in the space of a few pages, manages to alternately uphold primitive lifeways as exemplary of care for the Earth and condemn them for bringing on the most fundamental elements of capitalist exploitation.[8]

There has been a failure to come to grips with the tension between primitive culture and civilization, reflective of a long tradition in Western political thought. But now the stakes are considerably greater. Today, the radical break between nature and the city is paralleled by a similar radical discontinuity between previous modes of civilization and contemporary technological civilization, both in practice and in ideology. The traditional dialectic is broken. Cybernetic existence retains no sense of either nature or a primitive state. The fall from grace, even as metaphor, slips into the oblivion of the spectacle. The "end of nature" is boldly proclaimed across the board, from ethicists to environmental moderates to geo-engineers to postmodernists to neo-Marxists and neo-Stalinists.[9] Hyper-technological feats never before even possibly dreamed of, let alone engaged in, help give rise to and are reinforced by the idea that nature is dead and only civilization exists. What need is there for myths of emergence from a pristine, natural social order when the future promises limitless energy, endless technological fantasy and human immortality? Nuclear power (let alone terraced agriculture, pyramids or the steel plow) is child's play compared to the synthesizing of consciousness; new engineering at the genetic, geo, and nano scale; the singularity; and the indefinite extension of human life span. These "hyper-technologies" both help to constitute and reinforce the idea that humans, entirely by their own technological design, will live totally outside of nature. In fact, there is not and has never been any such thing as nature. Perhaps the mythic idea of nature will continue for some time as a relic, a basis for destroying any possibility of myth. The point is technological utopia: we have no place in existence other than the technosphere.

This unprecedented notion of civilization detached from nature creates an altogether new danger. Now, nothing, not even exalted human nature, is distinctly recognizable. Every thing becomes materiel or "standing reserve"[10] for integration into vast self-regulating systems. As Heidegger put it, "man in the midst of objectlessness is nothing but the orderer of the standing-reserve.... he comes to the very brink of a precipitous fall; that is, he comes to the point where he himself will have to be taken as standing-reserve." This fall into the machine world goes as unnoticed as the disappearance of myths, stories, and ideas that reminded us of another, original home for human beings. Thus, in the cybernetic age, the concept of "personnel" or "human resource management" shocks no one; it is banal. And the managers have no more recourse than the managed to traditional civilizational stories (let alone primitive myths). There is no history or mythic origin to be fulfilled, no lost, original state of nature to be redeemed. The nihilism inherent in this epoch is reflected in the steadily rotating recurrence of the technicized will to power.

The idea of an entirely engineered world broke the traditional dialectic. In this dialectic the image of an original state of nature was always distorted and de-privileged to serve the purposes of an equally distorted and exalted civilized order; now one side of the dialectic, nature, is obliterated; the other becomes a monstrosity. From out of this unprecedented danger arises the possibility for a more clear-eyed understanding of exactly what civilization is and what it left behind. Now that technique has been proclaimed the totality, it is possible for both sides of the dialectic to be grasped in a more essential light. No writer, living or dead, has undertaken this task in a more thorough and unflinching manner as John Zerzan.

In this and previous collections of essays Zerzan offers us an extraordinary survey of texts in philosophy, archeology and anthropology, social psychology, and arts and literature. Zerzan demonstrates that civilization threatens us, not just in terms of its technological gigantism and the global effects of technical failure, but more so in the way that it robs us, daily and ever more intensively, of a fundamental kinship with the natural world and with one another. Evolution is generally thought of in terms of a species adaptation to the environment. Civilization develops by fundamentally altering the environment. If this is to be called an adaptation then human beings (though agents of civilization) must adapt to the adaptation. Becoming civilized is a matter of compulsion. It entails the loss, not the attainment of freedom. It denies life; it does not fulfill it.

Civilization alters the environment mainly through the acquisition of energy resources, in earlier phases through deforestation, and now through the use of fossil fuels. But intensive energy use is necessitated by large-scale agriculture and the development of cities. Agriculture rests on the domestication of plants and animals, a process that developed only very gradually and probably in the context of climate change occurring 12 thousand years ago. Zerzan merely notes the obvious: humans, too, become domesticated, ruthlessly. Now the experience of being human must be subjected to the total control of a system bent on the total control of being itself. In this sense contemporary civilization is a difference in degree but of such an extent that it becomes a difference in kind.

We miss the whole point if we say merely that civilization is marked by agriculture and turns the vast majority of the population into agricultural and, later, wage-debtor slaves. Agriculture requires precise and rigid measurement systems for demarcating space (the field), time (the agricultural calendar), and the volume of production (accounting). Measurement requires the use of number, and number requires symbolic thought. More fundamentally still, these procedures require representational language. Zerzan contends that all of these elements are artifacts of civilization. Rendering them part and parcel of our cognitive orientation in the world is the source of our profound entrapment in the "iron cage." They are the psychological and intellectual determinants of our alienation from the authentic world of free, primitive human existence. Recent innovations like surveillance cameras and supermax prisons are obvious outward signs of control. But the most fundamental factors of our imprisonment in what is now becoming a total matrix of technological control are time, number, symbol, and representation. One might say that these are the "micro-microphysics" of institutionalized power relations.

The traditional, false nature-civilization dialectic reenters at this point. Aristotle distinguishes the social nature of human beings by our complex capacity for language. This is true as far as it goes. But this line of reasoning fails to distinguish between language that culminates in an abstract search for first principles and that form of intuitive language that involves a direct communication between human animals and our plant and non-human animal companions on Mother Earth. Stories of this type of "language older than words" are universal among primitive peoples.

For the Pythagoreans and other pre-Socratic philosophers, and for Plato, number or numerical ratio is not only a means of expressing the harmony of the universe, but is its essence. Numeracy, especially in geometry, is basic to being human and is a hallmark of advanced civilization. What then are we to make of accounts such as that of Thomas Jefferson Mayfield who, in 1850, at age seven, on the death of his mother, was left by his father to grow up with the Choinumni band of Yokuts Indians? Mayfield recalled an easily learned Yokuts number system that could be used to do calculations in an indefinitely large number of digits.[11] Why develop such a system in the absence of the need for a calendar or the astronomical calculations on which the calendar is designed? It is possible that the detailed familiarity with an extraordinary array of species of plants and animals and the means of maintaining an environment in which all species, including humans, could flourish negated the need to use numbers as a means of control. Given a way of life that M. Kat Anderson has so aptly described as "tending the wild," complex numeracy was perhaps a plaything or maybe a joke on how poorly a strict use of numbers could approximate a deeply practical and mythologically informed spiritual connection to Life.[12]

A detailed measurement of time is often pointed to as representing a higher order of civilized, human existence. A linear sense of time is, apparently, of a higher, more civilized sort. Tracing evolutionary progress depends upon it. It can be used both cosmologically to trace the age of the universe and, historically, to survey major human events and how they relate to one another. Now, time is measured by such extremes as light years and nanoseconds. But at what point do these measurements, defying as they do all human experience, slip over into a more primordial dream time of aboriginal peoples?[13] And if they never do, are we not cut off from a more fundamental sense of time that allows us to integrate with, rather than be cut off from reality? On this other "scale" of time great events and the spirits of ancestors apparently can be experienced simultaneously as past and as present. For some primitive peoples the future is thought of as "behind" oneself, having already occurred. It is not that primitive people have no language, obviously, or no conceptions of number and time. Rather, they may have experiences of language, number and time that do not undercut the identity of human consciousness and the natural lifeworld in which humans are co-participants. Zerzan's focus is exactly here, on the radical continuity between human perception, consciousness and nature. This continuity seems so evident in primitive cultures and so abandoned today. It is precisely in such abandonment that we experience the "disenchantment of the world."

In this sense, the ultimate bankruptcy of the traditional dialectic lies in Plato's separation of body and perception, on the one hand, and the mind or soul and consciousness, on the other. The debasement of the body as the source of ignorance and its association with the primitive, and the elevation of the mind and its association with enlightenment are, of course, the basis for the political dialectic of nature and the city. In Plato, the Form of the Good, the epistemological and ontological source of truth and reality, is represented metaphorically by the sun. The latter is alternately described as Lord, Father, and King of all light and seeing, physical and intellectual. By contrast "the body is the prison of the soul," the dungeon, a place of entrapment and darkness. The resonance of this metaphor points backwards to earlier civilizations" association of the sun god with the divine king and forward to the enlightenment. Even if it is only via negation, the figures of the body, Earth, mother, and fertility remain a part of the dialectic. Primitive peoples never divorced any of these realms and thus never separated themselves from the reality of which they (and we) and everything are a part, always, all of us, as both mind/spirit and body. But what is once divided must be repaired. As this would actually require the forbidden return to primitive consciousness and practice, civilization attempts substitutes.

For Zerzan, the remedy civilization unconsciously prescribes for our separation from nature and holds up as its greatest achievement is art, especially visual art. Not infrequently the 20,000-year-old cave paintings in Lascaux, France are pointed to as evidence of the first modern humans, our first actual human relations. There is truth to this, in that they may have been the first to express their anxiety at being cut off from reality and the first to try to repair the breach through art. The vividness of aesthetic work, the sense of presence, of a world revealing itself in the very act of creative power, for Zerzan, is a pale imitation of the lived, immediate sense of daily reality for primitive peoples. The cave paintings mark the initial demise of a way of life that predated them by scores of thousands of years. Art is shorthand for civilization; it is a psychological compensation for loss of identity and never actually fills the void. Only a return to the primitive can allay the anxiety that suffuses art.

Zerzan's uniqueness lies in his unrelenting rejection not only of all civilized norms and institutions, but even of the roots of such ideas and institutions—"objective" language, abstract notions of space and measured time, symbolic expression, especially art—basically any representational forms of consciousness. Modern forms of alienation, and they are obviously rampant, have their roots in a deep angst that is co-constituted with the basic premises and prerequisites of civilization. Civilization has its own trajectory: from the earliest cave paintings, humans have tried to repair the breach with nature by further control of nature. Each step away from immediate identification with our primordial, natural lifeworld merely deepens the crisis. Now, in the hyper-technological, an original state of nature is falling into oblivion. (A sun metaphor for knowledge is unnecessary in age of cyclotrons and an environment of compact fluorescent light.) Zerzan measures its disappearance, in part, by the sheer scale of psychopathology in modern existence—parents killing their own children, school shootings, workplace shootings, the mass addiction of young children to legal psychotropic drugs for the treatment of all manner of new social and psychological dysfunction, the mass addiction of children and adults to illegal drugs, and so on.

Many critics of industrial civilization use the metaphor of a speeding train heading for a wreck. By Zerzan's account we might say that civilization is like a vast hole, with the living participants being consigned, collectively, to the inescapable role of "digger." The rule is that salvation can be found only through more efficient and relentless means of digging; the participants experience the mute horror of watching natural light recede while engineers design artificial lighting and air conditioning systems. An increasingly powerful legal-bureaucratic-managerial authority promises a vast array of material pleasure as the reward for digging, poverty and insecurity for those who refuse to dig, and severe repression for those who sabotage the digging apparatus. When the workers dig deeply enough they will discover an underground river called Styx (hatred) and its confluence with other rivers, including Lethe (forgetfulness and oblivion), and these will mark their crossing over from life to death. And the shovels will be taken from their hands and replaced with oars, and their training in digging will suit them perfectly for rowing with metronomic precision. And they will pull endlessly along this dark river, forgetting there was ever even a world of sun, green earth, and air. And with these metaphors civilization will think that it is indicting the dark, prehistoric world. But really it is only indicting its own efforts at constructing an entirely man-made environment where "misery is the river of the world" and everybody rows.

To the civilization that would intentionally design such a present and future, Zerzan has always said, unequivocally, "Bring it down! Sabotage it! Don't merely visualize industrial collapse, collapse it!" His condemnation of civilization and his support for its saboteurs has won him, in general, silence from academic and popular environmentalist writers. For those detractors who have taken note of Zerzan's views, every kind of charge has been leveled at him including genocide (ad populum arguments being the better part of intellectual valor). Chomsky and Murray Bookchin, among others, contend that advocating the destruction of civilization amounts to a call for mass killing, inasmuch as it is only vast technological systems that can keep billions alive. It is, in my view, a shortcoming of his work that Zerzan has not written more about what a total frontal assault on civilization would entail. Where he has (for instance in "Postscript to Future Primitive, Re: The Transition") he points to current or potential practices that can bridge the gap between a de-commissioned civilization and a future primitive existence. These include growing food in cities, especially by employing permaculture techniques, treating cities like museums and using them as "moveable celebration sites," intentionally and radically reducing population as a cultural practice associated with recognizing natural limits, reducing population in colder climes where energy use is currently so intensive, increasing use of traditional health and healing practices, and the immersion of people in a whole array of spontaneous and communal activities from skill sharing to construction of simpler, more organically designed shelter. Needless to say, Zerzan's point is not to attack infrastructure and let everyone die. Anyway it debases humans to say that we can only live as appendages to vast systems.

Zerzan and others have pointed out, in rejoinder to Chomsky, that it is certain that when civilizations crash, sudden and abrupt population decreases occur. It is virtually certain that seven billion people and counting will not be able to be kept alive at the current increasing rate of resource use and climate change, especially as millions more each year adopt consumerist lifestyles. So the burden is on them to show that what they advocate can actually avert the real threat of a total, sudden collapse. Moreover, it is up to them to show how, if current technological civilization is to be maintained, its colossal degree of hierarchy and alienation can be addressed. Zerzan's betting that it can't, and the history of civilization tends to reinforce that view.

This gets to the real heart of the matter. The malignant reactions to Zerzan's work derive, I think, from his refusal to cop out on his own analysis. He promises no technological or social engineering magic that will lift us from the morass. He will not double down on the fake promises of civilization in order to extract another half-century of alienation. This constitutes a betrayal of 2500 years of social theory; the official voices of the left and right will not tolerate it. But a growing minority of anarchists—primitivists or not—and others will not keep digging; what we retain of our original condition, and it is much as Zerzan points out in the third section of this collection, rebels at further indoctrination and conformity. When the very concept of the living, natural world and human beings" fundamental belonging together with it is under attack from many quarters, not the least of which is an array of mainstream writers calling themselves "environmentalists," primitivism is a natural, necessary, and urgent response. Civilization versus primitivism mirrors the question of nomos versus physis, but in a new and raw way given the urgency of this latest crisis of civilization. With some notable exceptions, Zerzan's critics are devoted to saving civilization, not saving the earth. But civilization wars against Earth. In their own bias toward civilization, Zerzan's detractors fail to recognize that the actual roots of ecological crisis fundamentally threaten our own inner nature, not just the outer natural world of which we are part.

This failure of constructive dialogue is unfortunate. It undercuts the basis of social theory. And herein lies a great paradox regarding Zerzan: he is engaging in a quintessentially civilized practice, critical theory. It is a paradox, not a contradiction, any more so than his using a computer or publishing books.[14] But the danger in engaging in social theory, and this too is a legacy of civilization, is that it tends toward the discovery of absolute truths, which, once attained, close off discussion, critique and questioning. That is to say, it closes off freedom. If the threat of a "green fascism" exists it is not because of a need for totalitarian control to totally revolutionize society. Rather, total authority rests in the discovery of alleged universal truths, themselves reduced to useable ideologies; thus the way is opened for totalitarianism. Something very much like that exists and goes unchallenged in technological-industrial civilization with its right of property and technological inevitability. But what one of Zerzan's former colleagues at *Fifth Estate* pointed out more than a decade ago is, perhaps, only more accurate now.

Much of anarcho-primitivism today, however small the milieu may be, seems to falling into the thrall of a simplistic ideology that pretends to have a global response to an unprecedented crisis in what it means to be human.... It is a kind of "clash of civilizations" idea that compresses a multiplicity of human experience into a binary opposition...a reductionist legend in which primordial paradise is undermined by an ur-act of domestication.[15]

At its best anarcho-primitivists continue a rich anti-tradition by seeking to use the tools of civilization, including social theory, to smash institutions and return to nature. In doing so anti-civ theory would serve as a provisional basis for attack and might be maintained in a future primitive culture as a constant warning against the disastrous results of hubris, technical innovation, and centralized authority much in the way of coyote stories or iktome stories among many native peoples in North America. But across the millennia of civilization the tendency has nearly always been in the opposite direction, and we already see this in contemporary anarcho-primitivist thought and action.[16] This reverse movement includes the two most important elements of civilization itself: the discovery of "absolute truth" and its imposition on a mass level. Anti-civ would become a new, unquestioned "meta-narrative" that explains extraordinarily complex matters of civilization and primitive culture in a few sound bites.

This tendency can be seen in the Deep Green Resistance movement. In a recent article Derrick Jensen, Aric McBay, and Lierre Keith write, "Ninety-eight percent of the population will do nothing unless they are led, cajoled or forced. If the structural determinants are in place for them to live their lives without doing damage...then that's what happens."[17] It is down to the other two percent, who presumably have grasped the truth and know the solutions, to shift the society toward the "proper structural determinants."

I think Zerzan's theoretical insights into the real character of civilization are keen enough to detect the authoritarianism inherent in this perspective. The authors leave open the question of concrete steps to be taken. But anarchism is already foreclosed on as an option if a vanguard fighting force is oriented toward creating proper structural determinants for the masses.

Where Zerzan is more open to Watson's critique is in his wholesale denunciations of civilization. Zerzan's analysis runs the risk of becoming, simply, a reversal of the traditional false dialectic. Now it is civilization that is repugnant and irredeemable, while the primitive promises absolute fulfillment. One problem with this is that by succumbing to traditional logic, elements of civilization will always be retained because the primitive will necessarily derive its meaning from the negation of civilization. More problematic is that it assumes a universal standpoint: all civilization is evil. Obviously no one can say with certainty that every possible future civilization will retain the destructive elements of past civilizations or that no civilization can ever possibly be created that reconciles itself with primitive culture. Historical evidence suggests this to be sure. But the point of anarcho-primitivist critical theory is precisely to be another of the bridges to the future primitive.

In that respect, if it is to remain anarchistic it is bound to remain open to at least the possibility of retaining some features of civilization. At its best what it provides is the basis for rejecting ideas and practices that will reintroduce what we are only now coming to sense and know as the structural determinants that breed alienation in many wide-ranging forms. So types of technology or modes of practice might be retained but only if they can be reconciled with human freedom and identification with Earth as the place of all Life. As a bridge to the future anarcho-primitivism might begin, to lay out some basic, interrelated questions that can be used to appropriately judge human actions, given the knowledge of civilization's typical deep threats: Does the idea or practice in question create hierarchy, either between humans or between humans and non-human life? Asked another way, does it establish a realm of knowledge and technical sophistication that preclude others from making intelligent decisions about its effects? Does it introduce a dependency on abstract notions such as space and time that distort our relation to given natural reality? Does it involve the need for expansion of territory or use of resources in a way that systemically deprives other beings of life? For all of its problems otherwise, it would involve the maxim of Leopold's land ethic: "A thing is right when it tends to preserve the integrity, stability, and beauty of the biotic community. It is wrong when it tends otherwise."

This is a high and probably impossible standard for civilization to meet. But to assume that it is impossible is going too far. We find something like the possible reconciliation of civilization and the primitive in non-fiction (as in Paul Shepard's work, mentioned above) and in fiction, for example in Marge Piercy's *Woman on the Edge of Time*. Neither this novel nor anything else should be held up as a platform; but they remind us to keep open the possibility that some of the advantages of civilization could be integrated into a culture that is guided by the deeper insights of primitive life.

All of this probably overstates the role of choice. No one ever chose to be primitive or civilized. We can only choose how to respond to the conditions we confront. Primitive culture and civilization developed over long periods of time and always in the context of evolving ecological and social conditions. In their twilight and decline previous civilizations suffered from ecological decline and internal revolt. Choices regarding how to go forward emerged under conditions of serious strife. It would seem that this civilization is the first to take full empirical measure of its own impending decline. But in typical fashion its leading cultural figures refuse to hear the voices of those most certain to war against civilized order. These essays comprise another opportunity to listen, to respond, and, in the midst of gathering peril, to continue the search for a dignified, natural, and free human existence.

—*Michael Becker*

ENDNOTES

1. In this context it is worth pointing out briefly some of the intellectual forebears of anarcho-primitivism. Diogenes and the adherents of his primitivist philosophy consistently expressed utter contempt for the laws, institutions, customs, and manners that comprised ancient Athens and ancient Rome. They ate, shit, slept, and had sex openly; they accosted people in the marketplace and theatre and berated them for their pretension and hypocrisy. Condemned by their opponents as living a life fit for dogs, they adopted the label Cynics (dogs) and proceeded to bark at, urinate on and bite their opponents. Zerzan provides us a nice historical overview of anarchists with at least a primitivist bent, especially the Brothers and Sisters of the Free Spirit, in the fourteenth century: see "Revolt and Heresy in the Late Middle Ages" below. Radical Levellers and Diggers during the English Revolution similarly reflected a determination to live in accord with an earlier, simpler, free and egalitarian existence. And two centuries later the Luddites wrecked machines right across England.

2   Plato, *The Republic*, translated by Benjamin Jowett (New York: Anchor Books, 1973), 57. A state at "fever heat" is among the most honest depictions of civilization you will find in the Western canon; it conveys the delirious intensity and sickening pace of modernity. Only a student of Socrates could present such an ironic portrait of the *polis*.

3   John Locke, *The Second Treatise of Government*, edited with an introduction by C.B. McPherson (Cambridge: Hackett Publishing Co., 1980). 23.

4   Jean Jacques Tousseau, *The Social Contract and Discourse on the Origin of Inequality*, edited with an introduction by Lester G. Crocker (New York: Washington Square Press, 1976), 17–18.

5   Paul Shepherd, *The Tender Carnivore and the Sacred Game* (New York: Charles Scribner's Sons, 1973).

6   For various formulations of these arguments see articles by Milbrath, Pirages, and, especially, McLaughlin and Zimmerman in *Explorations in Environmental Political Theory*, ed. Joel Jay Kassiola (New York: M.E. Sharpe, 2003).

7   Bill Devall and George Sessions, *Deep Ecology* (Salt Lake City: Gibbs M. Smith Inc., 1985), 97.

8   In our "original condition" human intelligence and consciousness learned to take an ecocentric form, creating a "people who differentiate nature and know the individual plant species one by one, who live in the small, collectively managed communities that provide an immense range of opportunities for allopatric speciation, and who develop [an] existentially alive culture." Kovel necessarily claims that the "original" humans only learned individual plant species because hunting is said to be the cause of the earliest transition away from primitive innocence. Though he provides virtually no actual anthropological or archeological evidence for this and claims that it is "shrouded in an impenetrably distant past," he attributes the growth of

civilization, and ultimately its most exploitative form, capitalism, to the "death-dealing tools of the hunt," alleged sex-differentiation which hunting brought on, and the extension of hunting from animals to women and children captives from rival tribes. Joel Kovel, *The Enemy of Nature* (London: Zed Books, 2007), 120–127.

9   Paul Taylor's *Respect for Nature* is rather typical in defining nature as a place entirely untouched by human action. This amounts to an end to nature in that humans have no place or role in nature save to protect whatever wild nature remains. High civilization, by contrast, is precisely the ethical standard for determining when nature can be sacrificed. Obviously the more specific claim that nature has been eclipsed is found in McKibben's well-known text, *The End of Nature*. Another popular text, Stewart Brand's *Whole Earth Discipline*, opens with the caption "We are as gods and HAVE to get good at it [emphasis original]." Compared with Hawken and Lovins" *Natural Capitalism*, where salvation will be achieved through "higher efficiency in everything" and "biology-inspired industrial processes," Brand takes the step of reversing terms; he prefers to think of "ecosystems services as infrastructure." Timothy Morton, in *Ecology Without Nature*, seems to be on an interesting track in his claim that dispensing with the idea of nature is a prerequisite for rediscovering the sublime. But he seems to end up mainly with deconstructionist word games. In neo-Marxian thought, Steven Vogel has made the case for dropping the word "nature" with all its metaphysical ambiguities and instead focusing on the term "environment." Regarding the latter, we find, first, that the entire environment has, in fact, been altered by human activity. Secondly, our alienation stems not from separation from "nature" but from our lack of control over the built environment, the one and only environment that remains and, in any case, that in which we actually live, work, and breathe. Finally, in *Living in the End Times* the pop-philosopher Slovej Zizek asks us to accept that "nature no longer exists" and, further, to accept "our full alienation from nature." Science and technology are "the only solution...not to feel more organic with Mother Earth...we are already within technology." What we should do is "remain open and just patiently work; work how? Also with much stronger social discipline." He calls for a new sort of solidarity, proletarian discipline as a means of confronting ecological crisis.

10   Martin Heidegger, *The Question Concerning Technology*, translated with an introduction by William Lovitt (New York: Harper Torchbooks, 1982), 18.

11   Frank Latta, *Tailholt Tales* (New York: Brewer's Historical Press, 1976).

12   M. Kat Anderson, *Tending the Wild* (Berkeley, California: University of California Press, 2005).

13   Stanley Diamond, *In Search of the Primitive* (New Brunswick, New Jersey: Transaction Books, 1974).

14   There are many, apparently, who can't see the difference, that is, who dismiss Zerzan because he does not live in a cave and hunt with a stone knife. For them I can only recommend Bukowski's "Dinosauria, We."

15   David Watson, "Swamp Fever, Primitivism and the 'Ideological Vortex': Farewell to All That," in the Anarchist Library, theanarchistlibrary.org/HTML/ David_Watson__Swamp_Fever__Primitivism___the__Ideological_Vortex___

INTRODUCTION

Farewell_to_All_That.html (1997).

16   One of the less noted parts of Freddy Perlman's classic work *Against History, Against Leviathan* is his observation that "barbarians" in each so-called dark age ultimately failed to dismantle sovereign institutions and ideas and, instead, ultimately embraced the very cultural and political forms of sovereignty they originally fought against. They "re-caged" themselves rather than "re-wilding" themselves.

17   Derrick Jensen et al., "An Excerpt from *Deep Green Resistance*," in *Earth First! the Radical Environmental Journal*, 30th Anniversary Edition, vol. 1 (Samhain/Yule, 2010): 10.

PART ONE

FUTURE PRIMITIVE

CHAPTER ONE

FUTURE PRIMITIVE

DIVISION OF LABOR, which has had so much to do with bringing us to the present global crisis, works daily to prevent our understanding the origins of this horrendous present. Mary Lecron Foster (1990) surely errs on the side of understatement in allowing that anthropology is today "in danger of serious and damaging fragmentation." Shanks and Tilley (1987b) voice a rare, related challenge: "The point of archaeology is not merely to interpret the past but to change the manner in which the past is interpreted in the service of social reconstruction in the present." Of course, the social sciences themselves work against the breadth and depth of vision necessary to such a reconstruction. In terms of human origins and development, the array of splintered fields and sub-fields—anthropology, archaeology, paleontology, ethnology, paleobotany, ethnoanthropology, etc., etc.—mirrors the narrowing, crippling effect that civilization has embodied from its very beginning.

Nonetheless, the literature can provide highly useful assistance, if approached with an appropriate method and awareness and the desire to proceed past its limitations. In fact, the weakness of more or less orthodox modes of thinking can and does yield to the demands of an increasingly dissatisfied society. Unhappiness with contemporary life becomes distrust with the official lies that are told to legitimate that life, and a truer picture of human development emerges. Renunciation and subjugation in modern life have long been explained as necessary concomitants of "human nature." After all, our pre-civilized existence of deprivation, brutality, and ignorance made authority a benevolent gift that rescued us from savagery. "Cave man" and "Neanderthal" are still invoked to remind us where we would be without religion, government, and toil.

This ideological view of our past has been radically overturned in recent decades, through the work of academics like Richard Lee and Marshall Sahlins. A nearly complete reversal in anthropological orthodoxy has come about, with important implications. Now we can see that life before domestication/agriculture was in fact largely one of leisure, intimacy with nature, sensual wisdom, sexual equality, and health. This was our human nature, for a couple of million years, prior to enslavement by priests, kings, and bosses.

And lately another stunning revelation has appeared, a related one that deepens the first and may be telling us something equally important about who we were and what we might again become. The main line of attack against new descriptions of gatherer-hunter life has been, though often indirect or not explicitly stated, to characterize that life, condescendingly, as the most an evolving species could achieve at an early stage. Thus, the argument allows that there was a long period of apparent grace and pacific existence, but says that humans simply didn't have the mental capacity to leave simple ways behind in favor of complex social and technological achievement.

In another fundamental blow to civilization, we now learn that not only was human life once, and for so long, a state that did not know alienation or domination, but as the investigations since the '80s by archaeologists John Fowlett, Thomas Wynn, and others have shown, those humans possessed an intelligence at least equal to our own. At a stroke, as it were, the "ignorance" thesis is disposed of, and we contemplate where we came from in a new light.

To put the issue of mental capacity in context, it is useful to review the various (and again, ideologically loaded) interpretations of human origins and development. Robert Ardrey (1961, 1976) served up a bloodthirsty, macho version of prehistory, as have, to slightly lesser degrees, Desmond Morris and Lionel Tiger. Similarly, Freud and Konrad Lorenz wrote of the innate depravity of the species, thereby providing their contributions to hierarchy and power in the present.

Fortunately, a far more plausible outlook has emerged, one that corresponds to the overall version of Paleolithic life in general. Food sharing has for some time been considered an integral part of earliest human society (e.g. Washburn and DeVore, 1961). Jane Goodall (1971) and Richard Leakey (1978), among others, have concluded that it was the key element in establishing our uniquely *Homo* development at least as early as two million years ago. This emphasis, carried forward since the early '70s by Linton, Zihlman, Tanner, and Isaac, has become ascendant. One of the telling arguments in favor of the cooperation thesis, as against that of generalized violence and male domination, involves a diminishing, during early evolution, of the difference in size and strength between males and females. Sexual dimorphism, as it is called, was originally very pronounced, including such features as prominent canines or "fighting teeth" in males and much smaller canines for the female. The disappearance of large male canines strongly suggests that the female of the species exercised a selection for sociable, sharing males. Most apes today have significantly longer and larger canines, male to female, in the absence of this female choice capacity (Zihlman 1981, Tanner 1981).

Division of labor between the sexes is another key area in human beginnings, a condition once simply taken for granted and expressed by the term hunter-gatherer. Now it is widely accepted that gathering of plant foods, once thought to be the exclusive domain of women and of secondary importance to hunting by males, constituted the main food source (Johansen and Shreeve 1989). Since females were not significantly dependent on males for food (Hamilton 1984), it seems likely that rather than division of labor, flexibility and joint activity would have been central (Bender 1989). As Zihlman (1981) points out, an overall behavioral flexibility may have been the primary ingredient in early human existence. Joan Gero (1991) has demonstrated that stone tools were as likely to have been made by women as by men, and indeed Poirier (1987) reminds us that there is "no archaeological evidence supporting the contention that early humans exhibited a sexual division of labor." It is unlikely that food collecting involved much, if any, division of labor (Slocum 1975) and probably that sexual specialization came quite late in human evolution (Zihlman 1981, Crader and Isaac 1981).

So if the adaptation that began our species centered on gathering, when did hunting come in? Binford (1984) has argued that there is no indication of use of animal products (i.e. evidence of butchery practices) until the appearance, relatively quite recent, of anatomically modern humans. Electron microscope studies of fossil teeth found in East Africa (Walker 1984) suggest a diet composed primarily of fruit, while a similar examination of stone tools from a 1.5 million-year-old site at Koobi Fora in Kenya (Keeley and Toth 1981) shows that they were used on plant materials. The small amount of meat in the early Paleolithic diet was probably scavenged, rather than hunted (Ehrenberg 1989b).

The "natural" condition of the species was evidently a diet made up largely of vegetables rich in fiber, as opposed to the modern high-fat and animal protein diet with its attendant chronic disorders (Mendeloff 1977). Though our early forebears employed their "detailed knowledge of the environment and cognitive mapping" (Zihlman 1981) in the service of a plant-gathering subsistence, the archaeological evidence for hunting appears to slowly increase with time (Hodder 1991).

Much evidence, however, has overturned assumptions as to widespread prehistoric hunting. Collections of bones seen earlier as evidence of large kills of mammals, for example, have turned out to be, upon closer examination, the results of movement by flowing water or caches by animals. Lewis Binford's "Were There Elephant Hunters at Tooralba?" (1989) is a good instance of such a closer look, in which he doubts there was significant hunting until 200,000 years ago or sooner. Adrienne Zihlman (1981) has concluded that "hunting arose relatively late in evolution," and "may not extend beyond the last one hundred thousand years." And there are many (e.g. Straus 1986, Trinkhaus 1986) who do not see evidence for serious hunting of large mammals until even later, viz. the later Upper Paleolithic, just before the emergence of agriculture.

The oldest known surviving artifacts are stone tools from Hadar in eastern Africa. With more refined dating methods, they may prove to be 3.1 million years old (Klein 1989). Perhaps the main reason these may be classified as representing human effort is that they involve the crafting of one tool by using another, a uniquely human attribute so far as we know. *Homo habilis*, or "handy man," designates what has been thought of as the first known human species, its name reflecting association with the earliest stone tools (Coppens 1989). Basic wooden and bone implements, though more perishable and thus scantily represented in the archaeological record, were also used by *Homo habilis* as part of a "remarkably simple and effective" adaptation in Africa and Asia (Fagan 1990). Our ancestors at this stage had smaller brains and bodies than we do, but Poirier (1987) notes that "their postcranial anatomy was rather like modern humans," and Holloway (1972, 1974) allows that his studies of cranial endocasts from this period indicate a basically modern brain organization. Similarly, tools older than two million years have been found to exhibit a consistent right-handed orientation in the ways stone has been flaked off in their formation. Right-handedness as a tendency is correlated in moderns with such distinctly human features as pronounced lateralization of the brain and marked functional separation of the cerebral hemispheres (Holloway 1981a). Klein (1989) concludes that "basic human cognitive and communicational abilities are almost certainly implied."

Homo erectus is the other main predecessor to Homo sapiens, according to longstanding usage, appearing about 1.75 million years ago as humans moved out of forests into drier, more open African grasslands. Although brain size alone does not necessarily correlate with mental capacity, the cranial capacity of Homo erectus overlaps with that of moderns such that this species "must have been capable of many of the same behaviors" (Ciochon, Olsen and Tames 1990). As Johanson and Edey (1981) put it, "If the largest-brained erectus were to be rated against the smallest-brained sapiens—all their other characteristics ignored—their species names would have to be reversed." Homo Neanderthalus, which immediately preceded us, possessed brains somewhat larger than our own (Delson 1985, Holloway 1985, Donald 1991). Though of course the much-maligned Neanderthal has been pictured as a primitive, brutish creature—in keeping with the prevailing Hobbesian ideology—despite manifest intelligence as well as enormous physical strength (Shreeve 1991).

Recently, however, the whole species framework has become a doubtful proposition (Day 1987, Rightmire 1990). Attention has been drawn to the fact that fossil specimens from various Homo species "all show intermediate morphological traits," leading to suspicion of an arbitrary division of humanity into separate taxa (Gingerich 1979, Tobias 1982). Fagan (1989), for example, tells us that "it is very hard to draw a clear taxonomic boundary between Homo erectus and archaic Homo sapiens on the one hand, and between archaic and anatomically modern Homo sapiens on the other." Likewise, Foley (1989): "the anatomical distinctions between Homo erectus and Homo sapiens are not great." Jelinek (1978) flatly declares that "there is no good reason, anatomical or cultural" for separating erectus and sapiens into two species, and has concluded (1980a) that people from at least the Middle Paleolithic onward "may be viewed as *Homo sapiens*" (as does Hublin 1986). The tremendous upward revision of early intelligence, discussed below, must be seen as connected to the present confusion over species, as the once-prevailing overall evolutionary model gives way.

But the controversy over species categorization is only interesting in the context of how our earliest forebears lived. Despite the minimal nature of what could be expected to survive so many millennia, we can glimpse some of the texture of that life, with its often elegant, pre-division of labor approaches. The "tool kit" from the Olduvai Gorge area made famous by the Leakeys contains "at least six clearly recognizable tool types" dating from about 1.7 million years ago (M. Leakey, 1978). There soon appeared the Acheulian handaxe, with its symmetrical beauty, in use for about a million years. Teardrop-shaped, and possessed of a remarkable balance, it exudes grace and utility from an era much prior to symbolization. Isaac (1986) noted that "the basic needs for sharp edges that humans have can be met from the varied range of forms generated from "Oldowan" patterns of stone flaking," wondering how it came to be thought that "more complex equals better adapted." In this distant early time, according to cut-marks found on surviving bones, humans were using scavenged animal sinews and skins for such things as cord, bags, and rugs (Gowlett 1984). Further evidence suggests furs for cave wall coverings and seats, and seaweed beds for sleeping (Butzer 1970).

The use of fire goes back almost two million years (Kempe 1988) and might have appeared even earlier but for the tropical conditions of humanity's original African homeland, as Poirier (1987) implies. Perfected fire-making included the firing of caves to eliminate insects and heated pebble floors (Perles 1975, Lumley 1976), amenities that show up very early in the Paleolithic.

As John Gowlett (1986) notes, there are still some archaeologists who consider anything earlier than *Homo sapiens*, a mere 30,000 years ago, as greatly more primitive than we "fully human" types. But along with the documentation, referred to above, of fundamentally "modern" brain anatomy even in early humans, this minority must now contend with recent work depicting complete human intelligence as present virtually with the birth of the *Homo* species. Thomas Wynn (1985) judged manufacture of the Acheulian handaxe to have required "a stage of intelligence that is typical of fully modern adults." Gowlett, like Wynn, examines the required

6

"operational thinking" involved in the right hammer, the right force and the right striking angle, in an ordered sequence and with flexibility needed for modifying the procedure. He contends that manipulation, concentration, visualization of form in three dimensions, and planning were needed, and that these requirements "were the common property of early human beings as much as two million years ago, and this," he adds, "is hard knowledge, not speculation."

During the vast time-span of the Paleolithic, there were remarkably few changes in technology (Rolland 1990). Innovation, "over 2 1/2 million years measured in stone tool development was practically nil," according to Gerhard Kraus (1990). Seen in the light of what we now know of prehistoric intelligence, such "stagnation" is especially vexing to many social scientists. "It is difficult to comprehend such slow development," in the judgment of Wymer (1989). It strikes me as very plausible that intelligence, informed by the success and satisfaction of a gatherer-hunter existence, is the very reason for the pronounced absence of "progress." Division of labor, domestication, symbolic culture—these were evidently refused until very recently.

Contemporary thought, in its postmodern incarnation, would like to rule out the reality of a divide between nature and culture; given the abilities present among people before civilization, however, it may be more accurate to say that basically, they long chose nature over culture. It is also popular to see almost every human act or object as symbolic (e.g. Botscharow 1989), a position which is, generally speaking, part of the denial of a nature versus culture distinction. But it is culture as the manipulation of basic symbolic forms that is involved here. It also seems clear that reified time, language (written, certainly, and probably spoken language for all or most of this period), number, and art had no place, despite an intelligence fully capable of them.

I would like to interject, in passing, my agreement with Goldschmidt (1990) that "the hidden dimension in the construction of the symbolic world is time." And as Norman O. Brown put it, "life not repressed is not in historical time," which I take as a reminder that time as a materiality is not inherent in reality, but a cultural imposition, perhaps the first cultural imposition, on it. As this elemental dimension of symbolic culture progresses, so does, by equal steps, alienation from the natural.

Cohen (1974) has discussed symbols as "essential for the development and maintenance of social order." Which implies—as does, more forcefully, a great deal of positive evidence—that before the emergence of symbols there was no condition of disorder requiring them. In a similar vein, Lévi-Strauss (1953) pointed out that "mythical thought always progresses from the awareness of oppositions toward their resolution." So whence the absence of order, the conflicts or "oppositions?" The literature on the Paleolithic contains almost nothing that deals with this essential question, among thousands of monographs on specific features. A reasonable hypothesis, in my opinion, is that division of labor, unnoticed because of its glacially slow pace, and not sufficiently understood because of its newness, began to cause small fissures in the human community and unhealthy practices vis-à-vis nature. In the later Upper Paleolithic, "15,000 years ago, we begin to observe specialized collection of plants in the Middle East, and specialized hunting," observed Gowlett (1984). The sudden appearance of symbolic activities (e.g. ritual and art) in the Upper Paleolithic has definitely seemed to archaeologists one of prehistory's "big surprises" (Binford 1972b), given the absence of such behaviors in the Middle Paleolithic (Foster 1990, Kozlowski 1990). But signs of division of labor and specialization were making their presence felt as a breakdown of wholeness and natural order, a lack that needed redressing. What is surprising is that this transition to civilization can still be seen as benign. Foster (1990) seems to celebrate it by concluding that the "symbolic mode...has proved extraordinarily adaptive, else why has *Homo sapiens* become material master of the world?" He is certainly correct, as he is to recognize "the manipulation of symbols [to be] the very stuff of culture," but he appears oblivious to the fact that this successful adaptation has brought alienation and destruction of nature along to their present horrifying prominence.

It is reasonable to assume that the symbolic world originated in the formulation of language, which somehow appeared from a "matrix of extensive nonverbal communication" (Tanner and Zihlman 1976) and face-to-face contact. There is no agreement as to when language began, but no evidence exists of speech before the cultural "explosion" of the later Upper Paleolithic (Dibble 1984, 1989). It seems to have acted as an "inhibiting agent," a way of bringing life under "greater control" (Mumford 1972), stemming the flood of images and sensations to which the pre-modern individual was open. In this sense it would have likely marked an early turning away from a life of openness and communion with nature, toward one more oriented to the overlordship and domestication that followed symbolic culture's inauguration. It is probably a mistake, by the way, to assume that thought is advanced (if there were such a thing as "neutral" thought, whose advance could be universally appreciated) because we actually think in language; there is no conclusive evidence that we must do so (Allport 1983). There are many cases (Lecours and Joanette 1980, Levine et al. 1982), involving stroke and like impairments, of patients who have lost speech, including the ability to talk silently to themselves, who were fully capable of coherent thought of all kinds. These data strongly suggest that "human intellectual skill is uniquely powerful, even in the absence of language" (Donald 1991).

In terms of symbolization in action, Goldschmidt (1990) seems correct in judging that "the Upper Paleolithic invention of ritual may well have been the keystone in the structure of culture that gave it its great impetus for expansion." Ritual has played a number of pivotal roles in what Hodder (1990) termed "the relentless unfolding of symbolic and social structures" accompanying the arrival of cultural mediation. It was as a means of achieving and consolidating social cohesion that ritual was essential (Johnson 1982, Conkey 1985); totemic rituals, for example, reinforce clan unity.

The start of an appreciation of domestication, or taming of nature, is seen in a cultural ordering of the wild, through ritual. Evidently, the female as a cultural category, viz. seen as wild or dangerous, dates from this period. The ritual "Venus" figurines appear as of 25,000 years ago, and seem to be an example of earliest symbolic likeness of women for the purpose of representation and control (Hodder 1990). Even more concretely, subjugation of the wild occurs at this time in the first systematic hunting of large mammals; ritual was an integral part of this activity (Hammond 1974, Frison 1986).

Ritual, as shamanic practice, may also be considered as a regression from that state in which all shared a consciousness we would now classify as extrasensory (Leonard 1972). When specialists alone claim access to such perceptual heights as may have once been communal, further backward moves in division of labor are facilitated or enhanced. The way back to bliss through ritual is a virtually universal mythic theme, promising the dissolution of measurable time, among other joys. This theme of ritual points to an absence that it falsely claims to fill, as does symbolic culture in general.

9

Ritual as a means of organizing emotions, a method of cultural direction and restraint, introduces art, a facet of ritual expressiveness (Bender 1989). "There can be little doubt," to Gans (1985), "that the various forms of secular art derive originally from ritual." We can detect the beginning of an unease, a feeling that an earlier, direct authenticity is departing. La Barre (1972), I believe, is correct in judging that "art and religion alike arise from unsatisfied desire." At first, more abstractly as language, then more purposively as ritual and art, culture steps in to deal artificially with spiritual and social anxiety.

Ritual and magic must have dominated early (Upper Paleolithic) art and were probably essential, along with an increasing division of labor, for the coordination and direction of community (Wymer 1981). Similarly, Pfeiffer (1982) has depicted the famous Upper Paleolithic European cave paintings as the original form of initiating youth into now complex social systems; as necessary for order and discipline (see also Gamble 1982, Jochim 1983). And art may have contributed to the control of nature, as part of development of the earliest territorialism, for example (Straus 1990).

The emergence of symbolic culture, with its inherent will to manipulate and control, soon opened the door to domestication of nature. After two million years of human life within the bounds of nature, in balance with other wild species, agriculture changed our lifestyle, our way of adapting, in an unprecedented way. Never before has such a radical change occurred in a species so utterly and so swiftly (Pfeiffer 1977). Self-domestication through language, ritual, and art inspired the taming of plants and animals that followed. Appearing only 10,000 years ago, farming quickly triumphed; for control, by its very nature, invites intensification. Once the will to production broke through, it became more productive the more efficiently it was exercised, and hence more ascendant and adaptive.

Agriculture enables greatly increased division of labor, establishes the material foundations of social hierarchy, and initiates environmental destruction. Priests, kings, drudgery, sexual inequality, warfare are a few of its fairly immediate specific consequences (Ehrenberg 1986b, Wymer 1981, Festinger 1983). Whereas Paleolithic peoples enjoyed a highly varied diet, using several thousand species of plants for food, with farming these sources were vastly reduced (White 1959, Gouldie 1986).

Given the intelligence and the very great practical knowledge of Stone

Age humanity, the question has often been asked, "Why didn't agriculture begin, at say, 1,000,000 B.C. rather than about 8,000 B.C.?" I have provided a brief answer in terms of slowly accelerating alienation in the form of division of labor and symbolization, but given how negative the results were, it is still a bewildering phenomenon. Thus, as Binford (1968) put it, "The question to be asked is not why agriculture...was not developed everywhere, but why it was developed at all." The end of gatherer-hunter life brought a decline in size, stature, and skeletal robusticity (Cohen and Armelagos 1981, Harris and Ross 1981), and introduced tooth decay, nutritional deficiencies, and most infectious diseases (Larsen 1982, Buikstra 1976a, Cohen 1981). "Taken as a whole...an overall decline in the quality—and probably the length—of human life," concluded Cohen and Armelagos (1981).

Another outcome was the invention of number, unnecessary before the ownership of crops, animals, and land that is one of agriculture's hallmarks. The development of number further impelled the urge to treat nature as something to be dominated. Writing was also required by domestication, for the earliest business transactions and political administration (Larsen 1988). Lévi-Strauss has argued persuasively that the primary function of written communication was to facilitate exploitation and subjugation (1955); cities and empires, for example, would be impossible without it. Here we see clearly the joining of the logic of symbolization and the growth of capital.

Conformity, repetition, and regularity were the keys to civilization upon its triumph, replacing the spontaneity, enchantment, and discovery of the pre-agricultural human state that survived so very long. Clark (1979) cites a gatherer-hunter "amplitude of leisure," deciding "it was this and the pleasurable way of life that went with it, rather than penury and a day-long grind, that explains why social life remained so static." One of the most enduring and widespread myths is that there was once a Golden Age, characterized by peace and innocence, and that something happened to destroy this idyll and consign us to misery and suffering. Eden, or whatever name it goes by, was the home of our primeval forager ancestors, and expresses the yearning of disillusioned tillers of the soil for a lost life of freedom and relative ease.

The once rich environs people inhabited prior to domestication and agriculture are now virtually nonexistent. For the few remaining foragers there exist only the most marginal lands, those isolated places as yet unwanted by agriculture. And surviving gatherer-hunters, who have somehow managed to evade civilization's tremendous pressures to turn them into slaves (i.e. farmers, political subjects, wage laborers), have all been influenced by contact with outside peoples (Lee 1976, Mithen 1990).

Duffy (1984) points out that the present-day gatherer-hunters he studied, the Mbuti Pygmies of central Africa, have been acculturated by surrounding villager-agriculturalists for hundreds of years, and to some extent, by generations of contact with government authorities and missionaries. And yet it seems that an impulse toward authentic life can survive down through the ages: "Try to imagine," he counsels, "a way of life where land, shelter, and food are free, and where there are no leaders, bosses, politics, organized crime, taxes, or laws. Add to this the benefits of being part of a society where everything is shared, where there are no rich people and no poor people, and where happiness does not mean the accumulation of material possessions." The Mbuti have never domesticated animals or planted crops.

Among the members of non-agriculturalist bands resides a highly sane combination of little work and material abundance. Bodley (1976) discovered that the San (a.k.a. Bushmen) of the harsh Kalahari Desert of southern Africa work fewer hours, and fewer of their number work, than do the neighboring cultivators. In times of drought, moreover, it has been the San to whom the farmers have turned for their survival (Lee 1968). They spend "strikingly little time laboring and much time at rest and leisure," according to Tanaka (1980), while others (e.g. Marshall 1976, Guenther 1976) have commented on San vitality and freedom compared with sedentary farmers, their relatively secure and easygoing life.

Flood (1983) noted that to Australian aborigines "the labour involved in tilling and planting outweighed the possible advantages." Speaking more generally, Tanaka (1976) has pointed to the abundant and stable plant foods in the society of early humanity, just as "they exist in every modern gatherer society." Likewise, Festinger (1983) referred to Paleolithic access to "considerable food without a great deal of effort," adding that "contemporary groups that still live on hunting and gathering do very well, even though they have been pushed into very marginal habitats."

As Hole and Flannery (1963) summarized: "No group on earth has more leisure time than hunters and gatherers, who spend it primarily on games, conversation and relaxing." They have much more free time, adds Binford (1968), "than do modern industrial or farm workers, or even professors of archaeology."

The non-domesticated know that, as Vaneigem (1975) put it, only the present can be total. This by itself means that they live life with incomparably greater immediacy, density and passion than we do. It has been said that some revolutionary days are worth centuries; until then "We look before and after," as Shelley wrote, "And sigh for what is not...."

The Mbuti believe (Turnbull 1976) that "by a correct fulfillment of the present, the past and the future will take care of themselves." Primitive peoples do not live through memories, and generally have no interest in birthdays or measuring their ages (Cipriani 1966). As for the future, they have little desire to control what does not yet exist, just as they have little desire to control nature. Their moment-by-moment joining with the flux and flow of the natural world does not preclude an awareness of the seasons, but this does not constitute an alienated time consciousness that robs them of the present.

Though contemporary gatherer-hunters eat more meat than their pre-historic forebears, vegetable foods still constitute the mainstay of their diet in tropical and subtropical regions (Lee 1968a, Yellen and Lee 1976). Both the Kalahari San and the Hazda of East Africa, where game is more abundant than in the Kalahari, rely on gathering for 80 percent of their sustenance (Tanaka 1980). The !Kung branch of the San search for more than a hundred different kinds of plants (Thomas 1968) and exhibit no nutritional deficiency (Truswell and Hansen 1976). This is similar to the healthful, varied diet of Australian foragers (Fisher 1982, Flood 1983). The overall diet of gatherers is better than that of cultivators, starvation is very rare, and their health status generally superior, with much less chronic disease (Lee and Devore 1968a, Ackerman 1990).

Lauren van der Post (1958) expressed wonder at the exuberant San laugh, which rises "sheer from the stomach, a laugh you never hear among civilized people." He found this emblematic of a great vigor and clarity of senses that yet manages to withstand and elude the onslaught of civilization. Truswell and Hansen (1976) may have encountered it in the person of a San who had survived an unarmed fight with a leopard; although injured, he had killed the animal with his bare hands.

The Andaman Islanders, west of Thailand, have no leaders, no idea of symbolic representation, and no domesticated animals. There is also an absence of aggression, violence, and disease; wounds heal surprisingly quickly, and their sight and hearing are particularly acute. They are said to have declined since European intrusion in the mid-nineteenth century, but exhibit other such remarkable physical traits as a natural immunity to malaria, skin with sufficient elasticity to rule out post-childbirth stretch marks and the wrinkling we associate with aging, and an "unbelievable" strength of teeth: Cipriani (1966) reported seeing children of 10 to 15 years crush nails with them. He also testified to the Andamese practice of collecting honey with no protective clothing at all; "yet they are never stung, and watching them one felt in the presence of some age-old mystery, lost by the civilized world."

DeVries (1952) has cited a wide range of contrasts by which the superior health of gatherer-hunters can be established, including an absence of degenerative diseases and mental disabilities, and childbirth without difficulty or pain. He also points out that this begins to erode from the moment of contact with civilization.

Relatedly, there is a great deal of evidence not only for physical and emotional vigor among primitives but also concerning their heightened sensory abilities. Darwin described people at the southernmost tip of South America who went about almost naked in frigid conditions, while Peasley (1983) observed Aborigines who were renowned for their ability to live through bitterly cold desert nights "without any form of clothing." Lévi-Strauss (1979) was astounded to learn of a particular [South American] tribe which was able to "see the planet Venus in full daylight," a feat comparable to that of the North African Dogon who consider Sirius B the most important star; somehow aware, without instruments, of a star that can only be found with the most powerful of telescopes (Temple 1976). In this vein, Boyden (1970) recounted the Bushman ability to see four of the moons of Jupiter with the naked eye.

In The Harmless People (1959), Marshall told how one Bushman walked unerringly to a spot in a vast plain, "with no bush or tree to mark place," and pointed out a blade of grass with an almost invisible filament of vine around it. He had encountered it months before in the rainy season when it was green. Now, in parched weather, he dug there to expose a succulent root and quenched his thirst. Also in the Kalahari Desert, van der Post (1958) meditated upon San/Bushman communion with nature, a level of experience that "could almost be called mystical. For instance,

14

they seemed to know what it actually felt like to be an elephant, a lion, an antelope, a steenbuck, a lizard, a striped mouse, mantis, baobab tree, yellow-crested cobra or starry-eyed amaryllis, to mention only a few of the brilliant multitudes through which they moved." It seems almost pedestrian to add that gatherer-hunters have often been remarked to possess tracking skills that virtually defy rational explanation (e.g. Lee 1979).

Rohrlich-Leavitt (1976) noted, "The data show that gatherer-hunters are generally nonterritorial and bilocal; reject group aggression and competition; share their resources freely; value egalitarianism and personal autonomy in the context of group cooperation; and are indulgent and loving with children." Dozens of studies stress communal sharing and egalitarianism as perhaps the defining traits of such groups (e.g. Marshall 1961 and 1976, Sahlins 1968, Pilbeam 1972, Damas 1972, Diamond 1974, Lafitau 1974, Tanaka 1976 and 1980, Wiessner 1977, Morris 1982, Riches 1982, Smith 1988, Mithen 1990). Lee (1982) referred to the "universality among foragers" of sharing, while Marshall's classic 1961 work spoke of the "ethic of generosity and humility" informing a "strongly egalitarian" gatherer-hunter orientation. Tanaka provides a typical example: "The most admired character trait is generosity, and the most despised and disliked are stinginess and selfishness."

Baer (1986) listed "egalitarianism, democracy, personalism, individuation, nurturance" as key virtues of the non-civilized, and Lee (1988) cited "an absolute aversion to rank distinctions" among "simple foraging peoples around the world." Leacock and Lee (1982) specified that "any assumption of authority" within the group "leads to ridicule or anger among the !Kung, as has been recorded for the Mbuti (Turnbull 1962), the Hazda (Woodburn 1980) and the Montagnais-Naskapi (Thwaites 1906), among others."

"Not even the father of an extended family can tell his sons and daughters what to do. Most people appear to operate on their own internal schedules," reported Lee (1972) of the !Kung of Botswana. Ingold (1987) judged that "in most hunting and gathering societies, a supreme value is placed upon the principle of individual autonomy," similar to Wilson's finding (1988) of "an ethic of independence" that is "common to the focused open societies." The esteemed field anthropologist Radin (1953) went so far as to say: "Free scope is allowed for every conceivable kind of personality outlet or expression in primitive society. No moral judgment is passed on any aspect of human personality as such."

Turnbull (1976) looked on the structure of Mbuti social life as "an apparent vacuum, a lack of internal system that is almost anarchical." According to Duffy (1984), "the Mbuti are naturally acephalous—they do not have leaders or rulers, and decisions concerning the band are made by consensus." There is an enormous qualitative difference between foragers and farmers in this regard, as in so many others. For instance, agricultural Bantu tribes (e.g. the Saga) surround the San, and are organized by kingship, hierarchy and work; the San exhibit egalitarianism, autonomy, and sharing. Domestication is the principle which accounts for this drastic distinction.

Domination within a society is not unrelated to domination of nature. In gatherer-hunter societies, on the other hand, no strict hierarchy exists between the human and the non-human species (Noske 1989), and relations among foragers are likewise non-hierarchical. The non-domesticated typically view the animals they hunt as equals; this essentially egalitarian relationship is ended by the advent of domestication.

When progressive estrangement from nature became outright social control (agriculture), more than just social attitudes changed. Descriptions by sailors and explorers who arrived in "newly discovered" regions tell how wild mammals and birds originally showed no fear at all of the human invaders (Brock 1981). A few contemporary gatherers practiced no hunting before outside contact, but while the majority certainly do hunt, "it is not normally an aggressive act" (Rohrlich-Leavitt 1976). Turnbull (1965) observed Mbuti hunting as quite without any aggressive spirit, even carried out with a sort of regret. Hewitt (1986) reported a sympathy bond between hunter and hunted among the Xan Bushmen he encountered in the nineteenth century.

As regards violence among gatherer-hunters, Lee (1988) found that "the !Kung hate fighting, and think anybody who fought would be stupid." The Mbuti, by Duffy's account (1984), "look on any form of violence between one person and another with great abhorrence and distaste, and never represent it in their dancing or playacting." Homicide and suicide, concluded Bodley (1976), are both "decidedly uncommon" among undisturbed gatherer-hunters. The "warlike" nature of Native American peoples was often fabricated to add legitimacy to European aims of conquest (Kroeber 1961); the foraging Comanche maintained their nonviolent ways for centuries before the European invasion, becoming violent only upon contact with marauding civilization (Fried 1973).

The development of symbolic culture, which rapidly led to agriculture, is linked through ritual to alienated social life among extant foraging groups. Bloch (1977) found a correlation between levels of ritual and hierarchy. Put negatively, Woodburn (1968) could see the connection between an absence of ritual and the absence of specialized roles and hierarchy among the Hazda of Tanzania. Turner's study of the west African Ndembu (1957) revealed a profusion of ritual structures and ceremonies intended to redress the conflicts arising from the breakdown of an earlier, more seamless society. These ceremonies and structures function in a politically integrative way. Ritual is a repetitive activity for which outcomes and responses are essentially assured by social contract; it conveys the message that symbolic practice, via group membership and social rules, provides control (Cohen 1985). Ritual fosters the concept of control or domination, and has been seen to tend toward leadership roles (Hitchcock 1982) and centralized political structures (Lourandos 1985). A monopoly of ceremonial institutions clearly extends the concept of authority (Bender 1978), and may itself be the original formal authority.

Among agricultural tribes of New Guinea, leadership and the inequality it implies are based upon participation in hierarchies of ritual initiation or upon shamanistic spirit-mediumship (Kelly 1977, Modjeska 1982). In the role of shamans we see a concrete practice of ritual as it contributes to domination in human society.

Radin (1937) discussed "the same marked tendency" among Asian and North American tribal peoples for shamans or medicine men "to organize and develop the theory that they alone are in communication with the supernatural." This exclusive access seems to empower them at the expense of the rest; Lommel (1967) saw "an increase in the shaman's psychic potency...counterbalanced by a weakening of potency in other members of the group." This practice has fairly obvious implications for power relationships in other areas of life, and contrasts with earlier periods devoid of religious leadership.

The Batuque of Brazil are host to shamans who each claim control over certain spirits and attempt to sell supernatural services to clients, rather like priests of competing sects (S. Leacock 1988). Specialists of this type in "magically controlling nature...would naturally come to control men, too," in the opinion of Muller (1961). In fact, the shaman is often the most powerful individual in pre-agricultural societies (e.g. Sheehan 1985);

he is in a position to institute change. Johannessen (1987) offers the thesis that resistance to the innovation of planting was overcome by the influence of shamans, among the Indians of the American Southwest, for instance. Similarly, Marquardt (1985) has suggested that ritual authority structures have played an important role in the initiation and organization of production in North America. Another student of American groups (Ingold 1987) saw an important connection between shamans" role in mastering wildness in nature and an emerging subordination of women.

Berndt (1974a) has discussed the importance among Aborigines of ritual sexual division of labor in the development of negative sex roles, while Randolph (1988) comes straight to the point: "Ritual activity is needed to create "proper" men and women." There is "no reason in nature" for gender divisions, argues Bender (1989). "They have to be created by proscription and taboo, they have to be "naturalized" through ideology and ritual."

But gatherer-hunter societies, by their very nature, deny ritual its potential to domesticate women. The structure (non-structure?) of egalitarian bands, even those most oriented toward hunting, includes a guarantee of autonomy to both sexes. This guarantee is the fact that the materials of subsistence are equally available to women and men and that, further, the success of the band is dependent on cooperation based on that autonomy (Leacock 1978, Friedl 1975). The spheres of the sexes are often somewhat separate, but inasmuch as the contribution of women is generally at least equal to that of men, social equality of the sexes is "a key feature of forager societies" (Ehrenberg 1989b). Many anthropologists, in fact, have found the status of women in forager groups to be higher than in any other type of society (e.g. Fluer-Lobban 1979, Rohrlich-Leavitt, Sykes and Weatherford 1975, Leacock 1978).

In all major decisions, observed Turnbull (1970) of the Mbuti, "men and women have equal say, hunting and gathering being equally important." He made it clear (1981) that there is sexual differentiation—probably a good deal more than was the case with their distant forebears—"but without any sense of superordination or subordination." Men actually work more hours than women among the !Kung, according to Post and Taylor (1984).

It should be added, in terms of the division of labor common among contemporary gatherer-hunters, that this differentiation of roles is by no means universal. Nor was it when the Roman historian Tacitus wrote, of the Fenni of the Baltic region, that "the women support themselves by hunting, exactly like the men...and count their lot happier than that of others who groan over field labor." Or when Procopius found, in the sixth century A.D., that the Serithifinni of what is now Finland "neither till the land themselves, nor do their women work it for them, but the women regularly join the men in hunting."

The Tiwi women of Melville Island regularly hunt (Martin and Voorhies 1975) as do the Agta women in the Philippines (Estioko-Griffen and Griffen 1981). In Mbuti society, "there is little specialization according to sex. Even the hunt is a joint effort," reports Turnbull (1962), and Cotlow (1971) testifies that "among the traditional Eskimos it is (or was) a cooperative enterprise for the whole family group."

Darwin (1871) found another aspect of sexual equality: "...in utterly barbarous tribes the women have more power in choosing, rejecting, and tempting their lovers, or of afterwards changing their husbands, than might have been expected." The !Kung Bushmen and Mbuti exemplify this female autonomy, as reported by Marshall (1959) and Thomas (1965); "Women apparently leave a man whenever they are unhappy with their marriage," concluded Begler (1978). Marshall (1970) also found that rape was extremely rare or absent among the !Kung.

An intriguing phenomenon concerning gatherer-hunter women is their ability to prevent pregnancy in the absence of any contraception (Silberbauer 1981). Many hypotheses have been put forth and debunked, e.g. conception somehow related to levels of body fat (Frisch 1974, Leibowitz 1986). What seems a very plausible explanation is based on the fact that undomesticated people are very much more in tune with their physical selves. Foraging women's senses and processes are not alienated from themselves or dulled; control over childbearing is probably less than mysterious to those whose bodies are not foreign objects to be acted upon.

The Pygmies of Zaire celebrate the first menstrual period of every girl with a great festival of gratitude and rejoicing (Turnbull 1962). The young woman feels pride and pleasure, and the entire band expresses its happiness. Among agricultural villagers, however, a menstruating woman is regarded as unclean and dangerous, to be quarantined by taboo (Duffy 1984). The relaxed, egalitarian relationship between San men and women, with its flexibility of roles and mutual respect impressed Draper (1971, 1972, 1975); a relationship, she made clear, that endures as long as they remain gatherer-hunters and no longer.

Duffy (1984) found that each child in an Mbuti camp calls every man father and every woman mother. Forager children receive far more care, time, and attention than do those in civilization's isolated nuclear families. Post and Taylor (1984) described the "almost permanent contact" with their mothers and other adults that Bushman children enjoy. !Kung infants studied by Ainsworth (1967) showed marked precocity of early cognitive and motor skills development. This was attributed both to the exercise and stimulation produced by unrestricted freedom of movement, and to the high degree of physical warmth and closeness between !Kung parents and children (see also Konner 1976).

Draper (1976) could see that "competitiveness in games is almost entirely lacking among the !Kung," as Shostack (1976) observed "!Kung boys and girls playing together and sharing most games." She also found that children are not prevented from experimental sex play, consonant with the freedom of older Mbuti youth to "indulge in premarital sex with enthusiasm and delight" (Turnbull 1981). The Zuni "have no sense of sin," Ruth Benedict (1946) wrote in a related vein. "Chastity as a way of life is regarded with great disfavor...Pleasant relations between the sexes are merely one aspect of pleasant relations with human beings...Sex is an incident in a happy life."

Coontz and Henderson (1986) point to a growing body of evidence in support of the proposition that relations between the sexes are most egalitarian in the simplest foraging societies. Women play an essential role in traditional agriculture, but receive no corresponding status for their contribution, unlike the case of gatherer-hunter society (Chevillard and Leconte 1986, Whyte 1978). As with plants and animals, so are women subject to domestication with the coming of agriculture. Culture, securing its foundations with the new order, requires the firm subjugation of instinct, freedom, and sexuality. All disorder must be banished, the elemental and spontaneous taken firmly in hand. Women's creativity and their very being as sexual persons are pressured to give way to the role, expressed in all peasant religions, of Great Mother, that is, fecund breeder of men and food.

The men of the South American Munduruc, a farming tribe, refer to plants and sex in the same phrase about subduing women: "We tame them with the banana" (Murphy and Murphy 1985). Simone de Beauvoir (1949) recognized in the equation of the plow and the phallus a symbol of male authority over women. Among the Amazonian Jivaro, another agricultural group, women are beasts of burden and the personal property of men (Harner 1972); the "abduction of adult women is a prominent part of much warfare" by these lowland South American tribes (Ferguson 1988). Brutalization and isolation of women seem to be functions of agricultural societies (Gregor 1988), and the female continues to perform most or even all of the work in such groups (Morgan 1985).

Head-hunting is practiced by the above-mentioned groups, as part of endemic warfare over coveted agricultural land (Lathrap 1970); head-hunting and near-constant warring is also witnessed among the farming tribes of Highlands New Guinea (Watson 1970). Lenski and Lenski's 1974 researches concluded that warfare is rare among foragers but becomes extremely common with agrarian societies. As Wilson (1988) put it succinctly, "Revenge, feuds, rioting, warfare and battle seem to emerge among, and to be typical of, domesticated peoples."

Tribal conflicts, Godelier (1977) argues, are "explainable primarily by reference to colonial domination" and should not be seen as having an origin "in the functioning of pre-colonial structures." Certainly contact with civilization can have an unsettling, degenerative effect, but Godelier's Marxism (viz. unwillingness to question domestication/production), is, one suspects, relevant to such a judgment. Thus it could be said that the Copper Eskimos, who have a significant incidence of homicide within their group (Damas 1972), owe this violence to the impact of outside influences, but their reliance on domesticated dogs should also be noted.

Arens (1979) has asserted, paralleling Godelier to some extent, that cannibalism as a cultural phenomenon is a fiction, invented and promoted by agencies of outside conquest. But there is documentation of this practice (e.g. Poole 1983, Tuzin 1976) among, once again, peoples involved in domestication. The studies by Hogg (1966), for example, reveal its presence among certain African tribes, steeped in ritual and grounded in agriculture. Cannibalism is generally a form of cultural control of chaos, in which the victim represents animality, or all that should be tamed (Sanday 1986). Significantly, one of the important myths of Fiji Islanders, "How the Fijians first became cannibals," is literally a tale of planting (Sahlins 1983). Similarly, the highly domesticated and time-conscious Aztecs practiced human sacrifice as a gesture to tame unruly forces and uphold the social equilibrium of a very alienated society. As Norbeck (1961) pointed out, non-domesticated, "culturally impoverished" societies are devoid of cannibalism and human sacrifice.

As for one of the basic underpinnings of violence in more complex societies, Barnes (1970) found that "reports in the ethnographic literature of territorial struggles" between gatherer-hunters are "extremely rare." !Kung boundaries are vague and undefended (Lee 1979); Pandaram territories overlap, and individuals go where they please (Morris 1982); Hazda move freely from region to region (Woodburn 1968); boundaries and trespass have little or no meaning to the Mbuti (Turnbull 1966); and Australian Aborigines reject territorial or social demarcations (Gumpert 1981, Hamilton 1982). An ethic of generosity and hospitality takes the place of exclusivity (Steward 1968, Hiatt 1968).

Gatherer-hunter peoples have developed "no conception of private property," in the estimation of Kitwood (1984). As noted above in reference to sharing, and with Sansom's (1980) characterization of Aborigines as "people without property," foragers do not share civilization's obsession with externals.

"Mine and thine, the seeds of all mischief, have no place with them," wrote Pietro (1511) of the native North Americans encountered on the second voyage of Columbus. The Bushmen have "no sense of possession," according to Post (1958), and Lee (1972) saw them making "no sharp dichotomy between the resources of the natural environment and the social wealth." There is a line between nature and culture, again, and the non-civilized choose the former.

There are many gatherer-hunters who could carry all that they make use of in one hand, who die with pretty much what they had as they came into the world. Once humans shared everything; with agriculture, ownership becomes paramount and a species presumes to own the world. A deformation the imagination could scarcely equal.

Sahlins (1972) spoke of this eloquently: "The world's most primitive people have few possessions, but they are not poor. Poverty is not a certain small amount of goods, nor is it just a relation between means and ends; above all, it is a relation between people. Poverty is a social status. As such it is the invention of civilization."

The "common tendency" of gatherer-hunters "to reject farming until it was absolutely thrust upon them" (Bodley 1976) bespeaks a nature/culture divide also present in the Mbuti recognition that if one of them becomes a villager he is no longer an Mbuti (Turnbull 1976). They know that forager band and agriculturalist village are opposed societies with opposed values.

At times, however, the crucial factor of domestication can be lost sight of. "The historic foraging populations of the Western Coast of North America have long been considered anomalous among foragers," declared Cohen (1981); as Kelly (1991) also put it, "tribes of the Northwest Coast break all the stereotypes of hunter-gatherers." These foragers, whose main sustenance is fishing, have exhibited such alienated features as chiefs, hierarchy, warfare and slavery. But almost always overlooked are their domesticated tobacco and domesticated dogs. Even this celebrated "anomaly" contains features of domestication. Its practice, from ritual to production, with various accompanying forms of domination, seems to anchor and promote the facets of decline from an earlier state of grace.

Thomas (1981) provides another North American example, that of the Great Basin Shoshones and three of their component societies, the Kawich Mountain Shoshones, Reese River Shoshones, and Owens Valley Paiutes. The three groups showed distinctly different levels of agriculture, with increasing territoriality or ownership and hierarchy closely corresponding to higher degrees of domestication.

To "define" a disalienated world would be impossible and even undesirable, but I think we can and should try to reveal the unworld of today and how it got this way. We have taken a monstrously wrong turn with symbolic culture and division of labor, from a place of enchantment, understanding and wholeness to the absence we find at the heart of the doctrine of progress. Empty and emptying, the logic of domestication with its demand to control everything now shows us the ruin of the civilization that ruins the rest. Assuming the inferiority of nature enables the domination of cultural systems that soon will make the very Earth uninhabitable.

Postmodernism says to us that a society without power relations can only be an abstraction (Foucault, 1982). This is a lie unless we accept the death of nature and renounce what once was and what we can find again. Turnbull spoke of the intimacy between Mbuti people and the forest, dancing almost as if making love to the forest. In the bosom of a life of equals that is no abstraction, that struggles to endure, they were "dancing with the forest, dancing with the moon."

—1994

CHAPTER TWO

THE MASS PSYCHOLOGY OF MISERY

QUITE A WHILE AGO, just before the upheavals of the '60s—shifts that have not ceased, but have been forced in less direct, less public directions—Marcuse in his *One-Dimensional Man* described a populace characterized by flattened personality, satisfied and content. With the pervasive anguish of today, who could be so described? Therein lies a deep, if inchoate critique.

Much theorizing has announced the erosion of individuality's last remnants; but if this were so, if society now consists of the thoroughly homogenized and domesticated, how can there remain the enduring tension which must account for such levels of pain and loss? More and more people I have known have cracked up. It's going on to a staggering degree, in a context of generalized, severe emotional dis-ease.

Marx predicted, erroneously, that a deepening material immiseration would lead to revolt and to capital's downfall. Might it not be that an increasing psychic suffering is itself leading to the reopening of revolt—indeed, that this may even be the last hope of resistance?

And yet it is obvious that "mere" suffering is no guarantee of anything. "Desire does not 'want' revolution, it is revolutionary in its own right," as Deleuze and Guattari pointed out, while further on in *Anti-Oedipus*, remembering fascism, noting that people have desired against their own interests, and that tolerance of humiliation and enslavement remains widespread.

We know that behind psychic repression and avoidance stands social repression, even as massive denial shows at least some signs of giving way to a necessary confrontation with reality in all of its dimensions. Awareness of the social must not mean ignoring the personal, for that would only repeat, in its own terms, the main error of psychology. If in the nightmare of today each of us has his or her fears and limitations, there is no liberating route that forgets the primacy of the whole, including how that whole exists in each of us.

Stress, loneliness, depression, boredom—the madness of everyday life. Ever-greater levels of sadness, implying a recognition, on the visceral level at least, that things could be different. How much joy is there left in the technological society, this field of alienation and anxiety? Mental health epidemiologists suspect that no more than 20 percent of us are free of psychopathological symptoms. Thus we act out a "pathology of normalcy" marked by the chronic psychic impoverishment of a qualitatively unhealthy society.

Arthur Barsky's *Worried Sick* (1988) diagnoses an American condition where, despite all the medical "advances," the population has never felt such a "constant need for medical care." The crisis of the family and of personal life in general sees to it that the pursuit of health, and emotional health in particular, has reached truly industrial proportions. A work-life increasingly toxic, in every sense of the word, joins with the disintegration of the family to fuel the soaring growth of the corporate industrial health machine. But for a public in its misery dramatically more interested in health care than ever before, the dominant model of medical care is clearly only part of the problem, not its solution. Thus Thomas Bittker writes of "The Industrialization of American Psychiatry" (*American Journal of Psychiatry*, February 1985) and Gina Kolata discusses how much distrust of doctors exists, as medicine is seen as just another business (*New York Times*, February 20, 1990).

The mental disorder of going along with things as they are is now treated almost entirely by biochemicals, to reduce the individual's consciousness of socially induced anguish, tranquilizers are now the world's most widely prescribed drugs, and antidepressants set record sales as well. Temporary relief—despite side effects and addictive properties—is easily obtained, while we are all ground down a little more. The burden of simply getting by is "Why All Those People Feel They Never Have Any Time," according to Trish Hall (*New York Times*, January 2, 1988), who concluded that "everybody just seems to feel worn out" by it all.

An October 1989 Gallup poll found that stress-related illness is becoming the leading hazard in the nation's workplaces, and a month later an almost five-fold increase in California stress-related disability claims was reported to have occurred between 1982 and 1986. More recent figures estimate that almost two-thirds of new cases in employee assistance programs represent psychiatric or stress symptoms. In his *Modern Madness* (1986), Douglas La Bier asked, "What is it about work today that can cause such harm?" Part of the answer is found in a growing literature that reveals the Information Age "office of tomorrow" to be no better than the sweatshop of yesteryear. In fact, computerization introduces a neo-Taylorist monitoring of work that surpasses all earlier management control techniques. The "technological whip" now increasingly held over white-collar workers prompted Curt Supplee, in a January '90 *Washington Post* article, to judge, "We have seen the future, and it hurts." A few months earlier Sue Miller wrote in the *Baltimore Evening Sun* of another part of the job burnout picture, referring to a national clinical psychology study that determined that no less than a staggering 93 percent of American women "are caught up in a blues epidemic."

Meanwhile, the suicide and homicide rates are rising in the U.S. and 80 percent of the populace admit to having at least thought of suicide. Teenage suicide has risen enormously in the past three decades, and the number of teens locked up in mental wards has soared since 1970. So very many ways to gauge the pain: serious obesity among children has increased more than 50 percent in the last 15 to 20 years; severe eating disorders (bulimia and anorexia) among college women are now relatively common; sexual dysfunction is widespread; the incidence of panic and anxiety attacks is rising to the point of possibly overtaking depression as our most general psychological malady; isolation and a sense of meaninglessness continue to make even absurd cults and TV evangelism seem attractive to many.

The litany of cultural symptomatics is virtually endless. Despite its generally escapist function, much of contemporary film reflects the malaise; see Robert Phillip Kolker's *A Cinema of Loneliness: Penn, Kubrick, Scorsese, Spielberg, Altman*, for example. And many recent novels are even more unflinching in their depiction of the desolation and degradation of society, and the burnout of youth in particular, e.g. Bret Easton Ellis' *Less*

Than Zero, Fred Pfail's *Goodman 2020*, and *The Knockout Artist* by Harry Crews, to mention just a few.

In this context of immiseration, what is happening to prevailing values and mores is of signal interest in further situating our "mass psychology" and its significance. There are plenty of signs that the demand for "instant gratification" is more and more insistent, bringing with it outraged lamentations from both left and right and a further corrosion of the structure of repression.

Credit card fraud, chiefly the deliberate running up of bills, reached the billion-and-a-half-dollar level in 1988 as the personal bankruptcy solution to debt, which doubled between 1980 and 1990. Defaults on federal student loans more than quadrupled from 1983 to 1989.

In November 1989, in a totally unprecedented action, the U.S. Navy was forced to suspend operations worldwide for 48 hours owing to a rash of accidents involving deaths and injuries over the preceding three weeks. A total safety review was involved in the moratorium, which renewed discussion of drug abuse, absenteeism, unqualified personnel, and other problems threatening the Navy's very capacity to function.

Meanwhile, levels of employee theft reach ever-higher levels. In 1989 the Dallas Police Department reported a 29 percent increase in retail shrinkage over the previous five years, and a national survey conducted by London House said 62 percent of fast-food employees admitted stealing from employers. In early 1990 the FBI disclosed that shoplifting was up 35 percent since 1984, cutting heavily into retail profits.

November 1988 broke a 40-year mark for low voter turnout, continuing a downward direction in electoral participation that has plagued presidential elections since 1960. Average college entrance exam (SAT) scores declined throughout the '70s and early '80s, then rebounded very slightly, and in 1988 continued to fall. At the beginning of the '80s Arthur Levin's portrait of college students, *When Dreams and Heroes Died*, recounted "a generalized cynicism and lack of trust," while at the end of the decade Robert Nisbet's *The Present Age: Progress and Anarchy in North America* decried the disastrous effects that the younger generation's attitude of "hanging loose" was having on the system. George F. Will, for his part, reminded us all that social arrangements, including the authority of the government, rest "on a willingness of the public to believe in them," and Harvard economist Harvey Liebenstein's *Inside the Firm* echoed him in stressing that companies must depend on the kind of work their employees want to do.

The nation's high schools now graduate barely 70 percent of students who enter as freshmen, despite massive focus on the dropout rate problem. As Michael de Courcy Hinds put it (*New York Times*, February 17, 1990), "U.S. educators are trying almost anything to keep children in school," while an even more fundamental phenomenon is the rising number of people of all ages unwilling to learn to read and write. David Harman (*Illiteracy: A National Dilemma*, 1987) gave voice to how baffling the situation is, asking why has the acquisition of such skills, "seemingly so simple, been so evasive?"

The answer may be that literacy, like schooling, is increasingly seen to be valued merely for its contribution to the workplace. The refusal of literacy is but another sign of a deep turn-off from the system, part of the spreading disaffection. In mid-1988 a Hooper survey indicated that work now ranks eighth out of ten on a scale of important satisfactions in life, and 1989 showed the lowest annual productivity growth since the 1981–83 recession. The drug "epidemic," which cost the government almost $25 billion to combat in the '80s, threatens society most acutely at the level of the refusal of work and sacrifice. There is no "war on drugs" that can touch the situation while at the same time defending this landscape of pain and false values. The need for escape grows stronger and the sick social order feels consequent desertion, the steady corrosion of all that holds it up.

Unfortunately, the biggest "escape" of all is one that serves, in the main, to preserve the distorted present: what Sennett has called "the increasing importance of psychology in bourgeois life." This includes the extraordinary proliferation of new kinds of therapy since the '60s, and behind this phenomenon the rise of psychology as the predominant religion. In the Psychological Society the individual sees himself as a problem. This ideology constitutes a preeminent social imprisonment, because it denies the social; psychology refuses to consider that society as a whole shares fundamental responsibility for the conditions produced in every human being.

The ramifications of this ideology can be seen on all sides. For instance, the advice to those besieged by work stress to "take a deep breath, laugh, walk it off," etc. Or the moralizing exhortations to recycle, as if a personal ethics of consumption is a real answer to the global eco-crisis caused by industrial production. Or the 1990 California Task Force to Promote Self-Esteem as a solution to the major social breakdown in that state.

At the very center of contemporary life, this outlook legitimates alienation, loneliness, despair, and anxiety, because it cannot see the context for our malaise. It privatizes distress, and suggests that only non-social responses are attainable. This "bottomless fraud of mere inwardness," in Adorno's words, pervades every aspect of American life, mystifying experience and thus perpetuating oppression.

The widespread allegiance to a therapeutic worldview constitutes a culture tyrannized by the therapeutic in which, in the name of mental health, we are getting mental disease. With the expanding influence of behavioral experts, powerlessness and estrangement expand as well; modern life must be interpreted for us by the new expertise and its popularizers.

Gail Sheehy's *Passages* (1977), for example, considers life developments without reference to any social or historical context, thereby vitiating her concern for the "free and autonomous self." Arlie Russell Hochschild's *Managed Heart* (1983) focuses on the "commercialization of human feelings" in an increasingly service-sector economy, and manages to avoid any questioning of the totality by remaining ignorant of the fact of class society and the unhappiness it produces. *When Society Becomes an Addict* (1987) is Anne Wilson Schaef's completely incoherent attempt to deny, despite the title, the existence of society, by dealing strictly with the interpersonal. And these books are among the least escapist of the avalanche of "how-to" therapy books inundating the bookstores and supermarkets.

It is clear that psychology is part of the absence of community or solidarity, and of the accelerating social disintegration. The emphasis is on changing one's personality, and avoiding at all costs the facts of bureaucratic consumer capitalism and its meaning to our lives and consciousness. Consider Samuel Klarreich's *Stress Solution* (1988): "...I believe that we can largely determine what will be stressful, and how much it will interfere with our lives, by the views we uphold irrespective of what goes on in the workplace." Under the sign of productivity, the citizen is now trained as a lifelong inmate of an industrial world, a condition, as Ivan Illich noted, not unrelated to the fact that everyone tends toward the condition of therapy's patient, or at least tends to accept its worldview.

In the Psychological Society, social conflicts of all kinds are auto-matically shifted to the level of psychic problems, in order that they can be charged to individuals as private matters. Schooling produces near-universal resistance, which is classified, for example, as "hyperkinesis" and dealt with by drugs and/or psychiatric ideology. Rather than recognize the child's protest, his or her life is invaded still further, to ensure that no one eludes the therapeutic net.

It is clear that a retreat from the social, based largely on the experience of defeat and consequent resignation, promotes the personal as the only possible terrain of authenticity. A desperate denizen of the "singles world" is quoted by Louise Banikow: "My ambition is wholly personal now. All I want to do is fall in love." But the demand for fulfillment, however circumscribed by psychology, is that of a ravening hunger and a level of suffering that threaten to burst the bonds of the prescribed inner world. As noted above, indifference to authority, distrust of institutions, and a spreading nihilism mean that the therapeutic can neither satisfy the individual nor ultimately safeguard the social order. Toynbee noted that a decadent culture furthers the rise of a new church that extends hope to the proletariat while servicing only the needs of the ruling class. Perhaps sooner than later People will begin to realize that psychology is this Church, which may be the reason why so many voices of therapy now counsel their flocks against "unrealistic expectations" of what life could be.

For over half a century the regulative, hierarchical needs of a bureaucratic-consumerist system have sought modern means of control and prediction. The same consolatory ideology of the psychological outlook, in which the self is the overarching form of reality, has served these control needs and owes most of its assumptions to Sigmund Freud.

For Freud and his Wagnerian theory of warring instincts and the arbitrary division of the self into id, ego and superego, the passions of the individual were primordial and dangerous. The work of civilization was to check and harness them. The whole edifice of psychoanalysis, Freud said, is based upon the theory of necessary repression; domination is obviously assisted by this view. That human culture is established only by means of suffering, that constant renunciation of desire is inevitable for continuance of civilization, that work is sustained by the energy of stifled love—all this is required by the "natural aggressiveness" of "human nature," the latter an eternal and universal fact, of course. Understanding fully the deforming force of all this repression, Freud considered it likely that neurosis has come to characterize all of humanity. Despite his growing fear of fascism after

World War I, he nonetheless contributed to its growth by justifying the renunciation of happiness. Reich referred to Freud and Hitler with some bitterness, observing that "a few years later, a pathological genius—making the best of ignorance and fear of happiness—brought Europe to the verge of destruction with the slogan of 'heroic renunciation'."

With the Oedipus complex, inescapable source of guilt and repression, we see Freud again as the consummate Hobbesian. This universal condition is the vehicle whereby self-imposed taboos are learned via the (male) childhood experience of fear of the father and lust for the mother. It is based on Freud's reactionary fairy tale of a primal horde dominated by a powerful father who possessed all available women and who was killed and devoured by his sons. This was ludicrous anthropology even when penned, and fully exhibits one of Freud's most basic errors, that of equating society with civilization. There is now convincing evidence that precivilized life was a time of non-dominance and equality, certainly not the bizarre patriarchy Freud provided as origin of most of our sense of guilt and shame. He remained convinced of the inescapability of the Oedipal background, and the central validity of both the Oedipal complex and of guilt itself for the interests of culture.

Freud considered psychic life as shut in on itself, uninfluenced by society. This premise leads to a deterministic view of childhood and even infancy, along with such judgments as "the fear of becoming poor is derived from regressive anal eroticism." Consider his *Psychopathology of Everyday Life*, and its 10 editions between 1904 and 1924 to which new examples of "slips," or unintended revelatory usages of words, were continually added. We do not find a single instance, despite the upheavals of many of those years in and near Austria, of Freud detecting a "slip" that related to fear of revolution on the part of this bourgeois subjects, or even of any day-to-day social fears, such as related to strikes, insubordination, or the like. It seems more than likely that unrepressed slips concerning such matters were simply screened out as unimportant to his universalist, ahistorical views.

Also worth noting is Freud's "discovery" of the death instinct. In his deepening pessimism, he countered Eros, the life instinct, with Thanatos, a craving for death and destruction, as fundamental and ineradicable a part of the species as striving for life. "The aim of all life is death," simply put (1920). While it may be pedestrian to note that this discovery was accompanied by the mass carnage of World War I, an increasingly unhappy marriage, and the onset of cancer of the jaw, there is no mistaking the service this dystopian metaphysics performs in justifying authority. The assumption of the death instinct—that aggression, hatred, and fear will always be with us—militates against the idea that liberation is possible. In later decades, the death instinct-oriented work of Melanie Klein flourished in English ruling circles precisely because of its emphasis on social restraints in limiting aggressiveness. Today's leading neo-Freudian, Lacan, also seems to see suffering and domination as inevitable; specifically, he holds that patriarchy is a law of nature.

Marcuse, Norman O. Brown and others have re-theorized Freud in a radical direction by taking his ideas as descriptive rather than prescriptive, and there is a limited plausibility to an orientation that takes his dark views as valid only with respect to alienated life, rather than to any and all imaginable social worlds. There are even many Freudian feminists; their efforts to apply psychoanalytic dogma to the oppression of women, however, appear even more contrived.

Freud did identify the "female principle" as closer to nature, less sublimated, less diffused through repression than that of the male. But true to his overall values, he located an essential advance in civilization in the victory of male intellectuality over womanly sensuality. What is saddest about the various attempts to reappropriate Freud is the absence of a critique of civilization: his entire work is predicated on the acceptance of civilization as highest value. And basic in a methodological sense, regarding those who would merely reorient the Freudian edifice, is Foucault's warning that the will to any system "is to extend our participation in the present system."

In the area of gender difference, Freud straightforwardly affirmed the basic inferiority of the female. His view of women as castrated men is a case of biological determinism: anatomically they are simply less, and condemned by this to masochism and penis envy.

I make no pretense to completeness or depth in this brief look at Freud, but it should be already obvious how false was his disclaimer (*New Introductory Lectures*, 1933) that Freudianism posits any values beyond those inherent in "objective" science. And to this fundamental failing could be added the arbitrary nature of virtually all of his philosophy. Divorced as it pointedly is from gross social reality—further examples are legion, but seduction theory comes to mind, in which he declared that sexual abuse is, most importantly, fantasy—one Freudian inference could just as plausibly be replaced by a different one. Overall, we encounter, in the summary of Frederick Crews, "a doctrine plagued by mechanism, reification, and arbitrary universalism."

On the level of treatment, by his own accounts, Freud never was able to permanently cure a single patient, and psychoanalysis has proven no more effective since. In 1984 the National Institute of Mental Health estimated that over 40 million Americans are mentally ill, while a study by Regier, Boyd et al. (*Archives of General Psychiatry*, November 1988) showed that 15 percent of the adult population had a "psychiatric disorder." One obvious dimension of this worsening situation, in Joel Kovel's words, is the contemporary family, which "has fallen into a morass of permanent crisis," as indicated by the endless stream of emotionally disabled individuals it turns over to the mental health industry.

If alienation is the essence of all psychiatric conditions, psychology is the study of the alienated, but lacks the awareness that this is so. The effect of the total society, in which the individual can no longer recognize himself or herself, by the canons of Freud and the Psychological Society, is seen as irrelevant to diagnosis and treatment. Thus psychiatry appropriates disabling pain and frustration, redefines them as illnesses and, in some cases, is able to suppress the symptoms. Meanwhile, a morbid world continues its estranging technological rationality that excludes any continuously spontaneous, affective life: the person is subjected to a discipline designed, at the expense of the sensuous, to make him or her an instrument of production.

Mental illness is primarily an unconscious escape from this design, a form of passive resistance. R.D. Laing spoke of schizophrenia as a psychic numbing which feigns a kind of death to preserve something of one's inner aliveness. The representative schizophrenic is around 20, at the point of culmination of the long period of socialization that has prepared him to take up his role in the workplace. He is not "adequate" to this destiny. Historically, it is noteworthy that schizophrenia is very closely related to industrialism, as Torrey shows convincingly in his *Schizophrenia and Civilization* (1980).

In recent years Szasz, Foucault, Goffman, and others have called attention to the ideological preconceptions through which "mental illness" is seen. "Objective" language cloaks cultural biases, as in the case, for instance, of sexual "disorders": in the nineteenth century masturbation was treated as a disease, and it has only been within the past 20 years that the psychological establishment declassified homosexuality as illness.

And it has long been transparent that there is a class component to the origins and treatment of mental illness. Not only is what is called "eccentric" among the rich often termed psychiatric disorder—and treated quite differently—among the poor, but many studies since Hollingshead and Redlich's *Social Class and Mental Illness* (1958) have demonstrated how much more likely are the poor to become emotionally disabled. Roy Porter observed that because it imagines power, madness is both impotence and omnipotence, which serves as a reminder that due to the influence of alienation, powerlessness, and poverty, women are more often driven to breakdown than men. Society makes us all feel manipulated and thus mistrustful: "paranoid," and who could not be depressed? The gap between the alleged neutrality and wisdom of the medical model and the rising levels of pain and disease is widening, the credibility of the former visibly corroding.

It has been the failure of earlier forms of social control that has given psychological medicine, with its inherently expansionist aims, its upward trajectory in the past three decades. The therapeutic model of authority (and the supposedly value-free professional power that backs it up) is increasingly intertwined with state power, and has mounted an invasion of the self much more far-reaching than earlier efforts. "There are no limits to the ambition of psychoanalytic control; if it had its way, nothing would escape it," according to Guattari.

In terms of the medicalization of deviant behavior, a great deal more is included, than, say, the psychiatric sanctions on Soviet dissidents or the rise of a battery of mind control techniques, including behavior modification, in U.S. prisons. Punishment has come to include treatment, and treatment new powers of punishment; medicine, psychology, education and social work take over more and more aspects of control and discipline while the legal machinery grows more medical, psychological, pedagogical. But the new arrangements, relying chiefly on fear and necessitating more and more cooperation by the ruled in order to function, are no guarantee of civic harmony. In fact, with their overall failure, class society is running out of tactics and excuses, and the new encroachments have created new pockets of resistance.

The setup now usually referred to as "community mental health" can be legitimately traced to the establishment of the Mental Hygiene Movement in 1908. In the context of the Taylorist degradation of work called Scientific Management and a challenging tide of worker militancy, the new psychological offensive was based on the dictum that "individual unrest to a large degree means bad mental hygiene." Community psychiatry represents a later, nationalized form of this industrial psychology, developed to deflect radical currents away from social transformation objectives and back under the yoke of the dominating logic of productivity. By the 1920s, the workers had become the objects of social science professionals to an even greater degree, with the work of Elton Mayo and others, at a time when the promotion of consumption as a way of life came to be seen as itself a means of easing unrest, collective and individual. And by the end of the 1930s, industrial psychology had "already developed many of the central innovations which now characterize community psychology," according to Diana Ralph's *Work and Madness* (1983), such as mass psychological testing, the mental health team, auxiliary non-professional counselors, family and outpatient therapy, and psychiatric counseling to businesses.

The million-plus men rejected by the armed forces during World War II for "mental unfitness" and the steady rise, observable since the mid-'50s, in stress-related illnesses, called attention to the immensely crippling nature of modern industrial alienation. Government funding was called for, and was provided by the 1963 federal Community Mental Health Center legislation. Armed with the relatively new tranquilizing drugs to anaesthetize the poor as well as the unemployed, a state presence was initiated in urban areas hitherto beyond the reach of the therapeutic ethos. Small wonder that some black militants saw the new mental health services as basically refined police pacification and surveillance systems for the ghettos. The concerns of the dominant order, ever anxious about the masses, are chiefly served, however, here as elsewhere, by the strength of the image of what science has shown to be normal, healthy, and productive. Authority's best friend is relentless self-inspection according to the ruling canons of repressive normalcy in the Psychological Society.

The nuclear family once provided the psychic underpinning of what Norman O. Brown called "the nightmare of infinitely expanding technological progress." Thought by some to be a bastion against the outer world, it has always served as transmission belt for the reigning ideology, more specifically as the place in which the interiorizing psychology of women is produced, the social and economic exploitation of women is legitimated, and the artificial scarcity of sexuality is guarded.

Meanwhile, the state's concern with delinquent, uneducable and unsocializable children, as studied by Donzelot and others, is but one aspect of its overshadowing of the family. Behind the medicalized image of the good, the state advances and the family steadily loses its functions. Rothbaum and Weisz, in *Child Psychopathology and the Quest for Control* (1989), discuss the very rapid rise of their subject, while Castel, Castel and Lovell's earlier *The Psychiatric Society* (1982) could glimpse the nearing day "when childhood will be totally regimented by medicine and psychology." Some facets of this trend are no longer in the realm of conjecture; James R. Schiffman, for instance, wrote of one by-product of the battered family in his "Teen-Agers End Up in Psychiatric Hospitals in Alarming Numbers" (*Wall Street Journal*, Feb. 3, 1989).

Therapy is a key ritual of our prevailing psychological religion and a vigorously growing one. The American Psychiatric Association's membership jumped from 27,355 in 1983 to 36,223 by the end of the '80s, and in 1989 a record 22 million visited psychiatrists or other therapists covered to at least some extent by health insurance plans. Considering that only a small minority of those who practice the estimated 500 varieties of psychotherapy are psychiatrists or otherwise health insurance-recognized, even these figures do not capture the magnitude of therapy's shadow world.

Philip Rieff termed psychoanalysis "yet another method of learning how to endure the loneliness produced by culture," which is a good enough way to introduce the artificial situation and relationship of therapy, a peculiarly distanced, circumscribed and asymmetrical affair. Most of the time, one person talks and the other listens. The client almost always talks about himself and the therapist almost never does. The therapist scrupulously eschews social contact with clients, another reminder to the latter that they have not been talking to a friend, along with the strict time limits enclosing a space divorced from everyday reality. Similarly, the purely contractual nature of the therapeutic connection in itself guarantees that all therapy inevitably reproduces alienated society. To deal with alienation via a relationship paid for by the hour is to overlook the congruence of therapist and prostitute as regards the traits just enumerated.

Gramsci defined "intellectual" as the "functionary in charge of consent," a formulation which also fits the role of therapist. By leading others to concentrate their "desiring energy outside the social territory," as Guattari put it, he thereby manipulates them into accepting the constraints of society. By failing to challenge the social categories within which clients have organized their experiences, the therapist strengthens the hold of those categories. He tries, typically, to focus clients away from stories about work and into the so-called "real" areas—personal life and childhood.

Psychological health, as a function of therapy, is largely an educational procedure. The project is that of a shared system: the client is led to acceptance of the therapist's basic assumptions and metaphysics. Francois Roustang, in *Psychoanalysis Never Lets Go* (1983), wondered why a therapeutic method whose "explicit aim is the liberation of forces with a view toward being capable 'of enjoyment and efficiency" (Freud) so often ends in alienation either...because the treatment turns out to be interminable, or...(the client) adopts the manner of speech and thought, the theses as well as the prejudices of psychoanalysis."

Ever since Hans Lysenko's short but famous article of 1952, "The Effects of Psychotherapy," countless other studies have validated his finding: "Persons given intensive and prolonged psychotherapy are no better off than those in matched control groups given no treatment over the same time interval." On the other hand, there is no doubt that therapy or counseling does make many people feel better, regardless of specific results. This anomaly must be due to the fact that consumers of therapy believe they have been cared for, comforted, listened to. In a society growing ever colder, this is no small thing. It is also true that the Psychological Society conditions its subjects into blaming themselves and that those who most feel they need therapy tend to be those most easily exploited: the loneliest, most insecure, nervous, depressed, etc. It is easy to state the old dictum, "Natura sanat, medicus curat" (Nature heals, doctors/counselors/therapists treat); but where is the natural in the hyper-estranged world of pain and isolation we find ourselves in? And yet there is no getting around the imperative to remake the world. If therapy is to heal, make whole, what other possibility is there but to transform this world, which would of course also constitute a de-therapizing of society. It is clearly in this spirit that the Situationist International declared in 1963, "Sooner or later the S.I. must define itself as a therapeutic."

Unfortunately, the great communal causes later in the decade acquired a specifically therapeutic cast mainly in their degeneration, in the splintering of the '60s thrust into smaller, more idiosyncratic efforts. "The personal is the political" gave way to the merely personal, as defeat and disillusion overtook naive activism.

Conceived out of critical responses to Freudian psychoanalysis, which has shifted its sights toward ever-earlier phases of development in childhood and infancy, the Human Potential Movement began in the mid-'60s and acquired its characteristic features by the early '70s. With a post-Freudian emphasis on the conscious ego and its actualization, Human Potential set forth a smorgasbord of therapies, including varieties or amalgams of personal growth seminars, body awareness techniques, and Eastern spiritual disciplines. Almost buried in the welter of partial solutions lies a subversive potential: the notion that, as Adelaide Bry put it, life "can be a time of infinite and joyous possibility." The demand for instant relief from psychic immiseration underlined an increasing concern for the dignity and fulfillment of individuals, and Daniel Yankelovich (*New Rules*, 1981) saw the cultural centrality of this quest, concluding that by the end of the '70s, some 80 percent of Americans had become interested in this therapeutic search for transformation.

But the privatized approaches of the Human Potential Movement, high-water mark of contemporary Psychological Society, were obviously unable to deliver on their promises to provide any lasting, non-illusory breakthroughs. Arthur Janov recognized that "everyone in this society is in a lot of pain," but expressed no awareness at all of the repressive society generating it. His Primal Scream technique qualifies as the most ludicrous cure-all of the '70s. Scientology's promise of empowerment consisted mainly of bioelectronic feedback technologies aimed at socializing people to an authoritarian enterprise and worldview. The popularity of cult groups like the Moonies reminds one of a time-tested process for the uninitiated: isolation, deprivation, anticipation, and suggestion; brainwashing and the shamanic vision quest both use it.

Werner Erhard's est, speaking of intensive psychological manipulation, was one of the most popular and, in some ways, most characteristic Human Potential phenomena. Its founder became very wealthy by helping Erhard Seminars Training adepts "choose to become what they are." In a classic case of blaming the victim, est brought large numbers to a near-religious embrace of one of the system's basic lies: its graduates are obediently conformist because they "accept responsibility" for having created things as they are. Transcendental Meditation actually marketed itself in terms of the passive incorporation into society it helped its students achieve. TM's alleged usefulness for adjustment to the varied "excesses and stresses" of modern society was a major selling point to corporations, for example.

Trapped in a highly rationalized and technological world, Human Potential seekers naturally wanted personal development, emotional immediacy, and above all, a sense of having some control over their lives. Self-help best-sellers of the '70s, including *Power, Your Erroneous Zones, How to Take Charge of Your Life, Self-Creation, Looking Out for #1*, and *Pulling Your Own Strings*, focus on the issue of control. Preaching the gospel of reality as a personal construct, however, meant that control had to be narrowly defined. Once again acceptance of social reality as a given meant, for example, that "sensitivity training" would likely mean continued insensitivity to most of reality, an openness to more of the same alienation—more ignorance, more suffering.

The Human Potential Movement did at least raise publicly and widely the notion of an end to disease, however much it failed to make good on that claim. As more and more of everyday life has come under medical dominion and supervision, the almost bewildering array of new therapies was part of an undercutting of the older, mainly Freudian, "scientific" model for behavior. In the shift of therapeutic expectations, a radical hope appeared, which went beyond merely positive-thinking or empty confessionalist aspects and is different from quiescence.

A current form of self-help that clearly represents a step forward from both traditional therapy, commodified and under the direction of expertise, and the mass-marketed seminar-introduction sort of training, is the very popular "support group." Non-commercial and based on peer-group equality, support groups for many types of emotional distress have quadrupled in number in the past 10 years. Where these groups do not enforce the 12-step ideology of "anonymous" groups (e.g. Alcoholics Anonymous) based on the individual's subjection to a "Higher Power" (read: all constituted authority)—and most of them do not—they provide a great source of solidarity, and work against the depoliticizing force of illness or distress experienced in an isolated state.

If the Human Potential Movement thought it possible to re-create personality and thus transform life, New Ageism goes it one better with its central slogan, "Create your own reality." Considering the advancing, invasive desolation, an alternative reality seems desirable–the eternal consolation of religion. For the New Age, booming since the mid-1980s, is essentially a religious turning away from reality by people who are overloaded by feelings of helplessness and powerlessness, a more definitive turning away than that of the prevailing psychologistic evasion. Religion invents a realm of non-alienation to compensate for the actual one; New Age philosophy announces a coming new era of harmony and peace, obviously inverting the present, unacceptable state. An undemanding, eclectic, materialistic substitute religion where any balm, any occult nonsense—channeling, crystal healing, reincarnation, rescue by UFOs, etc.—goes. "It's true if you believe it."

Anything goes, so long as it goes along with what authority has ordained: anger is "unhealthy," "negativity" a condition to be avoided at all costs. Feminism and ecology are supposedly "roots" of the New Age scene, but likewise were militant workers a "root" of the Nazi movement (National Socialist German Workers Party, remember). Which brings to mind the chief New Age influence, Carl Jung. It is unknown or irrelevant to "nonjudgmental" bliss-seekers that in his attempt to resurrect all the old faiths and myths, Jung was less a psychologist than a figure of theology and reaction. Further, as president of the International Society for Psychotherapy from 1933 to 1939, he presided over its Nazified German section and co-edited the *Zentralblattfur Psychotherapie* (with M.H. Göring, cousin of the Reichsmarshall of the same name).

Still gathering steam, apparently, since the appearance of Otto Kernberg's *Borderline Conditions and Pathological Narcissism* (1975) and *The Culture of Narcissism* by Christopher Lasch (1978), is the idea that "narcissistic personality disorders" are the epitome of what is happening to all of us, and represent the "underlying character structure" of our age. Narcissus, the image of self-love and a growing demand for fulfillment, has replaced Oedipus, with its components of guilt and repression, as the myth of our time—a shift proclaimed and adopted far beyond the Freudian community.

In passing, it is noteworthy that this change, underway since the '60s, seems to connect more with the Human Potential search for self-development than with New Age whose devotees take their desires less seriously. Common New Age nostrums, e.g. "You are infinitely creative," "You have unlimited potential," smack of a vague wish-fulfillment sanitized against anger, by those who doubt their own capacities for change and growth. Though the concept of narcissism is somewhat elusive, clinically and socially, it is often expressed in a demanding, aggressive way that frightens various partisans of traditional authority. The Human Potential preoccupation with "getting in touch with one's feelings," it must be added, was not nearly as strongly self-affirming as narcissism is, where feelings— chiefly anger—are more powerful than those that need to be searched for.

Lasch's *Culture of Narcissism* remains extremely influential as a social analysis of the transition from Oedipus to Narcissus, given great currency and publicity by those who lament this turning away from internalized sacrifice and respect for authority. The "new leftist" Lasch proved himself a strict Freudian, and an overtly conservative one at that, looking back nostalgically at the days of the authoritarian conscience based on strong parental and social discipline. There is no trace of refusal in Lasch's work, which embraces the existing repressive order as the only available morality. Similar to his sour rejection of the "impulse-ridden" narcissistic personality is Neil Postman's *Amusing Ourselves to Death* (1985). Postman moralizes about the decline of political discourse, no longer "serious" but "shriveled and absurd," a condition caused by the widespread attitude that "amusement and pleasure" take precedence over "serious public involvement." Sennett and Bookchin can be mentioned as two other erstwhile radicals who see the narcissistic withdrawal from the present political framework as anything but positive or subversive. But even an orthodox Freudian like Russell Jacoby (*Telos*, Summer 1980) recognized that in the corrosion of sacrifice, "narcissism harbors a protest in the name of individual health and happiness," and Gilles Lipovetsky considered narcissism in France to have been born during the May '68 uprisings.

Thus narcissism is more than just the location of desire in the self, or the equally ubiquitous necessity to maintain feelings of self-identity and self-esteem. There are more and more "narcissistically troubled" people, products of the lovelessness and extreme alienation of modern divided society, and its cultural and spiritual impoverishment. Deep feelings of emptiness characterize the narcissist, coupled with a boundless rage, often just under the surface, at the sense of dependency felt because of dominated life, and the hollowness of one starved by a deficient reality.

Freudian theory attributes the common trait of defiance to an immature "clinging to anal eroticism," while ignoring Society just as Lasch expresses his fear of narcissistic resentment and insubordination" in a parallel defense of oppressive existence. The angry longing for autonomy and self-worth brings to mind another clash of values that relates to value itself. In each of us lives a narcissist who wants to be loved for himself or herself and not for his or her abilities, or even qualities. Value per se, intrinsic—a dangerously anti-instrumental, anti-capital orientation. To a Freudian therapist like Arnold Rothstein, this "expectation that the world should gratify him just because he wishes it" is repugnant. He prescribes lengthy psychoanalysis that will ultimately permit an acceptance of "the relative passivity, helplessness, and vulnerability implicit in the human condition."

Others have seen in narcissism the hunger for a qualitatively different world. Norman O. Brown referred to its project of "loving union with the world," while the feminist Stephanie Engel has argued that "the call back to the memory of original narcissistic bliss pushes us toward a dream of the future." Marcuse saw narcissism as an essential element of utopian thought, a mythic structure celebrating and yearning for completeness.

The Psychological Society offers, of course, every variety of commodity, from clothes and cars to books and therapies, for every lifestyle, in a vain effort to assuage the prevailing appetite for authenticity. Debord was right in his counsel that the more we capitulate to a recognition of self in the dominant images of need, the less we understand our own existence and desires. The images society provides do not permit us to find ourselves at home there, and one sees instead a ravening, infuriating sense of denial and loss, which nominates "narcissism" as a subversive configuration of misery.

Two centuries ago Schiller spoke of the "wound" civilization has inflicted on modern humanity: division of labor. In announcing the age of "psychological man," Philip Rieff discerned a culture "in which technics is invading and conquering the last enemy—man's inner life, the psyche itself." In the specialist culture of our bureaucratic-industrial age, the reliance on experts to interpret and evaluate inner life is in itself the most malignant and invasive reach of division of labor. As we have become more alien from our own experiences, which are processed, standardized, labeled, and subjected to hierarchical control, technology emerges as the power behind our misery and the main form of ideological domination. In fact, technology comes to replace ideology. The force deforming us stands increasingly revealed, while illusions are ground away by the process of immiseration.

43

Lasch and others may resent and try to discount the demanding nature of the contemporary "psychological" spirit, but what is contested has clearly widened for a great many, even if the outcome is equally unclear. Thus the Psychological Society may be failing to deflect or even defer conflict by means of its favorite question, "Can one change?" The real question is whether the world-that-enforces-our-inability-to-change can be forced to change, and beyond recognition.

CHAPTER THREE

TONALITY AND THE TOTALITY

THE DEFINING OF SENTIMENTS has always been a preoccupation of religions and governments. But for quite some time music, with its apparent indifference to external reality, has been developing an ideological power of expression hitherto unknown. Originally music was a utility to establish the rhythms of work, the rhythms of dances which were ritual observances. And we know that it was treated as a vital symbolic reinforcement of the "harmony" of ancient Chinese hierarchical society, just as to Plato and Aristotle it embodied key moral functions in the social order. The Pythagorean belief that "the whole cosmos is a harmony and a number" leapt from the fact of natural sonic phenomena to an all-encompassing philosophical idealism, and was echoed about a thousand years later by the seventh-century encyclopedist Isadore of Seville, who asserted that the universe "is held together by a certain harmony of sounds, and the heavens themselves are made to revolve" by its modulations. As Sancho Panza said to the duchess (another thousand years down the road), who was distressed at hearing the distant sound of an orchestra in the forest, "Where there is music, Madam, there could be no mischief."

Indeed, many things have been said to characterize the elusive element we know as music. Stravinsky, for example, was quite serious in denying its expressive, emotional aspect: "The phenomenon of music is given to us for the sole purpose of establishing order in things, and chiefly between man and time." It does seem clear that music calms the sense of time's oppressiveness, by offering, in its patterns of tensions and resolutions, a temporal counterworld. As Lévi-Strauss put it, "Because of the internal organization of the musical work, the act of listening to it immobilizes passing time; it catches and enfolds it as one catches and enfolds a cloth flapping in the wind."

But, contra Stravinsky, there is clearly more to music, more to its compelling appeal, of which Homer said, "We only hear, we know nothing." Part of its mysterious resonance, if you will, is its simultaneous universality and immediacy. Herein lies also its ambiguity, a cardinal feature of all art. An Eisenstadt photograph of 1934, entitled "The Room in which Beethoven was Born," testifies to the latter point; just as he was about to take the picture, a party of Nazis arrived and placed a commemorative wreath—shown in the foreground—before the room's bust of Beethoven.

So the great genre of inwardness that is music has been appropriated to many purposes and philosophies. To the Marxist Bloch, it is a realm where the utopian horizon already "begins at our feet." It lets us hear what we do not have, as in Marcuse's poetic formulation that music is "a remembrance of what could be." Although representation is already reconciliation with society, there is always a moment of longing in music. "Something is lacking, and sound at least states this lack clearly. Sound has itself something dark and thirsty about it and blows about instead of stopping in one place, like paint," to quote Bloch once more. Adorno insisted that the truth of music is "guaranteed more by its denial of any meaning in organized society," consonant with a retreat into aesthetics as his choice for the last repository of negation in an administered world.

Music, however, like all art, owes its existence to the division of labor in society. Although it is still generally seen in isolation, as personal creation and autonomous sphere, social meaning and values are always encoded in music. This truth coexists with the fact that music refers to nothing other than itself as is often said, and that what it signifies is, at base, always determined solely by its inner relationships. It is valid to point out, alter Adorno, that music can be understood as "a kind of analogue to that of social theory'" If it keeps open "the irrational doorways" through which we glimpse "the wildness and the pang of life," according to Aaron Copland, its ideological component must also be recognized, especially when it claims to transcend social reality and its antagonisms.

In "The Rational and Social Foundations of Music" Weber (as elsewhere) concerned himself with the disenchantment of the world, in this case searching out the irrational musical elements (e.g. the 7th chord) which seemed to him to have escaped the rationalistic equalization that characterizes the development of modern bureaucratic society. But if non-rationalized nature is a rebuke to equivalence, a reminder and remainder of non-identity, music, with its obsessive rules, is not such a reminder.

Research carried out at the University of Chicago demonstrated that there are more than 1300 discernible pitches available to melodic consciousness, yet only a very small fraction of them are allowed. Not even the 88 tones of the piano really come into play, considering the repetition of the octave structure—another aspect of the absence of free or natural music.

Not reducible to words, at once intelligible and untranslatable, music continues to refuse us complete access. Lévi-Strauss, introducing *The Raw and the Cooked*, even went so far as to isolate it as "the supreme mystery of the science of man [sic], a mystery that all the various disciplines come up against and which holds the key to their progress." This essay locates the fundamentals rather more simply, namely in the question of music's perennial combination of free expression with social regulation; more precisely in this case, with an historical treatment of that which is our sense of music, Western tonality. Put in context, its standardized grammar to a large extent answers the question of what it is that music says. And the depth of its authority may be understood as applicable to Nietzsche's fear that "We shall never be rid of God so long as we still believe in grammar."

But before situating tonality historically, a few words are in order toward defining this basic musical syntax, a cultural practice which has been termed one of the greatest intellectual achievements of Western civilization. First, it must be stressed that, contrary to the assertion of major theorists of tonal harmonics from Rameau to Schenker, tonality was not destined by the physical order of sounds. Tone, almost never found fixed at the same pitch in nature, is divested of any natural quality and shaped according to arbitrary laws; this standardization and strict distancing are elementary to harmonic progress, and tend toward an instrumental or mechanical expression and away from the human voice. As a result of the selection made in the sound continuum by an arbitrarily imposed scale, hierarchical relations are established among the notes.

Since the Renaissance (and until Schoenberg), Western music has been conceived on the basis of the diatonic scale, whose central element is the tonic triad, or defined key, which subordinates the other notes to it.

Tonality actually means the state of having a pitch—the tonic, as it is most simply called—that has authority over all the other tones; the systematics of this leading-note quality has been the preoccupation of our music. Schenker wrote of the tonic's "desire to dominate its fellow tones": in his choice of words we can already begin to see a connection between tonality and modern class society. The leading theorist of tonal authority, he referred to it in 1906 as "a sort of higher collective order, similar to a state, based on its own social contracts by which the individual tones are bound to abide."

There are many who still hold that the emergence of a tonal center in a work is an inevitable product of natural harmonic function and cannot be suppressed. Here we have an exact parallel to ideology, where the hegemony of the frame of reference that is tonality is treated as merely self-evident. The ideological miasma which helps make other social constructs seem natural and objective also hides the ruling prejudices that are imbedded in the essence of tonality. It is, nonetheless, as Arnold Schoenberg suggested, a "device" to produce unity. In fact, tonal music is full of illusion, such as that of false community, in which the whole is portrayed as being made up of autonomous voices; this impression transcends music to provide a legitimizing reflection of the general division of labor in divided society.

Dynamically speaking, tonality creates a sense of tension and release, of motion and repose, through the use of chordal dissonance and consonance. Movement away from the tonic is experienced as tension, returning as a homecoming, a resolution. All tonal music moves toward resolution in the cadence or close, with the tonic chord ruling all other harmonic combinations, drawing them to itself, and embodying authority, stability, repose. Supramusically, a nostalgically painful attitude of wandering and returning runs through the whole course of bourgeois culture, and is ably expressed by the very movement basic to tonality.

This periodic convergence toward a point of repose enabled increasingly extended musical structures, and the areas of tonal expectation and fulfillment came to be placed further apart. It is not surprising that as the dominant society must strive for agreement, assent—harmony— from its subjects through greater distances of alienation, tonality develops more distant departures from the certainty and repose of the tonic and thus lengthier delays in gratification. The forced march of progress finds its correspondence in the rationalized direction "compulsion of tonic" dominant harmony, complete with a persistent patriarchal character.

TONALITY AND THE TOTALITY

Three centuries of tonality also tend to bury awareness of its suppression of earlier rhythmic possibilities, its narrowing of the great inner variety of the rhythm to a schematic alternation of "stressed" and "unstressed." The rise of tonality similarly coincided with the coming to power of symmetrical thinking and the recapitulating musical structure, the possibility of attaining a certain closure by means of a certain uniformity. Chenneviére, in discussing tonality's newly simplified and intellectualized system of notation, discerned "a most radical impoverishment of occidental music," referring mainly to the symmetrical balancing of clause against clause and the emphasis on chordal repetition.

In the early nineteenth century, William Chappell published a collection of "national English airs" (popular songs) in which academic harmonic patterns were imposed on surviving folk melodies, older melodies suppressed and "irregular tunes squared off." The binarism of the basic major key/minor key had come to prevail and, as Busoni concluded, "The harmonic symbols have fenced in the expression of music." The emergence of tonality corresponded to that of nationalized and centralized hierarchy which came to pervade economic, political and cultural life. Ready-made structures of expressivity monopolize musical subjectivity and patterns of desire. Clifford Geertz makes this pertinent judgment: "One of the most significant facts about us may finally be that we all begin with the natural equipment to live a thousand lives but end in the end having lived only one."

Tonality in music may be likened to realism in literature and perspective in painting, but it is more deeply ingrained than either. This facilitates a would-be transcendence of class distinctions and social differences under the sign of a "universal" key-centered music, triumphant since tonality defined the realm of mass musical appreciation and consumption. There is no spoken language on the planet which even begins to compete with the accessibility tonality has provided as a means of human expression.

Any historical study that omits music risks a diminished understanding of society. Consider, for example, the ninth-century efforts of Charlemagne to establish uniformity in liturgical music throughout his empire for political reasons, or the tenth-century organ in Winchester Cathedral with its four hundred pipes: the height of Western technology to that time. It is at least arguable that music, in fact, provides a better key than any other to the understanding of the changing spirit of this civilization. To refocus on tonality, one can, using conventional periodization, locate perhaps its earliest roots in the transition between the Middle Ages and the Renaissance era.

If the eminent medievalist Bloch is correct in characterizing medieval society as unequal rather than hierarchical, there is a definite cogency to John Shepherd's interpretation of the faint beginnings of the tonal system as the encoding of a new hierarchical musical ideology out of a more mutual one which idealized its own, earlier society. The medieval outlook, based on its decentralized and localized character, was relatively tolerant of varying worldviews and musical forms, and did not consider them as basically destructive of its feudal ideological foundation. The emerging modern world, however, was typified by greater division of labor, abstraction, and an intolerant, totalizing character. Uniform printing, and a print literacy corrosive of oral, face-to-face traditions, explains some of the shift, as moveable type provided a model for the proto-industrial use of individuals as mechanically interacting parts of a machine. Indeed the invention of printing at about 1500 gave musical notation great scope, which made possible the role of composer, by the separation of creator and performer and the downgrading of the latter. Western culture thus soon produced the completely notated musical work, facilitating a formal theory of composition at the expense of an earlier predominance of improvisation along certain guidelines. In this way print literacy and its dynamic uniformity led to a growing harmonic explicitness.

Some musicologists have even located a recurrent urge to curb the "recalcitrant independence" of the individual parts of polyphonic multi-voiced music in the interests of harmony and order, dating back to the late thirteenth century. Ars nova, the principal musical form of the fourteenth century, illustrates some of the tendencies at work in this long transitional period of preharmonic polyphony. Early on, and especially in France, ars nova reached a stunning degree of rhythmic complexity that European music would not achieve again until Stravinsky's *Rite of Spring* five centuries later. But this very complexity, increasingly based on an abstract conception of time, led to an extraordinary refinement of notation, and hence pointed away from a music based on the singing voice and away from melodic subtlety and rhythmic flexibility. Formalization seems always to imply reduction, and in turn a nascent feeling for tonic-dominant relationships was manifest by the mid-fifteenth century.

The considerable loss of a spontaneous rhythmic sense after the

Middle Ages is evidence of increased domestication, just as two basic Renaissance characteristics, specialization of and within the orchestra and the formation of a class of narrowly focused virtuosi, also bespoke a greater division of labor at large. Similarly, new emphasis had been placed on the spectator, and by the late 1500s, music involving no spectacle other than that of men at work, not intended for provoking movement or for singing but made only for being passively consumed, first appeared.

Renaissance music remained for the most part and most importantly vocal, but during this period instrumental music became independent and first developed a number of autonomous forms known collectively as "absolute music." More and more secularized as well, European music under the unquestioned leadership of the Netherlands between 1400 and 1600 took on a mathematicized aspect quite compatible with the Dutch ascendancy within the rise of early mercantile capitalism. The power of sound achieved an intoxication born of the choral mass effects that are made possible when the many, formerly independent voices of a composition join into one body of harmony.

But a tonal harmonics present in some places was not yet a tonality present throughout. The modal scales, sufficient from the early Middle Ages to the latter part of the sixteenth century, expanded from eight to 12 modes and then began to break down and yield to two less fluid modes, major/minor scale binarism. "The restlessness and disenchantment of the late Renaissance," in Edward Lowinsky's words, called forth the coherence and unity of tonic-dominant structure as music's contribution to class society's cultural hegemony. Our modern harmonic sense, the conception of tone as the sum of many vertically grouped tones, is an idealization of hierarchized social harmony.

Peter Clark's *The European Crisis of the 1590s* quotes a Spanish writer of 1592: "England without God, Germany in schism, Flanders in rebellion, France with all these together." As the century drew to a close, surveyed Henry Karmen, "Probably never before in European history had so many popular uprisings coincided in time." Tonality was not yet victorious but would, fairly soon, come to reign among the dominant ideas of society, playing its part to channel and thereby pacify desire.

As polyphony faded, the modern key system began to emerge more distinctly in a new form in the opening years of the 1600s; namely, opera, first brought forth in Italy by Monteverdi. The conscious rhetorical presentation of emotion, it was the first secular musical structure in the West conceived on a scale sufficiently grand to rival that of religious music. With opera and elsewhere, the early phases of "the developing feeling for tonality," according to H.C. Colles, "already gave the new works an appearance of orderliness and stability which marked the inauguration of a new era in art."

The growing concern for a central tonality in the seventeenth century thrived on Descartes. With his mathematized, mechanistic rationalism and his specific attention to musical structure, Descartes advanced the new tonal system in the same spirit as he consciously put his scientific philosophy in the service of strong central government. To Adorno, polyphonic music contained nonreified, autonomous elements which made it perhaps best suited to express the "otherness" Cartesian consciousness was designed to eliminate.

The background to this development was a marked renewal of the social strife of the very late 1500s. Hobsbawm found in the 1600s the crisis par excellence; Parker and Smith (*The General Crisis of the Seventeenth Century*) saw this "explosion of political instability" in Europe as "directed overwhelmingly against the State, particularly during the period 1625–1675." The previous century had been largely the golden age of counterpoint, reaching its apogee with Palestrina and Lassus, its ideal a static social harmony to be imitated in music. The Baroque aesthetic corresponded to the crises beginning in the 1590s, and resuming in earnest with the general economic breakdown of 1620; it's nothing if not a rejection of classical calm and its polyphonic refinements. The essence of Baroque is to move with the turbulence so as to control it; hence it combines restless movement with formalism. Here the concerto comes of age, linked by more than etymology to consent, consensus. Derived from the Latin *concertare*, agreement reached with dissonant elements, it reflected, as a well-harmonized ensemble, the great demand of the system for authority equal to the social struggles.

Harmony is homophony, not polyphony; polyphony and harmony are in themselves irreconcilable. Instead of a form in which many voices are combined so that each retains its own character, with harmony we really hear only one tone. In the Baroque age of conflict homophony overtakes and supplants polyphony, with obvious ideological "overtones." Independent sounds merge to form a united block, whose function is background for the melody and also to register the tune in motion in its place within the tonal system. At this time harmony first established itself as essential to music, even changing the nature of melody in the process. Rhythm too was affected by harmony; indeed the division of music into bars was dictated by the new, ever-present harmonic rhythm.

Spengler judged that music overtook painting as the chief European art at about 1670. It prevailed at the very time when tonality was definitively realized; music was henceforth to be written in the idiom of fully established tonality, without challenge, for about two and a half centuries. The externalization of immediate subjective interests according to tonality's generalizing code corresponds, from this time as well, to the legal conception of the "reasonable man," Dunwell informs us, though one is tempted to rephrase it as "modern, domesticated," rather than "reasonable."

There are other striking temporal coincidences. John Wolf's The Emergence of the Great Powers, 1685-1715, among other historical studies, sets the moment of ascendant state power as paralleling that of central tonality. And as Bukhofzer wrote, "Both tonality and gravitation were discoveries of the baroque period made at exactly the same time." The significance of Newtonian physics is that universal gravitation offered a model emphasizing immutable law and resistance to change; its universally prevailing, ordered motions provided a unified cosmological exemplar for political and economic order—as did tonality. In the new harmonic system the principal tone, the one strongest and most dominant, gravitates downward and through, and becomes the bass, the fundamental tone of the chord; the laws of tonality can be read almost interchangeably, incredible as it may sound, with those of gravitation.

Mid- to late seventeenth century England exemplified more general social trends in music. The critics North and Mace wrote of the decline of the amateur viol player, and the tendency in composition wherein "Part writing gave way to fireworks and pattern making," to cite Peter Warlock. Family chamber music decreased; the habit of passive listening increased, against the breakup of village communalism with its songs and dances. Victorious tonality was a very important part of a major social and symbolic restructuring, and certainly not just in England.

Beginning in the Baroque era, the main vehicle of tonality was the sonata (i.e. "played" as opposed to the earlier, single-movement canzona or "sung"), which came to cover virtually any instrumental, multimovement composition that proceeds according to a formal plan. The sonata form was an organic outgrowth of harmonic tonality in that its symmetrics were basically related to the internal symmetrical organization of the grammar of tonality; its fundamental structure requires that music which appears first as a move away from the tonic toward a newly polarized key be reinterpreted finally with the original tonic area in order to restore the balance. Even the challenging finales of Mozart's operas, Rosen reminds us, have the symmetrical tonal structure of a sonata. By the end of the Baroque in the late eighteenth century, symmetry withheld and then finally granted had become one of music's cardinal satisfactions.

With its conflict of two themes, its keynote, development and reprise, the sonata form presupposes a capitalist dynamics; the equilibrium-oriented and totally undramatic fugue, high-water mark of an earlier counterpoint, reflected a more static hierarchical society. Fugal style was fulfilled just as tonality came to complete predominance and its movement is largely one of sequence. A classical sonata, on the other hand, is self-generating, moving forward as a revelation of its initially unseen inner potential. The fugue goes on obeying its initial law, like a calculation, as befits rationalist Enlightenment, whereas sonata themes exhibit a dynamic condition announcing the qualitative leap in domination of nature inaugurated by industrial capitalism.

In the early seventeenth century Rubens' studio became a factory; his output of over 1200 paintings was unprecedented in the history of art. One hundred fifty years later, utilizing the preordained sonata form, Haydn and Mozart could turn out 150 symphonies between them. Perhaps it is not suggesting too much, or denying the genius of some creators, to see in this mechanism a cultural prefiguring of mass production. A further characteristic is that sonata music, unlike the complicated late fugal style, had to be predictable, pleasing. Reminding one of tonality itself, "The sonata cycle affirms the happy ending, lends itself to reconciliation, to salvation from first and second movement strivings, torments, inner doubts" before it concludes, in the words of Robert Solomon.

The sonata form principle also involves the idea of gradually increasing activity, a cumulative dynamism that reaches out to exclude specificity, to dominate via generalization. It is for this effect that it embodies the crowning achievement of the emergence of generalizing forms in bourgeois evolution and so well expresses the drive toward "universal" values and world hegemony of European culture and capital.

In the eighteenth century the modern notion of music's autonomy began to form, with the claim (persisting today) to transcendental truth that attaches to Bach and Mozart especially. The proud solemnity of Handel's oratorios speaks of the rise of imperialist England and a desire to legitimate that rise, but Bach in particular most effectively articulated the social values of the emerging bourgeoisie as universal rationality, objectivity, truth.

The precursors of Bach had made evident a structuration proper to tonality, but it was he who brought that structuration to a precise perfection, combining the drama and goal orientation of the late Baroque with aspects of the earlier, soberer contrapuntal ideal. It is worth noting that the older, more statically mathematized forms survive in the eighteenth century, though they do not reign; this survival accounts for those sequential developments which Constant Lambert disrespectfully speaks of as the Bach "sewing machine," just as Wagner referred to Mozart as possessed of "sometimes an almost trivial regularity."

But if Bach represents the virtual apotheosis of harmonically based tonality there were some doubts expressed regarding this whole thrust. Rousseau, for example, saw harmony as only another symptom of Europe's cultural decay indeed as the death of music. He based this extreme view on harmony's depreciation of melody: its delimitation of the perception of musical sounds to the internal structuring of its elements and hence its truncation of the listener's experience. Goethe too had misgivings in terms of the artificiality and reification of fully developed tonality, but they were less clearly stated than Rousseau's.

By about 1800, tonal instrumental music reached the full command of its powers, a point that painting had arrived at almost three hundred years earlier. The greatest change in eighteenth-century tonality in part influenced by the establishment of equal temperament (the division of the octave into 12 precisely equal semitones) was an even more emphatic polarity between tonic and dominant and an enlargement of the range over which the key modulation obtains. At the beginning of the century the key relationship could already hold up over periods of eight or more bars without being sounded again, whereas Mozart, Haydn and Beethoven had, by the end of the century, extended the authority of harmonic relations to five or even ten minutes.

The widening of the tonal orbit, however, meant a consequent weakening in the gravitational pull of the tonic; with Beethoven, in the early Romantic era, some undermining of structural tonality can already be seen. What is new thematically in Beethoven is a climax of emotional expression as well as a greater range of emotions expressed, plus the centrality of the motif of the struggle for individual freedom, precisely as the defeat of the Luddites in England presaged the suppression of emotional expressivity and individual freedom in society at large. Much unlike say, Bach, he began from the fact of alienation and ultimately refused to reconcile in his music that which is unreconciled in society; this can be seen most clearly in his last quartets, which recall the incompleteness and anguish of the late music of Mozart.

The Romantic art par excellence, music came to be thought of as a uniquely privileged medium. Indeed, it was in the Beethovenian period, or shortly thereafter, that the composer was ceded the status of philosopher, contrasting sharply with the role of virtual servant that Haydn and Mozart had occupied. Perhaps the so-called "redemptive force" of music, to cross over to the social terrain, was nowhere more in evidence than with a performance of Auber's opera, *La Muette de Portici*, which provoked the outbreak of revolution in Brussels in 1830. Later in the century, Walter Pater's assessment that "All art constantly aspires towards the condition of music" bespoke not only music as the culmination of the arts but reflected its forcefulness at the height of tonality. It is also in this latter sense, as appreciation of tonality, that Schopenhauer celebrated music in a way unrivaled in philosophical writing, as more powerful than words and the direct expression of inner consciousness. Adorno spoke of the "bursting longing of Romanticism" and Marothy discussed its frequented themes of loneliness and nostalgia, the effort to capture the sense of something that is irretrievably lost. Along these lines, the drama of rescue was not only the literary fashion of the day but is often found in music, such as Beethoven's *Fidelio*. Schubert could ask whether there was such a thing as joyous music, as if in response to an industrializing Europe, and was answered by the elegiac, resigned Brahms and the pessimist Mahler in the later Romantic era.

Harmony was the special realm of the period; orchestral groupings favored the massed and unified deployment of each instrumental family to stretch and intensify the central concern with pitch relationships to convey meaning, over the other aspects of music. It was the age of great orchestral forces designed to exploit the compulsive powers of tone, proceeding via the coordination of diverse specialist function. In this manner, and with an increasingly systematic conception of musical structure, Romantic music paralleled the perfection of industrial method. As the nineteenth century progressed, a growing number of composers felt that musical language was becoming trapped under the syntactical and formal constraints of tonality, an overly standardized harmonic vocabulary bound to empty symmetrical regularities. Flattening out under the weight of its own habits, music seemed to be losing its former expressive power.

Like capital, then at the height of its initial expansiveness, the modern orchestra pursued the illusion of indefinite growth. But Romantic overstatement and giganticism (i.e. Mahler's *Symphony of a Thousand*) were used, more often than not, to create a limited range of homogenized sounds, a uniformity of timbre.

To speak of expansion calls to mind Wagner's attempt at a simple, economical repertoire opera—the resultant work was the five-hour, gorgeous agony of *Tristan and Isolde*. Or Wagner's Ring series, based on the Nibelungen myth, that epic of perpetual lust and death by which he desired to outdo all conceivable spectacles, and which most likely prompted Nietzsche to judge, "There is a deep significance in the fact that the rise of Wagner coincides with the rise of empire." An operatic portrait of Kaiser Wilhelm I beside a swan and wearing a Lohengrin helmet suggests the debt owed him for celebrating and reconsecrating the social order of the second German Reich. If *Tristan* was the prelude to the political development of Bismarckian Germany, the latter found its authoritarian and mystical justification in Parsifal's pseudo-erotic religiosity.

Wagner intended a merger of all the arts into a higher form of opera and in this project it seemed to him that he had superseded dogmatic religion. Such an aim projected the complete domination of the spectator by means of the grandeur and pomposity of his musical productions, their perfumed sultriness and bombardment of the senses. His boast was no less than that, owing to his neopagan, neonationalist achievement, "Church and state will be abolished," having outlived their usefulness. Thus his aims for art were more grandiose than those of industrial capitalism itself and spoke its language of power.

And yet Wagner also, and more importantly, represents the full decay of the classic harmonic system. Despite all the bombast and striving for a maximum of authority, his is the music of doubt. His music remained faithful to at least a latent foundation of tonality but, especially with Tristan, the enduring validity of tonal harmony was already disproved. Wagner had extended it to its ultimate limits and exhausted its last resources.

Part of Mahler's *Song of the Earth* is marked "without expression." It seems that romanticism after Wagner was turning to ashes, though at the same time something new was being foreshadowed. Harmony continued to show signs of collapse from within and increasing liberties were taken with the previously unlimited sovereignty of the major/minor tonal system (e.g. Debussy). Meanwhile, as capital required more "Third World" resources for its stability, music too turned imperialist in the sense of much needed folk transfusions (e.g. Bartok).

In 1908 Arnold Schoenberg's *Second Quartet in F Sharp Minor* attained the decisive break with harmonic development: it was the first atonal composition. Fittingly, the movement in question is begun by the soprano with the words: "Ich fühle Luft von anderen Planeten" ("I feel air from other planets").

Adorno saw the radical openness of atonal music as an "expression of unmitigated suffering, bound by no convention whatsoever" and as such "often hostile to culture" and "containing elements of barbarism." The rejection of tonality indeed enabled expression of the most intense subjectivity, the loneliness of the subject under technological domination. Nonetheless, the equivalences by which human emotion is universalized and objectified are still present, if released from the centralized control of the "laws of harmony." Schoenberg's "emancipation of the dissonance" allowed for the presentation of human passions with unprecedented immediacy via dissonant harmonies that have little or no tendency to resolve. The avoidance of tonal suggestion and resolution provides the listener with precious little support or security: Schoenberg's atonal work often seems almost hysterically emotional due to the absence of points of real repose. "It is driven frantically toward the unattainable," noted Leonard Meyer.

In this sense, atonality proved to be the most extreme manifestation of the general anti-authoritarian upheaval in society of the five or so years preceding World War I. Schoenberg's abandonment of tonality coincides with the abandonment of perspective in painting by Picasso and Kandinsky (in 1908). But with these "two great negative gestures" in culture, as they have been termed, it was the composer who found himself propelled into a public void. In his steadfast affirmation of alienation, his unwillingness to present any scene of human realization that was not feral, difficult, wild, Schoenberg's atonality was too much of a threat and challenge to find much acceptance. The expressionist painter August Macke wrote to his colleague Franz Marc following an evening of Schoenberg's chamber music in 1911: "Can you imagine music in which tonality has been completely abandoned? I was reminded constantly of Kandinsky's large compositions which are written, as it were, in no single key...this music which lets every tone stand by itself." Unfortunately, their feeling for such a radically libertarian approach was not shared by many, nor exposed to many.

As Macke's letter implies, before the atonal breakout, music had achieved meaning through the defined relations of chords to a tonal center. Schoenberg's Theory of Harmony summed up the old system well: "It has always been the referring of all results to a center, to an emanating point... Tonality does not serve: on the contrary it demands to be served."

Some defenders of tonality, on the other hand, have adopted a frankly socially authoritarian point of view, feeling that more than just changes in music were at stake. Levarie and Levy's *Musical Morphology* (1983), for example, proceeded from the philosophical thesis that "Chaos is nonbeing" to the political stance that "The revolt against tonality... is an egalitarian revolution." They further pronounced atonality to be "a general contemporary phenomenon," nothing with displeasure how "Obsessive fear of tonality reveals a deep aversion to the concept of hierarchy and rank." This stance is reminiscent of Hindemith's conclusion that it is impossible to deny the validity of hierarchical tone relationships and that there is therefore "no such thing as atonal music." Such comments obviously seek to defend more than the dominant musical form: they would preserve authority, standardization, hierarchy and whatever cultural grammar guarantees a world defined by such values.

Schoenberg's atonal experiment suffered as part of the defeat that World War I and its aftermath meted out for social dissonance. By the early 1920s he had given up the systemless radicalism of atonality. not a single "free" note survived. In the absence of a tonal center he inserted the totally rule-governed 32-tone set, which, as Adorno judged, "virtually extinguishes the subject." Dodecaphony, or serialism as it is also called, constituted a new compliance in the place of tonality, corresponding to a new phase of increasingly systematized industrialism introduced with

FUTURE PRIMITIVE REVISITED

World War I. Schoenberg forged new laws to control what was liberated by the destruction of the old tonal rules of resolution, new laws that guarantee a more complete circulation among all 12 pitches and may be said to speak to capital's growing need for improved recirculation. Serial technique is a kind of total integration in which movement is strictly controlled, as in a bureaucratically enforced mode. Its conceptual drawback for the dominant order is that while greater circulation is achieved via its new standardized demands (none of the tones is to be repeated before the other 11 have been heard), the concentrated control actually allows for very little production. This is seen most clearly in the extreme understatement and brevity in much of the work of Webern, Schoenberg's most successful disciple; at times there are as many pauses as notes, while the second of Webern's early *Three Pieces for Cello and Piano*, for example, lasts only 13 seconds.

The old harmonic system and its major/minor key points of reference provided easily understood places of departure and destination. Serialism accords equal use to each note, making any chord feasible: this conveys a somewhat homeless, fragmentary sense, suitable to an age of more diffuse, traditionless domination.

As of World War I, art music in general began to fragment. Stravinsky led the neoclassicist tendency, which reaffirmed a tonal center despite the prevailing winds of change. Grounded firmly in the eighteenth century, it seemed to increasing numbers of composers, especially after World War II, to be no solution to music's theoretical problems. Serialist figure Pierre Boulez termed its rather flagrantly anachronistic character and refusal of development a "mockery." Neoclassical music seemed to share at least something with the new serialist movement, however: an often stark, austere character, in line with the general trend toward contraction and pessimism. Benjamin Britten seemed preoccupied with the problem of suffering, while many of Aaron Copland's works evoke the loneliness of industrial cities, whose very energy is bereft of real vitality. Another major traditionalist, Vaughan Williams, ended his masterful *Sixth Symphony* with what can only be described as an objective statement of utter nihilism.

Meanwhile, by the 1950s, serialism came to be regarded as overdetermined, its discipline too severe, so much so that it occasioned "chance" music (also called aleatory music or indeterminacy). Closely identified popularly with John Cage, chance seemed another part of the larger swing away from the subject—which electronic or computer-generated composition would take even further—whereby the human voice disappears and even the performer is often eliminated. Paradoxically, the aesthetic effects produced by random methods are the same as those realized by totally ordered music. The minimalism of Reich, Glass and others seems a mass-marketed neoconservatism in its pleasant, repetitious poverty of ideas. Iannis Xenakis, imitating the brutalism of his teacher Le Corbusier, may be said to stand for the height of the cybernetizing, computer-worshipping approach: he has sought an "alloy of music and technology" based on his research into "logico-mathematical invariants."

Art music is today bewildered by a scattering influence, the absence of any unifying, common-practice language. And yet the main thrust of all of it—if one can use the word thrust in such an enervated context— is a cold expressionlessness wholly befitting the enormous increase in alienation, objectification and reification of worldwide late capitalism. A divided society must finally make do with a divided art: the landscape does not "harmonize." It is an era that perhaps cannot even be given a musical ending anymore; it has certainly become both too unruly and too bleak to be composed and brought to any tonal, cadenced close. When art and even symbolization itself seem false to many, the question occurs, where do the forces lie by which music can be kept alive, where is the enchantment?

"All art is mortal, not merely the individual artifacts but the arts themselves," wrote Spengler. Art—with music in the forefront—may, as Hegel speculated it would, be already well within the age of its demise. Samuel Lipman's *Music After Modernism* (1979) pronounced music's terminal illness, its status as "living on the capital of the explosion of creativity which lasted from before Bach to World War I." The failure of tonality's "creativity" is of course part of an overall entropy in which capital, in Lipman's accidental accuracy of words, turns toxic and unmistakably self-destructive. Adorno saw that "There are fewer and fewer works from the past that continue to be any good. It is as if the entire supply of culture is dwindling." Some would merely hold on to the museum pieces of tonality at all costs and deplore the lack of their resupply. This is the meaning of virtually all the standard laments on the subject, such as Constant Lambert's *Music Ho! A Study of Music in Decline* (1934) or *The Agony of Modern Music* (1955) in which Henry Pleasants told us that "The vein which for three hundred years offered a seemingly inexhaustible yield of beautiful music has run out," or Roland Stromberg in *After Everything* (1975): "It is hard ...

not to think that serious music has reached the state of total decay." But the same death verdict also comes from non-antiquarians: a 1983 lecture by noted serialist composer Milton Babbitt was called "The Unlikely Survival of Serious Music." Earlier, Babbitt, in the face of the unpopularity of contemporary art music posed, defiantly and unrealistically, the "complete elimination of the public and social aspects of musical composition" and penned an article entitled "Who Cares If You Listen?"

The lack of a public for "difficult" music is obvious and noteworthy. If Bloch was correct to judge "All we hear is ourselves," it may also be correct to conclude that the listener does not want that element in music that is a confrontation with our age. Adorno referred to Schoenberg's music as the reflection of a broken and empty world, evoking a reply from Milan Rankovic that "Such a reflection cannot be loved because it reproduces the same emptiness in the spirit of the listener." A further question, relating to the limits of art itself, is whether estrangement in music could ever prove effective in the struggle against the estrangement of society.

Modern music, however splintered and removed from the old tonal paradigm, has obviously not effaced the popularity of the Baroque, Classical and Romantic masters. And in the area of music education tonality continues to prevail at all levels; undergraduates in composition classes are instructed that the dominant "demands" resolution, that it "must resolve" to the tonic, etc., and the students' musical sense itself is appraised in terms of the once-unchallenged harmonic categories and rules. Tonality, as should be clear by now, is an ideology in purely musical terms, and one that perseveres.

One wonders, in fact, why art music, where traditions are revered, should have made the break that it has, while all of pop music (and almost all jazz, which inherited its harmonic system from classic European tonality), where traditions are often despised, has held back. There is no form of popular music in the industrial world that exists outside the province of mass tonal consciousness. As Richard Norton said so well: "It is the tonality of the church, school, office, parade, convention, cafeteria, workplace, airport, airplane, automobile, truck, tractor, lounge, lobby, bar, gym, brothel, bank, and elevator. Afraid of being without it on foot, humans are presently strapping it to their bodies in order to walk to it, run to it, work to it, and relax to it. It is everywhere. It is music and it writes the songs."

It is also as totally integrated into commercialized mass production as any product of the assembly line. The music never changes from the seemingly eternal formula, despite superficial variations; the "good" song, the harmonically marketable song, is one that contains fewer different chords than a fourteenth-century ballad. Its expressive potential exists solely within the limited confines of consumer choice, wherein, according to Horkheimer and Adorno, "Something is provided for everyone so that none shall escape." As a one-dimensional code of consumer society, it is a training course in passivity.

Music, reduced to background noise which no longer takes itself seriously, is at the same time a central, omnipresent element of environment, more so than ever before. The immersion in tonality is at once distraction and pervasive control, as the silence of isolation and boredom must be filled in. It comforts us, denying that the world is as reified as it is, reduced to making believe that—as Beckett put it in *Endgame*—anything is happening, that anything changes. Pop music also provides a pleasure of identification, the immediate experience of collective identity that only massified culture, unconscious of the authoritarian ideology which is tonality, can provide.

Rock music was a "revolution" compared with earlier pop music only in the sense of lyrics and tempo (and volume)—no tonal revolution had even been dimly conceived. Studies have shown that all types of (tonal) music calm the unruly; consider how punk has standardized and clichéd the musical sneer. It is not only the music of overt pacification, like New Age composition, which denies the negative as dangerous and evil in the same way that Socialist Realism did, and likewise aids and abets the daily oppression. Just as surely it will take more than rockers smashing their guitars on stage, even though the limits of tonality may be behind such acts, to signal a new age.

Like language, tonality is historically characterized by its unfreedom. We are made tonal by society: only in the elimination of that society will occur the superseding of all grammars of domination.

CHAPTER FOUR

THE CATASTROPHE OF POSTMODERNISM

POSTMODERNISM. Originally a theme within aesthetics, it has colonized "ever wider areas," according to Ernesto Laclau, "until it has become the new horizon of our cultural, philosophical, and political experience." "The growing conviction," as Richard Kearney has it, "that human culture as we have known it...is now reaching its end." It is, especially in the U.S., the intersection of poststructuralist philosophy and a vastly wider condition of society: both specialized ethos and, far more importantly, the arrival of what modern industrial society has portended. Postmodernism is contemporaneity, a morass of deferred solutions on every level, featuring ambiguity, the refusal to ponder either origins or ends, as well as the denial of oppositional approaches, "the new realism." Signifying nothing and going nowhere, pm [postmodernism] is an inverted millenarianism, a gathering fruition of the technological "life"-system of universal capital. It is not accidental that Carnegie Mellon University, which in the '80s was the first to require that all students be equipped with computers, is establishing "the nation's first poststructuralist undergraduate curriculum."

Consumer narcissism and a cosmic "what's the difference?" mark the end of philosophy as such and the etching of a landscape, according to Kroker and Cook, of "disintegration and decay against the background radiation of parody, kitsch and burnout." Henry Kariel concludes that "for postmodernists, it is simply too late to oppose the momentum of industrial society." Surface, novelty, contingency—there are no grounds available for criticizing our crisis. If the representative postmodernist resists summarizable conclusions, in favor of an alleged pluralism and openness of perspective, it is also reasonable (if one is allowed to use such a word) to predict that if and when we live in a completely pm culture, we would no longer know how to say so.

THE PRIMACY OF LANGUAGE AND THE END OF THE SUBJECT

In terms of systematic thought, the growing preoccupation with language is a key factor accounting for the pm climate of narrowed focus and retreat. The so-called "descent into language," or the "linguistic turn" has levied the postmodernist-poststructuralist assumption that language constitutes the human world and the human world constitutes the whole world. For most of this century language has been moving to center stage in philosophy, among figures as diverse as Wittgenstein, Quine, Heidegger, and Gadamer, while growing attention to communication theory, linguistics, cybernetics, and computer languages demonstrates a similar emphasis over several decades in science and technology. This very pronounced turn toward language itself was embraced by Foucault as a "decisive leap towards a wholly new form of thought." Less positively, it can be at least partially explained in terms of pessimism following the ebbing of the oppositional moment of the '60s. The '70s witnessed an alarming withdrawal into what Edward Said called the "labyrinth of textuality," as contrasted with the sometimes more insurrectionary intellectual activity of the preceding period.

Perhaps it isn't paradoxical that "the fetish of the textual," as Ben Agger judged, "beckons in an age when intellectuals are dispossessed of their words." Language is more and more debased; drained of meaning, especially in its public usage. No longer can even words be counted on, and this is part of a larger anti-theory current, behind which stands a much larger defeat than the '60s: that of the whole train of Enlightenment rationality. We have depended on language as the supposedly sound and transparent handmaiden of reason and where has it gotten us? Auschwitz, Hiroshima, mass psychic misery, impending destruction of the planet, to name a few. Enter postmodernism, with its seemingly bizarre and fragmented turns and twists. Edith Wyschograd's *Saints and Postmodernism* (1990) not only testifies to the ubiquity of the pm "approach"—there are apparently no fields outside its ken—but also comments cogently on the new direction: "postmodernism as a "philosophical" and "literary" discursive style cannot straightforwardly appeal to the techniques of reason, themselves the instruments of theory, but must forge new and necessarily arcane means for undermining the pieties of reason."

The immediate antecedent of postmodernism/poststructuralism, reigning in the '50s and much of the '60s, was organized around the centrality it accorded the linguistic model. Structuralism provided the premise that language constitutes our only means of access to the world of objects and experience and its extension, that meaning arises wholly from the play of differences within cultural sign systems. Lévi-Strauss, for example, argued that the key to anthropology lies in the uncovering of unconscious social laws (e.g. those that regulate marriage ties and kinship), which are structured like language. It was the Swiss linguist Saussure who stressed, in a move very influential to postmodernism, that meaning resides not in a relationship between an utterance and that to which it refers, but in the relationship of signs to one another. This Saussurian belief in the enclosed, self-referential nature of language implies that everything is determined within language, leading to the scrapping of such quaint notions as alienation, ideology, repression, etc. and concluding that language and consciousness are virtually the same.

On this trajectory, which rejects the view of language as an external means deployed by consciousness, appears the also very influential neo-Freudian, Jacques Lacan. For Lacan, not only is consciousness thoroughly permeated by language and without existence for itself apart from language, even the "unconscious is structured like a language."

Earlier thinkers, most notably Nietzsche and Heidegger, had already suggested that a different language or a changed relationship to language might somehow bring new and important insights. With the linguistic turn of more recent times, even the concept of an individual who thinks as the basis of knowledge becomes shaky. Saussure discovered that "language is not a function of the speaking subject," the primacy of language displacing who it is that gives voice to it. Roland Barthes, whose career joins the structuralist and poststructuralist periods, decided "It is language that speaks, not the author," paralleled by Althusser's observation that history is "a process without a subject."

If the subject is felt to be essentially a function of language, its stifling mediation and that of the symbolic order in general ascends toward the top of the agenda. Thus does postmodernism flail about trying to communicate what lies beyond language, "to present the unpresentable." Meanwhile, given the radical doubt introduced as to the availability to us of a referent in the world outside of language, the real fades from consideration. Jacques Derrida, the pivotal figure of the postmodernism ethos, proceeds as if the connection between words and the world were arbitrary. The object world plays no role for him. The exhaustion of modernism and the rise of postmodernism.

EXHAUSTED MODERNISM AND THE RISE OF POSTMODERNISM

But before turning to Derrida, a few more comments on precursors and the wider change in culture. Postmodernism raises questions about communication and meaning, so that the category of the aesthetic, for one, becomes problematic. For modernism, with its sunnier belief in representation, art and literature held at least some promise for providing a vision of fulfillment or understanding. Until the end of modernism, "high culture" was seen as a repository of moral and spiritual wisdom. Now there seems to be no such belief, the ubiquity of the question of language perhaps telling as to the vacancy left by the failure of other candidates of promising starting points of human imagination. In the '60s modernism seems to have reached the end of its development, the austere canon of its painting (e.g. Rothko, Reinhardt) giving way to pop art's uncritical espousal of the consumer culture's commercial vernacular. Postmodernism, and not just in the arts, is modernism without the hopes and dreams that made modernity bearable.

A widespread "fast food" tendency is seen in the visual arts, in the direction of easily consumable entertainment. Howard Fox finds that "theatricality may be the single most pervasive property of postmodern art." A decadence or exhaustion of development is also detected in the dark paintings of an Eric Fischl, where often a kind of horror seems to lurk just below the surface. This quality links Fischl, America's quintessential pm painter, to the equally sinister *Twin Peaks* and pm's quintessential television figure, David Lynch. The image, since Warhol, is self-consciously a mechanically reproducible commodity and this is the bottom-line reason for both the depthlessness and the common note of eeriness and foreboding.

Postmodern art's oft-noted eclecticism is an arbitrary recycling of fragments from everywhere, especially the past, often taking the form of parody and kitsch. Demoralized, derealized, dehistoricized: art that can no longer take itself seriously. The image no longer refers primarily to some "original," situated elsewhere in the "real" world; it increasingly refers only to other images. In this way it reflects how lost we are, how removed from nature, in the ever more mediated world of technological capitalism.

The term postmodernism was first applied, in the '70s, to architecture. Christopher Jencks wrote of an anti-planning, pro-pluralism approach, the abandoning of modernism's dream of pure form in favor of listening to "the multiple languages of the people." More honest are Robert Venturi's celebration of Las Vegas and Piers Gough's admission that postmodern architecture is no more caring for people than was modernist architecture. The arches and columns laid over modernist boxes are a thin façade of playfulness and individuality, which scarcely transforms the anonymous concentrations of wealth and power underneath.

Postmodernist writers question the very grounds for literature instead of continuing to create the illusion of an external world. The novel redirects its attention to itself; Donald Barthelme, for example, writes stories that seem to always remind the reader that they are artifices. By protesting against statement, point of view and other patterns of representation, pm literature exhibits its discomfort with the forms that tame and domesticate cultural products. As the wider world becomes more artificial and meaning less subject to our control, the new approach would rather reveal the illusion even at the cost of no longer saying anything. Here as elsewhere art is struggling against itself, its prior claims to help us understand the world evaporating while even the concept of imagination loses its potency.

For some the loss of narrative voice or point of view is equivalent to the loss of our ability to locate ourselves historically. For postmodernists this loss is a kind of liberation. Raymond Federman, for instance, glories in the coming fiction that "will be seemingly devoid of any meaning... deliberately illogical, irrational, unrealistic, non sequitur, and incoherent."

Fantasy, on the rise for decades, is a common form of the postmodern, carrying with it the reminder that the fantastic confronts civilization with the very forces it must repress for its survival. But it is a fantasy that, paralleling both deconstruction and high levels of cynicism and resignation in society, does not believe in itself to the extent of very much understanding or communicating. Pm writers seem to smother in the folds of language, conveying little else than their ironic stance regarding more traditional literature's pretensions to truth and meaning. Perhaps typical is Laurie Moore's 1990 novel *Like Life*, whose title and content reveal a retreat from living and an inversion of the American Dream, in which things can only get worse.

THE CELEBRATION OF IMPOTENCE

Postmodernism subverts two of the overarching tenets of Enlightenment humanism: the power of language to shape the world and the power of consciousness to shape a self. Thus we have the postmodernist void, the general notion that the yearning for emancipation and freedom promised by humanist principles of subjectivity cannot be satisfied. Pm views the self as a linguistic convention; as William Burroughs put it, "Your "I" is a completely illusory concept."

It is obvious that the celebrated ideal of individuality has been under pressure for a long time. Capitalism in fact has made a career of celebrating the individual while destroying him/her. And the works of Marx and Freud have done much to expose the largely misdirected and naive belief in the sovereign, rational Kantian self in charge of reality, with their more recent structuralist interpreters, Althusser and Lacan, contributing to and updating the effort. But this time the pressure is so extreme that the term "individual" has been rendered obsolete, replaced by "subject," which always includes the aspect of being subjected (as in the older "a subject of the king," for example).

Even some libertarian radicals, such as the Interrogations group in France, join in the postmodernist chorus to reject the individual as a criterion for value due to the debasing of the category by ideology and history.

So pm reveals that autonomy has largely been a myth and cherished ideals of mastery and will are similarly misguided. But if we are promised herewith a new and serious attempt at demystifying authority, concealed behind the guises of a bourgeois humanist "freedom," we actually get a dispersal of the subject so radical as to render it impotent, even nonexistent, as any kind of agent at all. Who or what is left to achieve a liberation, or is that just one more pipe dream? The postmodern stance wants it both ways: to put the thinking person "under erasure," while the very existence of its own critique depends on discredited ideas like subjectivity. Fred Dallmayr, acknowledging the widespread appeal of contemporary anti-humanism, warns that primary casualties are reflection and a sense of values. To assert that we are instances of language foremost is obviously to strip away our capacity to grasp the whole, at a time when we are urgently required to do just that. Small wonder that to some, pm amounts, in practice, to merely a liberalism without the subject, while feminists who try to define or reclaim an authentic and autonomous female identity would also likely be unpersuaded.

The postmodern subject, what is presumably left of subjecthood, seems to be mainly the personality constructed by and for technological capital, described by the Marxist literary theorist Terry Eagleton as a "dispersed, decentered network of libidinal attachments, emptied of ethical substance and psychical interiority, the ephemeral function of this or that act of consumption, media experience, sexual relationship, trend or fashion." If Eagleton's definition of today's non-subject as announced by pm is unfaithful to their point of view, it is difficult to see where, to find grounds for a distancing from his scathing summary. With postmodernism even alienation dissolves, for there is no longer a subject to be alienated! Contemporary fragmentation and powerlessness could hardly be heralded more completely, or existing anger and disaffection more thoroughly ignored.

DERRIDA, DECONSTRUCTION AND DIFFÉRANCE

Enough, for now, on background and general traits. The most influential specific postmodern approach has been Jacques Derrida's, known since the '60s as deconstruction. Postmodernism in philosophy means above all the writings of Derrida, and this earliest and most extreme outlook has found a resonance well beyond philosophy, in the popular culture and its mores.

Certainly the "linguistic turn" bears on the emergence of Derrida, causing David Wood to call deconstruction "an absolutely unavoidable move in philosophy today," as thought negotiates its inescapable predicament as written language. That language is not innocent or neutral but bears a considerable number of presuppositions it has been his career to develop, exposing what he sees as the fundamentally self-contradictory nature of human discourse. The mathematician Kurt Gödel's "Incompleteness Theorem" states that any formal system can be either consistent or complete, but not both. In rather parallel fashion, Derrida claims that language is constantly turning against itself so that, analyzed closely, we can neither say what we mean or mean what we say. But like semiologists before him, Derrida also suggests, at the same time, that a deconstructive method could demystify the ideological contents of all texts, interpreting all human activities as essentially texts. The basic contradiction and cover-up strategy inherent in the metaphysics of language in its widest sense might be laid bare and a more intimate kind of knowing result.

What works against this latter claim, with its political promise constantly hinted at by Derrida, is precisely the content of deconstruction; it sees language as a constantly moving independent force that disallows a stabilizing of meaning or definite communication, as referred to above. This internally-generated flux he called "différance" and this is what calls the very idea of meaning to collapse, along with the self-referential nature of language, which, as noted previously, says that there is no space outside of language, no "out there" for meaning to exist in anyway. Intention and the subject are overwhelmed, and what is revealed are not any "inner truths" but an endless proliferation of possible meanings generated by différance, the principle that characterizes language. Meaning within language is also made elusive by Derrida's insistence that language is metaphorical and cannot therefore directly convey truth, a notion taken from Nietzsche, one which erases the distinction between philosophy and literature. All these insights supposedly contribute to the daring and subversive nature of deconstruction, but they surely provoke some basic questions as well. If meaning is indeterminate, how are Derrida's argument and terms not also indeterminate, un-pin-downable? He has replied to critics, for example, that they are unclear as to his meaning, while his "meaning" is that there can be no clear, definable meaning. And though his entire project is in an important sense aimed at subverting all systems" claims to any kind of transcendent truth, he raises différance to the transcendent status of any philosophical first principle.

For Derrida, it has been the valorizing of speech over writing that has caused all of Western thought to overlook the downfall that language itself causes philosophy. By privileging the spoken word a false sense of immediacy is produced, the invalid notion that in speaking the thing itself is present and representation overcome. But speech is no more "authentic" than the written word, not at all immune from the built-in failure of language to accurately or definitely deliver the (representational) goods. It is the misplaced desire for presence that characterizes Western metaphysics, an unreflected desire for the success of representation. It is important to note that because Derrida rejects the possibility of an unmediated existence, he assails the efficacy of representation but not the category itself. He mocks the game but plays it just the same. Différance (later simply "difference") shades into indifference, due to the unavailability of truth or meaning, and joins the cynicism at large.

Early on, Derrida discussed philosophy's false steps in the area of presence by reference to Husserl's tortured pursuit of it. Next he developed his theory of "grammatology," in which he restored writing to its proper primacy as against the West's phonocentric, or speech-valued, bias. This was mainly accomplished by critiques of major figures who committed the sin of phonocentrism, including Rousseau, Heidegger, Saussure, and Lévi-Strauss, which is not to overlook his great indebtedness to the latter three of these four.

As if remembering the obvious implications of his deconstructive approach, Derrida's writings shift in the '70s from the earlier, fairly straightforward philosophical discussions. Glas (1974) is a mishmash of Hegel and Gent, in which argument is replaced by free association and bad puns. Though baffling to even his warmest admirers, Glas certainly is in keeping with the tenet of the unavoidable ambiguity of language and a will to subvert the pretensions of orderly discourse. Spurs (1978) is a book-length study of Nietzsche that ultimately finds its focus in nothing Nietzsche published, but in a handwritten note in the margin of one of his notebooks: "I have forgotten my umbrella." Endless, undecidable possibilities exist as to the meaning or importance—if any—of this scrawled comment. This, of course, is Derrida's point, to suggest that the same can be said for everything Nietzsche wrote. The place for thought, according to deconstruction, is clearly (er, let us say unclearly) with the relative, the fragmented, the marginal.

Meaning is certainly not something to be pinned down, if it exists at all. Commenting on Plato's *Phaedrus*, the master of de-composition goes so far as to assert that "like any text [it] couldn't not be involved, at least in a virtual, dynamic, lateral manner, with all the words that composed the system of the Greek language."

Related is Derrida's opposition to binary opposites, like literal/ metaphorical, serious/playful, deep/superficial, nature/culture, ad infinitum. He sees these as basic conceptual hierarchies, mainly smuggled in by language itself, which provide the illusion of definition or orientation. He further claims that the deconstructive work of overturning these pairings, which valorize one of the two over the other, leads to a political and social overturning of actual, non-conceptual hierarchies. But to automatically refuse all binary oppositions is itself a metaphysical proposition; it in fact bypasses politics and history out of a failure to see in opposites, however imprecise they may be, anything but a linguistic reality. In the dismantling of every binarism, deconstruction aims at "conceiving difference without opposition." What in a smaller dosage would seem a salutary approach, a skepticism about neat, either/or characterizations, proceeds to the very questionable prescription of refusing all unambiguity. To say that there can be no yes or no position is tantamount to a paralysis of relativism, in which "impotence" becomes the valorized partner to "opposition."

Perhaps the case of Paul De Man, who extended and deepened Derrida's seminal deconstructive positions (surpassing him, in the opinion of many), is instructive. Shortly after the death of De Man in 1985, it was discovered that as a young man he had written several anti-Semitic, pro-Nazi newspaper articles in occupied Belgium. The status of this brilliant Yale deconstructor, and indeed to some, the moral and philosophical value of deconstruction itself, were called into question by the sensational revelation. De Man, like Derrida, had stressed "the duplicity, the confusion, the untruth that we take for granted in the use of language." Consistent with this, albeit to his discredit, in my opinion, was Derrida's tortuous commentary on De Man's collaborationist period: in sum, "how can we judge, who has the right to say?" A shabby testimony for deconstruction, considered in any way as a moment of the anti-authoritarian.

Derrida announced that deconstruction "instigates the subversion of every kingdom." In fact, it has remained within the safely academic realm of inventing ever more ingenious textual complications to keep itself in business and avoid reflecting on its own political situation. One of Derrida's most central terms, dissemination, describes language, under the principle of difference, as not so much a rich harvest of meanings but a kind of endless loss and spillage, with meaning appearing everywhere and evaporating virtually at once. This flow of language, ceaseless and unsatisfying, is a most accurate parallel to that of the heart of consumer capital and its endless circulation of non-significance. Derrida thus unwittingly eternalizes and universalizes dominated life by rendering human communication in its image. The "every kingdom" he would see deconstruction subverting is instead extended and deemed absolute.

Derrida represents both the well-travelled French tradition of *explication de texte* and a reaction against the Gallic veneration of Cartesian classicist language with its ideals of clarity and balance. Deconstruction emerged also, to a degree, as part of the original element of the near-revolution of 1968, namely the student revolt against rigidified French higher education. Some of its key terms (e.g. dissemination) are borrowed from Blanchot's reading of Heidegger, which is not to deny a significant originality in Derridean thought. Presence and representation constantly call each other into question, revealing the underlying system as infinitely fissured, and this in itself is an important contribution.

Unfortunately, to transform metaphysics into the question of writing, in which meanings virtually choose themselves and thus one discourse (and therefore mode of action) cannot be demonstrated to be better than another, seems less than radical. Deconstruction is now embraced by the heads of English departments, professional societies, and other bodies-in-good-standing because it raises the issue of representation itself so weakly. Derrida's deconstruction of philosophy admits that it must leave intact the very concept whose lack of basis it exposes. While finding the notion of a language-independent reality untenable, neither does deconstruction promise liberation from the famous "prison house of language." The essence of language, the primacy of the symbolic, are not really tackled, but are shown to be as inescapable as they are inadequate to fulfillment. No exit; as Derrida declared: "It is not a question of releasing oneself into an unrepressive new order (there are none)."

THE CRISIS OF REPRESENTATION

If deconstruction's contribution is mainly just an erosion of our assurance of reality, it forgets that reality—advertising and mass culture to mention just two superficial examples—has already accomplished this. Thus this quintessentially postmodern point of view bespeaks the movement of thinking from decadence to its elegiac, or post-thought phase, or as John Fekete summarized it, "a most profound crisis of the Western mind, a most profound loss of nerve."

Today's overload of representation serves to underline the radical impoverishment of life in technological class society—technology is deprivation. The classical theory of representation held that meaning or truth preceded and prescribed the representations that communicated it. But we may now inhabit a postmodern culture where the image has become less the expression of an individual subject than the commodity of an anonymous consumerist technology. Ever more mediated, life in the Information Age is increasingly controlled by the manipulation of signs, symbols, marketing and testing data, etc. Our time, says Derrida, is "a time without nature."

All formulations of the postmodern agree in detecting a crisis of representation. Derrida, as noted, began a challenge of the nature of the philosophical project itself as grounded in representation, raising some unanswerable questions about the relationship between representation and thought. Deconstruction undercuts the epistemological claims of representation, showing that language, for example, is inadequate to the task of representation. But this undercutting avoids tackling the repressive nature of its subject, insisting, again, that pure presence, a space beyond representation, can only be a utopian dream. There can be no unmediated contact or communication, only signs and representations; deconstruction is a search for presence and fulfillment interminably, necessarily, deferred.

Jacques Lacan, sharing the same resignation as Derrida, at least reveals more concerning the malign essence of representation. Extending Freud, he determined that the subject is both constituted and alienated by the entry into the symbolic order, namely, into language. While denying the possibility of a return to a pre-language state in which the broken promise of presence might be honored, he could at least see the central, crippling stroke that is the submission of free-ranging desires to the symbolic world, the surrender of uniqueness to language. Lacan termed jouissance unspeakable because it could properly occur only outside of language: that happiness which is the desire for a world without the fracture of money or writing, a society without representation.

The inability to generate symbolic meaning is, somewhat ironically, a basic problem for postmodernism. It plays out its stance at the frontier between what can be represented and what cannot, a half-way resolution (at best) that refuses to refuse representation. (Instead of providing the arguments for the view of the symbolic as repressive and alienating, the reader is referred to the first five essays of my *Elements of Refusal* [Left Bank Books, 1988], which deal with time, language, number, art, and agriculture as cultural estrangements owing to symbolization.) Meanwhile an estranged and exhausted public loses interest in the alleged solace of culture, and with the deepening and thickening of mediation emerges the discovery that perhaps this was always the meaning of culture. It is certainly not out of character, however, to find that postmodernism does not recognize reflection on the origins of representation, insisting as it does on the impossibility of unmediated existence.

In response to the longing for the lost wholeness of pre-civilization, postmodernism says that culture has become so fundamental to human existence that there is no possibility of delving down under it. This, of course, recalls Freud, who recognized the essence of civilization as a suppression of freedom and wholeness, but who decided that work and culture were more important. Freud at least was honest enough to admit the contradiction or non-reconciliation involved in opting for the crippling nature of civilization, whereas the postmodernists do not.

Floyd Merrell found that "a key, perhaps the principal key to Derridean thought" was Derrida's decision to place the question of origins off limits. And so while hinting throughout his work at a complicity between the fundamental assumptions of Western thought and the violences and repressions that have characterized Western civilization, Derrida has centrally, and very influentially, repudiated all notions of origins. Causative thinking, after all, is one of the objects of scorn for postmodernists. "Nature" is an illusion, so what could "unnatural" mean? In place of the situationists' wonderful "Under the pavement it's the beach," we have Foucault's famous repudiation, in *The Order of Things*, of the whole notion of the "repressive hypothesis." Freud gave us an understanding of culture as stunting and neurosis-generating; pm tells us that culture is all we can ever have, and that its foundations, if they exist, are not available to our understanding. Postmodernism is apparently what we are left with when the modernization process is complete and nature is gone for good.

Not only does pm echo Beckett's comment in *Endgame*, "there's no more nature," but it also denies that there ever was any recognizable space outside of language and culture. "Nature," declared Derrida in discussing Rousseau, "has never existed." Again, alienation is ruled out; that concept necessarily implies an idea of authenticity which postmodernism finds unintelligible. In this vein, Derrida cited "the loss of what has never taken place, of a self-presence which has never been given but only dreamed of…" Despite the limitations of structuralism, Lévi-Strauss' sense of affiliation with Rousseau, on the other hand, bore witness to his search for origins. Refusing to rule out liberation, either in terms of beginnings or goals, Lévi-Strauss never ceased to long for an "intact" society, a non-fractured world where immediacy had not yet been broken. For this Derrida, pejoratively to be sure, presents Rousseau as a utopian and Lévi-Strauss as an anarchist, cautioning against a "step further toward a sort of original anarchy," which would be only a dangerous delusion.

The real danger consists in not challenging, at the most basic level, the alienation and domination threatening to completely overcome nature, what is left of the natural in the world and within ourselves. Marcuse discerned that "the memory of gratification is at the origin of all thinking, and the impulse to recapture past gratification is the hidden driving power behind the process of thought." The question of origins also involves the whole question of the birth of abstraction and indeed of philosophical conceptuality as such, and Marcuse came close, in his search for what would constitute a state of being without repression, to confronting culture itself. He certainly never quite escaped the impression "that something essential had been forgotten" by humanity. Similar is the brief pronouncement by Novalis, "Philosophy is homesickness." By comparison, Kroker and Cook are undeniably correct in concluding that "the postmodern culture is a forgetting, a forgetting of origins and destinations."

BARTHES, FOUCAULT AND LYOTARD

Turning to other poststructuralist/postmodern figures, Roland Barthes, earlier in his career a major structuralist thinker, deserves mention. His *Writing Degree Zero* expressed the hope that language can be used in a utopian way and that there are controlling codes in culture that can be broken. By the early '70s, however, he fell into line with Derrida in seeing language as a metaphorical quagmire, whose metaphoricity is not recognized. Philosophy is befuddled by its own language and language in general cannot claim mastery of what it discusses. With *The Empire of Signs* (1970), Barthes had already renounced any critical, analytical intention. Ostensibly about Japan, this book is presented "without claiming to depict or analyze any reality whatsoever." Various fragments deal with cultural forms as diverse as haiku and slot machines, as parts of a sort of anti-utopian landscape wherein forms possess no meaning and all is surface. *Empire* may qualify as the first fully postmodern offering, and by the mid-'70s its author's notion of the pleasure of the text carried forward the same Derridean disdain for belief in the validity of public discourse. Writing had become an end in itself, a merely personal aesthetic the overriding consideration. Before his death in 1980, Barthes had explicitly denounced "any intellectual mode of writing," especially anything smacking of the political. By the time of his final work, *Barthes by Barthes*, the hedonism of words, paralleling a real-life dandyism, considered concepts not in terms of their validity or invalidity but only for their efficacy as tactics of writing.

In 1985 AIDS claimed the most widely known influence on postmodernism, Michel Foucault. Sometimes called "the philosopher of the death of man" and considered by many the greatest of Nietzsche's modern disciples, his wide-ranging historical studies (e.g. on madness, penal practices, sexuality) made him very well known and in themselves suggest differences between Foucault and the relatively more abstract and ahistorical Derrida. Structuralism, as noted, had already forcefully devalued the individual on largely linguistic grounds, whereas Foucault characterized "man (as) only a recent invention, a figure not yet two centuries old, a simple fold in our knowledge that will soon disappear." His emphasis lies in exposing "man" as that which is represented and brought forth as an object, specifically as a virtual invention of the modern human sciences. Despite an idiosyncratic style, Foucault's works were much more popular than those of Horkheimer and Adorno (e.g. *The Dialectic of Enlightenment*) and Erving Goffman, in the same vein of revealing the hidden agenda of bourgeois rationality. He pointed to the "individualizing" tactic at work in the key institutions in the early 1800s (the family, work, medicine, psychiatry, education), bringing out their normalizing, disciplinary roles within emerging capitalist modernity, as the "individual" is created by and for the dominant order.

Foucault, typically pm, rejects originary thinking and the notion that there is a "reality" behind or underneath the prevailing discourse of an era. Likewise, the subject is a delusion essentially created by discourse, an "I" created out of the ruling linguistic usages. And so his detailed historical narratives, termed "archaeologies" of knowledge, are offered instead of theoretical overviews, as if they carried no ideological or philosophical assumptions. For Foucault there are no foundations of the social to be apprehended outside the contexts of various periods, or epistemes, as he called them; the foundations change from one episteme to another. The prevailing discourse, which constitutes its subjects, is seemingly self-forming; this is a rather unhelpful approach to history resulting primarily from the fact that Foucault makes no reference to social groups, but focuses entirely on systems of thought. A further problem arises from his view that the episteme of an age cannot be known by those who labor within it. If consciousness is precisely what, by

Foucault's own account, fails to be aware of its relativism or to know what it would have looked like in previous epistemes, then Foucault's own elevated, encompassing awareness is impossible. This difficulty is acknowledged at the end of *The Archaeology of Knowledge* (1972), but remains unanswered, a rather glaring and obvious problem.

The dilemma of postmodernism is this: how can the status and validity of its theoretical approaches be ascertained if neither truth nor foundations for knowledge are admitted? If we remove the possibility of rational foundations or standards, on what basis can we operate? How can we understand what the society is that we oppose, let alone come to share such an understanding? Foucault's insistence on a Nietzschean perspectivism translates into the irreducible pluralism of interpretation. He relativized knowledge and truth only insofar as these notions attach to thought-systems other than his own, however. When pressed on this point, Foucault admitted to being incapable of rationally justifying his own opinions. Thus the liberal Habermas claims that postmodern thinkers like Foucault, Deleuze, and Lyotard are "neoconservative" for offering no consistent argumentation to move in one social direction rather than another. The pm embrace of relativism (or "pluralism') also means there is nothing to prevent the perspective of one social tendency from including a claim for the right to dominate another, in the absence of the possibility of determining standards.

The topic of power, in fact, was a central one to Foucault and the ways he treated it are revealing. He wrote of the significant institutions of modern society as united by a control intentionality, a "carceral continuum" that expresses the logical finale of capitalism, from which there is no escape. But power itself, he determined, is a grid or field of relations in which subjects are constituted as both the products and the agents of power. Everything thus partakes of power and so it is no good trying to find a "fundamental," oppressive power to fight against. Modern power is insidious and "comes from everywhere." Like God, it is everywhere and nowhere at once.

Foucault finds no beach underneath the paving stones, no "natural" order at all. There is only the certainty of successive regimes of power, each one of which must somehow be resisted. But Foucault's characteristically pm aversion to the whole notion of the human subject makes it quite difficult to see where such resistance might spring from, notwithstanding his view that there is no resistance to power that is not a variant of power itself. Regarding the latter point, Foucault reached a further dead-end in considering the relationship of power to knowledge. He came to see them as inextricably and ubiquitously linked, directly implying one another. The difficulties in continuing to say anything of substance in light of this interrelationship caused Foucault to eventually give up on a theory of power. The determinism involved meant, for one thing, that his political involvement became increasingly slight. It is not hard to see why Foucaultism was greatly boosted by the media, while the situationists, for example, were blacked out.

Castoriadis once referred to Foucault's ideas on power and opposition to it as, "Resist if it amuses you—but without a strategy, because then you would no longer be proletarian, but power." Foucault's own activism had attempted to embody the empiricist dream of a theory—and ideology—free approach, that of the "specific intellectual" who participates in particular, local struggles. This tactic sees theory used only concretely, as ad hoc "tool kit" methods for specific campaigns. Despite the good intentions, however, limiting theory to discrete, perishable instrumental "tools" not only refuses an explicit overview of society but accepts the general division of labor which is at the heart of alienation and domination. The desire to respect differences, local knowledge and the like refuses a reductive, totalitarian-tending overvaluing of theory, but only to accept the atomization of late capitalism with its splintering of life into the narrow specialties that are the province of so many experts. If "we are caught between the arrogance of surveying the whole and the timidity of inspecting the parts," as Rebecca Comay aptly put it, how does the second alternative (Foucault's) represent an advance over liberal reformism in general? This seems an especially pertinent question when one remembers how much Foucault's whole enterprise was aimed at disabusing us of the illusions of humanist reformers throughout history. The "specific intellectual" in fact turns out to be just one more expert, one more liberal attacking specifics rather than the roots of problems. And looking at the content of his activism, which was mainly in the area of penal reform, the orientation is almost too tepid to even qualify as liberal. In the '80s "he tried to gather, under the aegis of his chair at the College de France, historians, lawyers, judges, psychiatrists and doctors concerned with law and punishment," according to Keith Gandal. All the cops. "The work I did on the historical relativity of the prison form," said Foucault, "was an incitation to try to think of other forms of punishment." Obviously, he accepted the legitimacy of this society and of punishment; no less unsurprising was his corollary dismissal of anarchists as infantile in their hopes for the future and faith in human potential.

The works of Jean-François Lyotard are significantly contradictory to each other—in itself a pm trait—but also express a central postmodern theme: that society cannot and should not be understood as a whole. Lyotard is a prime example of anti-totalizing thought to the point that he has summed up postmodernism as "incredulity toward metanarratives" or overviews. The idea that it is unhealthy as well as impossible to grasp the whole is part of an enormous reaction in France since the '60s against Marxist and Communist influences. While Lyotard's chief target is the Marxist tradition, once so very strong in French political and intellectual life, he goes further and rejects social theory in toto. For example, he has come to believe that any concept of alienation—the idea that an original unity, wholeness, or innocence is fractured by the fragmentation and indifference of capitalism—ends up as a totalitarian attempt to unify society coercively. Characteristically, his mid-'70s Libidinal Economy denounces theory as terror.

One might say that this extreme reaction would be unlikely outside of a culture so dominated by the Marxist left, but another look tells us that it fits perfectly with the wider, disillusioned postmodern condition. Lyotard's wholesale rejection of post-Kantian Enlightenment values does, after all, embody the realization that rational critique, at least in the form of the confident values and beliefs of Kantian, Hegelian and Marxist metanarrative theory, has been debunked by dismal historical reality. According to Lyotard, the pm era signifies that all consoling myths of intellectual mastery and truth are at an end, replaced by a plurality of "language-games," the Wittgensteinian notion of "truth" as provisionally shared and circulating without any kind of epistemological warrant or philosophical foundation. Language-games are a pragmatic, localized, tentative basis for knowledge; unlike the comprehensive views of theory or historical interpretation, they depend on the agreement of participants for their use-value. Lyotard's ideal is thus a multitude of "little narratives" instead of the "inherent dogmatism" of metanarratives or grand ideas. Unfortunately, such a pragmatic approach must accommodate to things as they are, and depends upon prevailing consensus virtually by definition.

Thus Lyotard's approach is of limited value for creating a break from the everyday norms. Though his healthy, anti-authoritarian skepticism sees totalization as oppressive or coercive, what he overlooks is that the Foucaultian relativism of language-games, with their freely contracted agreement as to meaning, tends to hold that everything is of equal validity. As Gerard Raulet concluded, the resultant refusal of overview actually obeys the existing logic of homogeneity rather than somehow providing a haven for heterogeneity.

To find progress suspect is, of course, prerequisite to any critical approach, but the quest for heterogeneity must include awareness of its disappearance and a search for the reasons why it disappeared. Postmodern thought generally behaves as if in complete ignorance of the news that division of labor and commodification are eliminating the basis for cultural or social heterogeneity. Pm seeks to preserve what is virtually nonexistent and rejects the wider thinking necessary to deal with impoverished reality. In this area it is of interest to look at the relationship between pm and technology, which happens to be of decisive importance to Lyotard.

Adorno found the way of contemporary totalitarianism prepared by the Enlightenment ideal of triumph over nature, also known as instrumental reason. Lyotard sees the fragmentation of knowledge as essential to combatting domination, which disallows the overview necessary to see that, to the contrary, the isolation that is fragmented knowledge forgets the social determination and purpose of that isolation. The celebrated "heterogeneity" is nothing much more than the splintering effect of an overbearing totality he would rather ignore. Critique is never more discarded than in Lyotard's postmodern positivism, resting as it does on the acceptance of a technical rationality that forgoes critique. Unsurprisingly, in the era of the decomposition of meaning and the renunciation of seeing what the ensemble of mere "facts" really add up to, Lyotard embraces the computerization of society. Rather like the Nietzschean Foucault, Lyotard believes that power is more and more the criterion of truth. He finds his companion in the postmodern pragmatist Richard Rorty who likewise welcomes modern technology and is deeply wedded to the hegemonic values of present-day industrial society.

In 1985 Lyotard put together a spectacular high-tech exhibition at the Pompidou Center in Paris, featuring the artificial realities and microcomputer work of such artists as Myron Krueger. At the opening, its planner declared, "We wanted...to indicate that the world is not evolving toward greater clarity and simplicity, but rather toward a new degree of complexity in which the individual may feel very lost but in which he can in fact become more free." Apparently overviews are permitted if they coincide with the plans of our masters for us and for nature. But the more specific point lies with "immateriality," the title of the exhibit and a Lyotardian term which he associates with the erosion of identity, the breaking down of stable barriers between the self and a world produced by our involvement in labyrinthine technological and social systems. Needless to say, he approves of this condition, celebrating, for instance, the "pluralizing" potential of new communications technology—of the sort that de-sensualizes life, flattens experience and eradicates the natural world. Lyotard writes: "All peoples have a right to science," as if he has the very slightest understanding of what science means. He prescribes "public free access to the memory and data banks." A horrific view of liberation, somewhat captured by: "Data banks are the encyclopedia of tomorrow; they are "nature" for postmodern men and women."

Its usually very opaque jargon aside, pm partakes of fast-food consumerism. It is also, maybe even more fundamentally, the embrace of technology. The expression, as Lorenzo Simpson puts it so well in his *Technology, Time, and the Conversations of Modernity*, of a world "being thoroughly dominated and domesticated by technology." In sum, "the realization of the universalization of the technological attitude, its completion."

Frank Lentricchia termed Derrida's deconstructionist project "an elegant, commanding overview matched in philosophic history only by Hegel." It is an obvious irony that the postmodernists require a general theory to support their assertion as to why there cannot and should not be general theories or metanarratives. Sartre, gestalt theorists and common sense tell us that what pm dismisses as "totalizing reason" is in fact inherent in perception itself: one sees a whole, as a rule, not discrete fragments. Another irony is provided by Charles Altieri's observation of Lyotard, "that this thinker so acutely aware of the dangers inherent in master narratives nonetheless remains completely committed to the authority of generalized abstraction." Pm announces an anti-generalist bias, but its practitioners, Lyotard perhaps especially, retain a very high level of abstraction in discussing culture, modernity and other such topics which are of course already vast generalizations.

"A liberated humanity," wrote Adorno, "would by no means be a totality." Nonetheless, we are currently stuck with a social world that is one and which totalizes with a vengeance. Postmodernism, with its celebrated fragmentation and heterogeneity, may choose to forget about the totality, but the totality will not forget about us.

DELEUZE, GUATTARI AND BAUDRILLARD

Gilles Deleuze's "schizo-politics" flow, at least in part, from the prevailing pm refusal of overview, of a point of departure. Also called "nomadology," employing "rhizomatic writing," Deleuze's method champions the deterritorialization and decoding of structures of domination, by which capitalism will supersede itself through its own dynamic. With his sometime partner Felix Guattari, with whom he shares a specialization in psychoanalysis, he hopes to see the system's schizophrenic tendency intensified to the point of shattering. Deleuze seems to share, or at least comes very close to, the absurdist conviction of Yoshimoto Takai that consumption constitutes a new form of resistance.

This brand of denying the totality by the radical strategy of urging it to dispose of itself also recalls the impotent pm style of opposing representation: meanings do not penetrate to a center, they do not represent something beyond their reach. "Thinking without representing," is Charles Scott's description of Deleuze's approach. Schizo-politics celebrates surfaces and discontinuities; nomadology is the opposite of history.

Deleuze also embodies the postmodern "death of the subject" theme, in his and Guattari's best-known work, *Anti-Oedipus*, and subsequently. "Desiringmachines," formed by the coupling of parts, human and nonhuman, with no distinction between them, seek to replace humans as the focus of his social theory. In opposition to the illusion of an individual subject in society, Deleuze portrays a subject no longer even recognizably anthropocentric. One cannot escape the feeling, despite his supposedly radical intention, of an embrace of alienation, even a wallowing in estrangement and decadence.

In the early '70s Jean Baudrillard exposed the bourgeois foundations of marxism, mainly its veneration of production and work, in his *Mirror of Production* (1972). This contribution hastened the decline of marxism and the Communist Party in France, already in disarray after the reactionary role played by the Left against the upheavals of May '68. Since that time, however, Baudrillard has come to represent the darkest tendencies of postmodernism and has emerged, especially in America, as a pop star to the ultra-jaded, famous for his fully disenchanted views of the contemporary world. In addition to the unfortunate resonance between the almost hallucinatory morbidity of Baudrillard and a culture in decomposition, it is also true that he (along with Lyotard) has been magnified by the space he was expected to fill following the passing, in the '80s, of relatively deeper thinkers like Barthes and Foucault.

Derrida's deconstructive description of the impossibility of a referent outside of representation becomes, for Baudrillard, a negative metaphysics in which reality is transformed by capitalism into simulations that have no backing. The culture of capital is seen as having gone beyond its fissures and contradictions to a place of self-sufficiency that reads like a rather science-fiction rendering of Adorno's totally administered society. And there can be no resistance, no "going back," in part because the alternative would be that nostalgia for the natural, for origins, so adamantly ruled out by postmodernism.

"The real is that of which it is possible to give an equivalent reproduction." Nature has been so far left behind that culture determines materiality; more specifically, media simulation shapes reality. "The simulacrum is never that which conceals the truth—it is the truth which conceals that there is none. The simulacrum is true." Debord's "society of the spectacle"—but at a stage of implosion of self, agency, and history into the void of simulations such that the spectacle is in service to itself alone.

It is obvious that in our "Information Age," the electronic media technologies have become increasingly dominant, but the overreach of Baudrillard's dark vision is equally obvious. To stress the power of images should not obscure underlying material determinants and objectives, namely profit and expansion. The assertion that the power of the media now means that the real no longer exists is related to his claim that power "can no longer be found anywhere"; and both claims are false. Intoxicating rhetoric cannot erase the fact that the essential information of the Information Age deals with the hard realities of efficiency, accounting, productivity and the like. Production has not been supplanted by simulation, unless one can say that the planet is being ravaged by mere images, which is not to say that a progressive acceptance of the artificial does not greatly assist the erosion of what is left of the natural.

Baudrillard contends that the difference between reality and representation has collapsed, leaving us in a "hyperreality" that is always and only a simulacrum. Curiously, he seems not only to acknowledge the inevitability of this development, but to celebrate it. The cultural, in its widest sense, has reached a qualitatively new stage in which the very realm of meaning and signification has disappeared. We live in "the age of events without consequences" in which the "real" only survives as formal category, and this, he imagines, is welcomed. "Why should we think that people want to disavow their daily lives in order to search for an alternative? On the contrary, they want to make a destiny of it...to ratify monotony by a grander monotony." If there should be any "resistance," his prescription for that is similar to that of Deleuze, who would prompt society to become more schizophrenic. That is, it consists wholly in what is granted by the system: "You want us to consume—O.K., let's consume always more, and anything whatsoever; for any useless and absurd purpose." This is the radical strategy he names "hyperconformity."

At many points, one can only guess as to which phenomena, if any, Baudrillard's hyperbole refers. The movement of consumer society toward both uniformity and dispersal is perhaps glimpsed in one passage...but why bother when the assertions seem all too often cosmically inflated and ludicrous. This most extreme of the postmodern theorists, now himself a top-selling cultural object, has referred to the "ominous emptiness of all discourse," apparently unaware of the phrase as an apt reference to his own vacuities.

Japan may not qualify as "hyperreality," but it is worth mentioning that its culture seems to be even more estranged and postmodern than that of the U.S. In the judgment of Masao Miyoshi, "the dispersal and demise of modern subjectivity, as talked about by Barthes, Foucault, and many others, have long been evident in Japan, where intellectuals have chronically complained about the absence of selfhood." A flood of largely specialized information, provided by experts of all kinds, highlights the Japanese high-tech consumer ethos, in which the indeterminacy of meaning and a high valuation of perpetual novelty work hand in hand. Yoshimoto Takai is perhaps the most prolific national cultural critic; somehow it does not seem bizarre to many that he is also a male fashion model, who extols the virtues and values of shopping.

Yasuo Tanaka's hugely popular *Somehow, Crystal* (1980) was arguably the Japanese cultural phenomenon of the '80s, in that this vacuous, unabashedly consumerist novel, awash with brand names (a bit like Bret Easton Ellis' 1991 *American Psycho)*, dominated the decade. But it is cynicism, even more than superficiality, that seems to mark that full dawning of postmodernism which Japan seems to be: how else does one explain that the most incisive analyses of pm there—*Now is the Meta-Mass Age*, for example—are published by the Parco Corporation, the country's trendiest marketing and retailing outlet. Shigesatu Itoi is a top media star, with his own television program, numerous publications, and constant appearances in magazines. The basis of this idol's fame? Simply that he wrote a series of state-of-the-art (flashy, fragmented, etc.) ads for Seibu, Japan's largest and most innovative department store chain. Where capitalism exists in its most advanced, postmodern form, knowledge is consumed in exactly the way that one buys clothes. "Meaning" is passé, irrelevant; style and appearance are all.

We are fast arriving at a sad and empty place, which the spirit of postmodernism embodies all too well. "Never in any previous civilization have the great metaphysical preoccupations, the fundamental questions of being and the meaning of life, seemed so utterly remote and pointless," in Frederic Jameson's judgment. Peter Sloterdijk finds that "the discontent in culture has assumed a new quality: it appears as universal, diffuse cynicism." The erosion of meaning, pushed forward by intensified reification and fragmentation, causes the cynic to appear everywhere. Psychologically "a borderline melancholic," he is now "a mass figure."

The postmodern capitulation to perspectivism and decadence does not tend to view the present as alienated—surely an old-fashioned concept— but rather as normal and even pleasant. Robert Rauschenberg: "I really feel sorry for people who think things like soap dishes or mirrors or Coke bottles are ugly, because they're surrounded by things like that all day long, and it must make them miserable." It isn't just that "everything is culture," the culture of the commodity, that is offensive; it is also the pm affirmation of what is by its refusal to make qualitative distinctions and judgments. If the postmodern at least does us the favor, unwittingly, of registering the decomposition and even depravity of a cultural world that accompanies and abets the current frightening impoverishment of life, that may be its only "contribution."

We are all aware of the possibility that we may have to endure, until its self-destruction and ours, a world fatally out of focus. "Obviously, culture does not dissolve merely because persons are alienated," wrote John Murphy, adding, "A strange type of society has to be invented, nonetheless, in order for alienation to be considered normative."

Meanwhile, where are vitality, refusal, the possibility of creating a non-mutilated world? Barthes proclaimed a Nietzschean "hedonism of discourse"; Lyotard counselled, "Let us be pagans." Such wild barbarians! Of course, their real stuff is blank and dispirited, a thoroughly relativized academic sterility. Postmodernism leaves us hopeless in an unending mall; without a living critique; nowhere.

CHAPTER FIVE

THE NIHILIST'S DICTIONARY

1. NICEISM

Nice-ism n. *tendency, more or less socially codified, to approach reality in terms of whether others behave cordially; tyranny of decorum which disallows thinking or acting for oneself; mode of interaction based upon the above absence of critical judgement or autonomy.*

All of us prefer what is friendly, sincere, pleasant—nice. But in an immiserated world of pervasive and real crisis, which should be causing all of us to radically reassess everything, the nice can be the false.

The face of domination is often a smiling one, a cultured one. Auschwitz comes to mind, with its managers who enjoyed their Goethe and Mozart. Similarly, it was not evil-looking monsters who built the A-bomb but nice liberal intellectuals. Ditto regarding those who are computerizing life and those who in other ways are the mainstays of participation in this rotting order, just as it is the nice businessperson (self-managed or otherwise) who is the backbone of a cruel work-and-shop existence by concealing its real horrors.

Cases of niceism include the peaceniks, whose ethic of niceness puts them—again and again and again-in stupid ritualized, no-win situations, those Earth First!ers who refuse to confront the thoroughly reprehensible ideology at the top of "their" organization, and *Fifth Estate*, whose highly important contributions now seem to be in danger of an eclipse by liberalism. All the single-issue causes, from ecologism to feminism, and all the militancy in their service, are only ways of evading the necessity of a qualitative break with more than just the excesses of the system.

The nice as the perfect enemy of tactical or analytical thinking: Be agreeable; don't let having radical ideas make waves in your personal behavior. Accept the pre-packaged methods and limits of the daily strangulation. Ingrained deference, the conditioned response to "play by the rules"—authority's rules—this is the real Fifth Column, the one within us.

In the context of a mauled social life that demands the drastic as a minimum response toward health, niceism becomes more and more infantile, conformist and dangerous. It cannot grant joy, only more routine and isolation. The pleasure of authenticity exists only against the grain of society. Niceism keeps us all in our places, confusedly reproducing all that we supposedly abhor. Let's stop being nice to this nightmare and all who would keep us in it.

2. TECHNOLOGY

Tech-nol-o-gy n. According to Webster's: *industrial or applied science. In reality: the ensemble of division of labor/production/industrialism and its impact on us and on nature. Technology is the sum of mediations between us and the natural world and the sum of those separations mediating us from each other. It is all the drudgery and toxicity required to produce and reproduce the stage of hyper-alienation we live in. It is the texture and the form of domination at any given stage of hierarchy and commodification.*

Those who still say that technology is "neutral," "merely a tool," have not yet begun to consider what is involved. Junger, Adorno and Horkheimer, Ellul and a few others over the past decades—not to mention the crushing, all but unavoidable truth of technology in its global and personal toll—have led to a deeper approach to the topic. Thirty-five years ago the esteemed philosopher Jaspers wrote that "Technology is only a means, in itself neither good nor evil. Everything depends upon what man makes of it, for what purpose it serves him, under what conditions he places it." The archaic sexism aside, such superficial faith in specialization and technical progress is increasingly seen as ludicrous. Infinitely more on target was Marcuse when he suggested in 1964 that "the very concept of technical reason is perhaps ideological. Not only the application of technology, but technology itself is domination... methodical, ascientific, calculated, calculating control." Today we experience that control as a steady reduction of our contact with the living world, a speeded-up Information Age emptiness drained by computerization and poisoned by the dead, domesticating imperialism of high-tech method. Never before have people been so infantilized, made so dependent on the machine for everything; as the Earth rapidly approaches its extinction due to technology, our souls are shrunk and flattened by its pervasive rule. Any sense of wholeness and freedom can only return by the undoing of the massive division of labor at the heart of technological progress. This is the liberatory project in all its depth.

Of course, the popular literature does not yet reflect a critical awareness of what technology is. Some works completely embrace the direction we are being taken, such as McCorduck's *Machines Who Think* and Simons" *Are Computers Alive?*, to mention a couple of the more horrendous. Other, even more recent books seem to offer a judgment that finally flies in the face of mass pro-tech propaganda, but fail dismally as they reach their conclusions. Murphy, Mickunas and Pilotta edited *The Underside of High-Tech: Technology and the Deformation of Human Sensibilities*, whose ferocious title is completely undercut by an ending that technology will become human as soon as we change our assumptions about it! Very similar is Siegel and Markoff's *The High Cost of High Tech*; after chapters detailing the various levels of technological debilitation, we once again learn that it's all just a question of attitude: "We must, as a society, understand the full impact of high technology if we are to shape it into a tool for enhancing human comfort, freedom and peace." This kind of cowardice and/or dishonesty owes only in part to the fact that major publishing corporations do not wish to publicize fundamentally radical ideas.

The above-remarked flight into idealism is not a new tactic of avoidance. Martin Heidegger, considered by some the most original and deep thinker of this century, saw the individual becoming only so much raw material for the limitless expansion of industrial technology. Incredibly, his solution was to find in the Nazi movement the essential "encounter between global technology and modern man." Behind the rhetoric of National Socialism, unfortunately, was only an acceleration of technique, even into the sphere of genocide as a problem of industrial production. For the Nazis and the gullible, it was, again a question of how technology is understood ideally, not as it really is. In 1940, the General Inspector for the German Road System put it this way: "Concrete and stone are material things. Man gives them form and spirit. National Socialist technology possesses in all material achievement ideal content."

The bizarre case of Heidegger should be a reminder to all that good intentions can go wildly astray without a willingness to face technology and its systematic nature as part of practical social reality. Heidegger feared the political consequences of really looking at technology critically; his apolitical theorizing thus constituted a part of the most monstrous development of modernity, despite his intention.

EarthFirst! claims to put nature first, to be above all petty "politics." But it could well be that behind the macho swagger of a Dave Foreman (and the "deep ecology" theorists who also warn against radicals) is a failure of nerve like Heidegger's, and the consequence, conceivably, could be similar.

3. CULTURE

Cul-ture n. commonly rendered as the sum of the customs, ideas, arts, patterns, etc. of a given society. Civilization is often given as a synonym, reminding us that cultivation—as in domestication—is right in there, too. The Situationists, in 1960, had it that "culture can be defined as the ensemble of means through which society thinks of itself and shows itself to itself." Getting warmer, Barthes remarked that it is "a machine for showing you desire. To desire, always to desire but never to understand."

Culture was more respected once, seemingly, something to "live up to." Now, instead of concern for how we fail culture, the emphasis is on how culture has failed us. Definitely something at work that thwarts us, does not satisfy and this makes itself more evident as we face globally and within us the death of nature. Culture, as the opposite of nature, grows discordant, sours, fades as we strangle in the thinner and thinner air of symbolic activity. High culture or low, palace or hovel, it's the same prison-house of consciousness; the symbolic as the repressive.

It is inseparable from the birth and continuation of alienation surviving, as ever, as compensation, a trade of the real for its objectification. Culture embodies the split between wholeness and the parts of the whole turning into domination. Time, language, number, art—cultural impositions that have come to dominate us with lives of their own.

Magazines and journals now teem with articles lamenting the spread of cultural illiteracy and historical amnesia, two conditions that underline a basic dis-ease in society. In our postmodern epoch the faces of fashion range from blank to sullen, as hard drug use, suicide, and emotional disability rates continue to soar. About a year ago I got a ride from Berkeley to Oregon with a U.C. senior and somewhere along the drive I asked her, after talking about the '60s, among other things, to describe her own generation. She spoke of her co-students in terms of loveless sex, increasing heroin use, and "a sense of despair masked by consumerism."

Meanwhile, massive denial continues. In a recent collection of essays on culture, D.J. Enright offers the sage counsel that "the more commonly personal misery and discontent are aired, the more firmly these ills tighten their grip on us." Since anxiety first sought deliverance via cultural form and expression, in the symbolic approach to authenticity, our condition has probably not been this transparently bankrupt. Robert Harbison's *Deliberate Regression* is another work displaying complete ignorance regarding the fundamental emptiness of culture: "the story of how enthusiasm for the primitive and the belief that salvation lies in unlearning came to be a force in almost every held of thought is exceedingly strange."

Certainly the ruins are there for everyone to see. From exhausted art in the form of the recycled mish-mash of postmodernism, to the poststructuralist technocrats like Lyotard, who finds in data banks "the Encyclopedia of tomorrow...'nature" for postmodern man," including such utterly impotent forms of "opposition" as "micropolitics" and "schizopolitics," there is little but the obvious symptoms of a general fragmentation and despair. Peter Sloterdijk (*Critique of Cynical Reason*) points out that cynicism is the cardinal, pervasive outlook, for now the best that negation has to offer.

But the myth of culture will manage to survive as long as our immiseration fails to force us to confront it, and so cynicism will remain as long as we allow culture to remain in lieu of unmediated life.

4. FERAL

Fer-al adj. *wild, or existing in a state of nature, as freely occurring animals or plants; having reverted to the wild state from domestication.*

We exist in a landscape of absence wherein real life is steadily being drained out by debased work, the hollow cycle of consumerism and the mediated emptiness of high-tech dependency. Today it is not only the stereotypical yuppie workaholic who tries to cheat despair via activity, preferring not to contemplate a fate no less sterile than that of the planet and (domesticated) subjectivity in general. We are confronted, nonetheless, by the ruins of nature and the ruin of our own nature, the sheer enormity of the meaninglessness and the inauthentic amounting to a weight of lies. It's still drudgery and toxicity for the vast majority, while a poverty more absolute than financial renders more vacant the universal Dead Zone of civilization. "Empowered" by computerization? Infantilized, more like. An Information Age characterized by increased communication? No, that would presuppose experience worth communicating. A time of unprecedented respect for the individual? Translation: wage-slavery needs the strategy of worker self-management at the point of production to stave off the continuing productivity crisis, and market research must target each "lifestyle" in the interest of a maximized consumer culture.

In the upside-down society the solution to massive alienation-induced drug use is a media barrage, with results as embarrassing as the hundreds of millions futilely spent against declining voter turnout. Meanwhile, TV, voice and soul of the modern world, dreams vainly of arresting the growth of illiteracy and what is left of emotional health by means of propaganda spots of 30 seconds or less. In the industrialized culture of irreversible depression, isolation, and cynicism, the spirit will die first, the death of the planet an afterthought. That is, unless we erase this rotting order, all of its categories and dynamics.

Meanwhile, the parade of partial (and for that reason false) oppositions proceeds on its usual routes. There are the Greens and their like who try to extend the life of the racket of electoralism, based on the lie that there is validity in any person representing another; these types would perpetuate just one more home for protest, in lieu of the real thing. The peace "movement" exhibits, in its every (uniformly pathetic) gesture, that it is the best friend of authority, property and passivity. One illustration will suffice: in May 1989, on the 20th anniversary of Berkeley's People's Park battle, a thousand people rose up admirably, looting 28 businesses and injuring 15 cops; declared peace-creep spokesperson Julia Talley, "These riots have no place in the peace movement." Which brings to mind the fatally misguided students in Tiananmen Square, after the June 3 massacre had begun, trying to prevent workers from fighting the government troops. And the general truth that the university is the number one source of that slow strangulation known as reform, the refusal of a qualitative break with degradation. Earth First! recognizes that domestication is the fundamental issue (e.g. that agriculture itself is malignant) but many of its partisans cannot see that our species could become wild.

Radical environmentalists appreciate that the turning of national forests into tree farms is merely a part of the overall project that also seeks their own suppression. But they will have to seek the wild everywhere rather than merely in wilderness as a separate preserve.

Freud saw that there is no civilization without the forcible renunciation of instincts, without monumental coercion. But, because the masses are basically "lazy and unintelligent," civilization is justified, he reasoned. This model or prescription was based on the idea that pre-civilized life was brutal and deprived—a notion that has been, amazingly, reversed in the past 20 years. Prior to agriculture, in other words, humanity existed in a state of grace, ease and communion with nature that we can barely comprehend today.

The vista of authenticity emerges as no less than a wholesale dissolution of civilization's edifice of repression, which Freud, by the way, described as "something which was imposed on a resisting majority by a minority which understood how to obtain possession of the means to power and coercion." We can either passively continue on the road to utter domestication and destruction or turn in the direction of joyful upheaval, passionate and feral embrace of wildness and life that aims at dancing on the ruins of clocks, computers and that failure of imagination and will called work. Can we justify our lives by anything less than such a politics of rage and dreams?

5. DIVISION OF LABOR

Di-vi-sion of la-bor n. *1. the breakdown into specific, circumscribed tasks for maximum efficiency of output which constitutes manufacture; cardinal aspect of production. 2. the fragmenting or reduction of human activity into separated toil that is the practical root of alienation; that basic specialization which makes civilization appear and develop.*

The relative wholeness of pre-civilized life was first and foremost an absence of the narrowing, confining separation of people into differentiated roles and functions. The foundation of our shrinkage of experience and powerlessness in the face of the reign of expertise, felt so acutely today, is the division of labor. It is hardly accidental that key ideologues of civilization have striven mightily to valorize it. In Plato's *Republic*, for example, we are instructed that the origin of the state lies in that "natural" inequality of humanity that is embodied in the division of labor. Durkheim celebrated a fractionated, unequal world by divining that the touchstone of "human solidarity," its essential moral value is—you guessed it. Before him, according to Franz Borkenau, it was a great increase in division of labor occurring around 1600 that introduced the abstract category of work, which may be said to underlie, in turn, the whole modern, Cartesian notion that our bodily existence is merely an object of our (abstract) consciousness.

In the first sentence of *The Wealth of Nations* (1776), Adam Smith foresaw the essence of industrialism by determining that division of labor represents a qualitative increase in productivity. 20 years later Schiller recognized that division of labor was producing a society in which its members were unable to develop their humanity. Marx could see both sides: "as a result of division of labor," the worker is "reduced to the condition of a machine." But decisive was Marx's worship of the fullness of production as essential to human liberation. The immiseration of humanity along the road of capital's development he saw as a necessary evil.

Marxism cannot escape the determining imprint of this decision in favor of division of labor, and its major voices certainly reflect this acceptance. Lukacs, for instance, chose to ignore it, seeing only the "reifying effects of the dominant commodity form" in his attention to the problem of proletarian consciousness. E.P. Thompson realized that with the factory system, "the character-structure of the rebellious pre-industrial labourer or artisan was violently recast into that of the submissive individual worker." But he devoted amazingly little attention to division of labor, the central mechanism by which this transformation was achieved. Marcuse tried to conceptualize a civilization without repression, while amply demonstrating the incompatibility of the two. In bowing to the "naturalness" inherent in division of labor, he judged that the "rational exercise of authority" and the "advancement of the whole" depend upon it—while a few pages later (in *Eros and Civilization*) granting that one's "labor becomes the more alien the more specialized the division of labor becomes."

Ellul understood how "the sharp knife of specialization has passed like a razor into the living flesh," how division of labor causes the ignorance of a "closed universe" cutting off the subject from others and from nature. Similarly did Horkheimer sum up the debilitation: "thus, for all their activity individuals are becoming more passive; for all their power over nature they are becoming more powerless in relation to society and themselves." Along these lines, Foucault emphasized productivity as the fundamental contemporary repression.

But recent Marxian thought continues in the trap of having, ultimately, to elevate division of labor for the sake of technological progress. Braverman's in many ways excellent *Labor and Monopoly Capital* explores the degradation of work, but sees it as mainly a problem of loss of "will and ambition to wrest control of production from capitalist hands." And Schwabbe's *Psychosocial Consequences of Natural and Alienated Labor* is dedicated to the ending of all domination in production and projects a self-management of production. The reason, obviously, that he ignores division of labor is that it is inherent in production; he does not see that it is nonsense to speak of liberation and production in the same breath.

The tendency of division of labor has always been the forced labor of the interchangeable cog in an increasingly autonomous, impervious-to-desire apparatus. The barbarism of modern times is still the enslavement to technology, that is to say, to division of labor. "Specialization," wrote Giedion, "goes on without respite," and today more than ever can we see and feel the barren, de-eroticized world it has brought us to. Robinson Jeffers decided, "I don't think industrial civilization is worth the distortion of human nature, and the meanness and loss of contact with the earth, that it entails."

Meanwhile, the continuing myths of the "neutrality" and "inevitability" of technological development are crucial to fitting everyone to the yoke of division of labor. Those who oppose domination while defending its core principle are the perpetuators of our captivity. Consider Guattari, that radical post-structuralist, who finds that desire and dreams are quite possible "even in a society with highly developed industry and highly developed public information services, etc." Our advanced French opponent of alienation scoffs at the naive who detect the "essential wickedness of industrial societies," but does offer the prescription that "the whole attitude of specialists needs questioning." Not the existence of specialists, of course, merely their "attitudes."

To the question, "How much division of labor should we jettison?" returns, I believe, the answer, "How much wholeness for ourselves and the planet do we want?"

6. PROGRESS

Prog-ress n. 1.[archaic] official journey, as of a ruler. 2. historical development, in the sense of advance or improvement. 3. forward course of history or civilization, as in horror show or death-trip.

Perhaps no single idea in Western civilization has been as important as the notion of progress. It is also true that, as Robert Nisbet has put it, "Everything now suggests that Western faith in the dogma of progress is waning rapidly in all levels and spheres in this final part of the twentieth century."

In the anti-authoritarian milieu, too, progress has fallen on hard times. There was a time when the syndicalist blockheads, like their close Marxist relatives, could more or less successfully harangue as marginal and insignificant those disinterested in organizing their alienation via unions, councils and the like. Instead of the old respect for productivity and production (the pillars of progress), a Luddite prescription for the factories is ascendant and anti-work a cardinal starting point of radical dialogue. We even see certain aging leopards trying to change their spots: the Industrial Workers of the World, embarrassed by the first word of their name may yet move toward refusing the second (though certainly not as an organization).

The eco-crisis is clearly one factor in the discrediting of progress, but how it remained an article of faith for so many for so long is a vexing question. For what has progress meant, after all? Its promise began to realize itself, in many ways, from history's very beginning. With the emergence of agriculture and civilization commenced, for instance, the progressive destruction of nature; large regions of the Near East, Africa and Greece were rather quickly rendered desert wastelands.

In terms of violence, the transformation from a mainly pacific and egalitarian gatherer-hunter mode to the violence of agriculture/civilization was rapid. "Revenge, feuds, warfare, and battle seem to emerge among, and to be typical of, domesticated peoples," according to Peter Wilson. And violence certainly has made progress along the way, needless to say, from state weapons of mega-death to the recent rise in outburst murders and serial killers.

Disease itself is very nearly an invention of civilized life; every known degenerative illness is part of the toll of historical betterment. From the wholeness and sensual vitality of prehistory, to the present vista of endemic ill-health and mass psychic misery—more progress.

The pinnacle of progress is today's Information Age, which embodies a progression in division of labor, from an earlier time of the greater possibility of unmediated understanding, to the stage where knowledge becomes merely an instrument of the repressive totality, to the current cybernetic era where data is all that's really left. Progress has put meaning itself to flight.

Science, the model of progress, has imprisoned and interrogated nature, while technology has sentenced it (and humanity) to forced labor. From the original dividing of the self that is civilization, to Descartes" splitting of the mind from the rest of objects (including the body), to our arid, high-tech present—a movement indeed wondrous. Two centuries ago the first inventors of industrial machinery were spat on by the English textile workers subjected to it and thought villainous by just about everyone but their capitalist paymasters. The designers of today's computerized slavery are lionized as cultural heroes, though opposition is beginning to mount.

In the absence of greater resistance, the inner logic of class society's development will culminate in a totally technicized life as its final stage. The equivalence of the progress of society and that of technology is becoming ever more apparent by the fact of their immanent convergence. *Theses on the Philosophy of History*, Walter Benjamin's last and best work, contains this lyrically expressed insight:

"A Klee painting named *Angelus Novus* shows an angel looking as though he is about to move away from something he is fixedly contemplating. His eyes are staring, his mouth is open, his wings are spread. This is how one pictures the angel of history. His face is turned toward the past. Where we perceive a chain of events, he sees one single catastrophe which keeps piling wreckage upon wreckage and hurls it in front of his feet. The angel would like to stay, awaken the dead, and make whole what has been smashed. But a storm is blowing from Paradise; it has got caught in his wings with such violence that the angel can no longer close them. This storm irresistibly propels him into the future to which his back is turned, while the pile of debris before him grows skyward. This storm is what we call progress."

7. ARTIFICIAL INTELLIGENCE, ARTIFICIAL LIFE

Though somewhat slowed in the past decade, the pursuit of Artificial Intelligence proceeds apace toward the highest moment of science and technology so far. The achievement of AI would mark a qualitative change in the actions, culture and self-perception of the human race, and what underlines this is how far this departure has already taken place.

Marvin Minsky described the brain as a three-pound computer made of meat, an outlook echoed since by AI theorists, such as the Churchills. The computer is constantly serving as a metaphor for the human mind or brain, so much so that we tend to see ourselves as thinking machines. Note how many mechanical terms have crept into the common vocabulary of human cognition.

It is the whole train of mass production, with its linearism and homogenization, that carries forward toward the currency of machine models, toward the non-individual and non-sensual and away from the sense of the natural and the whole. With the movement of AI (and robotics) the human becomes inessential. *Humanness* becomes inessential.

The computational metaphor that sees mind as an information-processing or symbol-manipulating machine has produced a psychology which looks to machines for central concepts. Cognitive psychology ground itself in the mathematical orientation of information theory and computer science. Indeed, the field of AI is now co-extensive with that of cognitive psychology and philosophy of mind. Computer modeling reigns from academic disciplines even to popular usage.

In 1981 Aaron Sloman and Monica Croucher wrote "Why Robots Will Have Emotions," which calls to mind *Psychology Today* for December 1983, dedicated to the "Affectionate Machine," a limitless tribute to the promise of AI. In the January 1990 *Scientific American*, John Searle asks, "Is the Brain's Mind a Computer Program?" while Patricia Smith Churchill and Paul Churchill pose the standard "Could a Machine Think?" The tentative answers are, I believe, less important than the presence of such questions.

Decades ago, Adorno could already see the contemporary diminishing and deforming of the individual at the hands of high tech, and its impact on critical thought. "The computer—which thinking wants to make its own equal and to whose greater glory it would like nothing better than to eliminate itself—is the bankruptcy petition of consciousness." Even earlier (1950), Alan Turing predicted that by the year 2000 "the use of words and general educated opinion will have altered so much that one will be able to speak of machines thinking" without fear of contradiction. His forecast clearly dealt not with the state of machines but with a prevailing future ethos. Growing alienation brings a sea change regarding the whole subject, which ultimately includes a redefinition of what it means to be human. Finally, perhaps, even "emotions" of computers will be recognized and will be confused with what is left of human sensibilities.

Meanwhile, the computer simulations of physicist Steven Wolfram supposedly replicate freely-occurring physical processes, leading to the dubious conclusion that nature itself is one vast computer. On a more tangible, if even eerier plane, is the effort to create synthetic life via computer simulation, the progress of which was the big news from the second Artificial Life Conference at Santa Fe in February 1990. What it means to be alive is also undergoing a cultural redefinition.

Relatedly, another wonderful development is the Human Genome Project of the National Institutes of Health, a $3 billion government attempt to decipher the three-billion-digit genetic sequence that encodes human growth. The massive Genome Project is yet another example of the dehumanizing paradigms engulfing us: one Nobel laureate has asserted that knowing that whole sequence would tell us what human beings really *are*. Add to this awful reductionism the potential vistas the project opens up for genetic engineering.

Computerized neuroscience, joined by AI, is pointed toward an interface of the artificial and the human on a deep neurological level. The trend, if unchecked, proposes nothing less than the cyborganization of the species, including the possibility of permanent genetic changes in us.

In the February 5, 1990 *Forbes*, David Churchbuck wrote of "The Ultimate Computer Game: Why Settle for the Real Thing if You Can Live in a Dream that Is Safer, Cheaper and Easier to Manipulate? Computers Will Soon Make Such a World Possible." His lengthy subtitle refers to the advent of "cyberspace" games that simulate total environments, a quantum leap from video games! Quite a testimony to increasing passivity and isolation in an increasingly artificial and empty world. Those who still see technology as "neutral," a mere "tool" existing apart from the dominant values and social system are criminally blind to the will to nullify of a death-trip culture.

8. COMMUNITY

Com-mu-ni-ty n. *1. a body of people having the same interests. 2. [Ecol.] an aggregate of organisms with mutual relations. 3. a concept invoked to establish solidarity, often when the basis for such affiliation is absent or when the actual content of that affiliation contradicts the stated political goal of solidarity.*

Community, by which one obviously means more than, say, neighborhood, is a very elusive term but a continuing touchstone of radical value. In fact, all manner of folks resort to it, from the pacifist encampments near nuclear test sites to "serve the people" leftists with their sacrifice-plus-manipulation approach to the proto-fascist Afrikaaner settlers. It is invoked for a variety of purposes or goals, but as a liberatory notion is a fiction.

Everyone feels the *absence* of community, because human fellowship must struggle, to even remotely exist, against what "community" is in reality. The nuclear family, religion, nationality, work, school, property, the specialism of roles—some combination of these seems to comprise every surviving community since the imposition of civilization. So we are dealing with an illusion, and to argue that some qualitatively higher form of community is allowed to exist within civilization is to affirm civilization. Positivity furthers the lie that the authentically social can coexist with domestication. In this regard, what really accompanies domination, as community, is at best middle-class, respect-the-system protest.

Fifth Estate, for example, undercuts its (partial) critique of civilization by upholding community and ties to it in its every other sentence. At times it seems that the occasional Hollywood film (e.g. *Emerald Forest, Dances With Wolves*) outdoes our anti-authoritarian journals in showing that a liberatory solidarity springs from non-civilization and its combat with the "community" of industrial modernity.

Jacques Camatte discussed capital's movement from the stage of formal domination to that of real domination. But there appear to be significant grounds from which to project the continuing erosion of support for existing community and a desire for genuine solidarity and freedom. As Fredy Perlman put it, near the end of his exceptional *Against His-Story, Against Leviathan!*: "What is known is that Leviathan, the great artifice, single and world-embracing for the first time, in His-story, is decomposing... It is a good time for people to let go of its sanity, its masks and armors, and go mad, for they are already being ejected from its pretty polis."

The refusal of community might be termed a self-defeating isolation but it appears preferable, healthier, than declaring our allegiance to the daily fabric of an increasingly self-destructive world. Magnified alienation is not a condition chosen by those who insist on the truly social over the falsely communal. It is present in any case, due to the content of community. Opposition to the estrangement of civilized, pacified existence should at least amount to naming that estrangement instead of celebrating it by calling it community.

The defense of community is a conservative gesture that faces away from the radical break required. Why defend that to which we are held hostage?

In truth, there is no community. And only by abandoning what is passed off in its name can we move on to redeem a vision of communion and vibrant connectedness in a world that bears no resemblance to this one. Only a negative "community," based explicitly on contempt for the categories of existent community, is legitimate and appropriate to our aims.

9. SOCIETY

So-ci-e-ty n. *from L.* socius, *companion. 1. an organized aggregate of interrelated individuals and groups. 2. totalizing racket, advancing at the expense of the individual, nature and human solidarity.*

Society everywhere is now driven by the treadmill of work and consumption. This harnessed movement, so very far from a state of companionship, does not take place without agony and disaffection. Having more never compensates for being less, as witness rampant addiction to drugs, work, exercise, sex, etc. Virtually anything can be and is overused in the desire for satisfaction in a society whose hallmark is denial of satisfaction. But such excess at least gives evidence of the hunger for fulfillment, that is, an immense dissatisfaction with what is before us.

Hucksters purvey every kind of dodge, for example. New Age panaceas, disgusting materialistic mysticism on a mass scale: sickly and self-absorbed, apparently incapable of looking at any part of reality with courage or honesty. For New Age practitioners, psychology is nothing short of an ideology and society is irrelevant.

Meanwhile, Bush, surveying "generations born numbly into despair," was predictably loathsome enough to blame the victimized by citing their "moral emptiness." The depth of immiseration might best be summed up by the federal survey of high schoolers released 9/19/91, which found that 27 percent of them "thought seriously" about suicide in the preceding year.

It could be that the social, with its growing testimony to alienation— mass depression, the refusal of literacy, the rise of panic disorders, etc.— may finally be registering politically. Such phenomena as continually declining voter turnout and deep distrust of government led the Kettering Foundation in June '91 to conclude that "the legitimacy of our political institutions is more at issue than our leaders imagine," and an October study of three states (as reported by columnist Tom Wicker, 10/14/91) to discern "a dangerously broad gulf between the governors and the governed."

The longing for nonmutilated life and a nonmutilated world in which to live it collides with one chilling fact: underlying the progress of modern society is capital's insatiable need for growth and expansion. The collapse of state capitalism in Eastern Europe and the USSR leaves only the "triumphant" regular variety, in command but now confronted insistently with far more basic contradictions than the ones it allegedly overcame in its pseudo-struggle with "socialism." Of course, Soviet industrialism was not qualitatively different from any other variant of capitalism, and far more importantly, no system of production (division of labor, domination of nature, and work-and-pay slavery in more or less equal doses) can allow for either human happiness or ecological survival.

We can now see an approaching vista of all the world as a toxic, ozone-less deadness. Where once most people looked to technology as a promise, now we know for certain that it will kill us. Computerization, with its congealed tedium and concealed poisons, expresses the trajectory of society, engineered sleekly away from sensuous existence and finding its current apotheosis in Virtual Reality.

The escapism of VR is not the issue, for which of us could get by without escapes? Likewise, it is not so much a diversion from consciousness as it is itself a consciousness of complete estrangement from the natural world. Virtual Reality testifies to a deep pathology, reminiscent of the Baroque canvases of Rubens that depict armored knights mingling with but separated from naked women. Here the "alternative" technojunkies of *Whole Earth Review*, pioneer promoters of VR, show their true colors. A fetish of "tools," and a total lack of interest in critique of society's direction, lead to glorification of the artificial paradise of VR.

The consumerist void of high-tech simulation and manipulation owes its dominance to two increasing tendencies in society, specialization of labor and the isolation of individuals. From this context emerges the most terrifying aspect of evil: it tends to be committed by people who are not particularly evil. Society, which in no way could survive a conscious inspection is arranged to prevent that very inspection.

The dominant, oppressive ideas do not permeate the whole of society, rather their success is assured by the fragmented nature of opposition to them. Meanwhile, what society dreads most are precisely the lies it suspects it is built upon. This dread or avoidance is obviously not the same as beginning to subject a deadening force of circumstances to the force of events.

Adorno noted in the '60s that society is growing more and more entrapping and disabling. He predicted that eventually talk of causation within society would become meaningless: society itself is the cause. The struggle toward a society—if it could still be called that-of the face-to-face, in and of the natural world, must be based on an understanding of society today as a monolithic, all-encompassing death march.

PART TWO

THE WAY WE USED TO BE

CHAPTER SIX

THE WAY
WE USED TO BE

HOW LONG AGO did our humanness begin? Evidence keeps pushing back the dates by which we exhibited various capacities and achievements. It has reached the point, with almost certainly more revelations to come, of presenting us with grounds for a new understanding of humanity in the neighborhood of two million years ago.

This critical overview focuses on *Homo erectus*, who followed *Homo habilis*, the earliest human species, and survived for about 1.5 million years. But it must be taken into account from the start that the taxonomic framework itself, looking at life as basically taxa or species, is not only questionable but somewhat confused. D.W. Cameron points out the "explosion" in the recognition of new hominid species and the questions this introduces.[1] Separate species vs. continuity of species is an issue, for example. Xinzhi Wu and Poirier point to "a long recognized general morphological similarity between Chinese H. erectus and subsequent H. sapiens in China,"[2] suggesting that a reasonable classification for the populations of more than the last one million years would be to include them all within our own species, *Homo sapiens*. "Does *Homo erectus* exist as a true taxon or should it be sunk into *Homo sapiens*?" asks Wenke.[3] Perspectives, by the way, that imply the earlier and earlier emergence of human aptitudes. Taxonomic boundaries, then, are rather subjective constructs influenced by archaeological discoveries.

There are still a few who do not see "fully modern" hunter-gatherers in the picture until about 40,000 years ago,[4] but such a view is being rapidly revised. An Ethiopian site yielded this *Science Daily* headline: "The Oldest

Homo sapiens: Fossils Push Human Emergence Back to 195,000 Years Ago."[5] Even "early *H. erectus*," Gilbert asserts, is "very similar postcranially to modern humans."[6] Colin Tudge tells us, "There is no God-given law that says that *Homo sapiens* was or is the only bona fide species of human being," adding that "the very first people who were more or less like ourselves...date from about five hundred thousand years ago."[7]

But so often they were ignored altogether by researchers and scholars or looked at as strictly lower forms, consonant, for example, with the Aristotelian "Great Chain of Being" ranking all creatures along a continuum, from "beasts" to "higher" mankind, to the angels, etc. Similarly, some view *Homo erectus* as a creature of great but unrealized potential, failing to see our very early forebears on their own terms, for what they were in themselves.

Nadia Seremetakis cited a once whole sensory state and our separation from that primal and originary experience.[8] Who we are and what we are doing here might be enriched by considering what obtained at the beginning, and for so vastly long a time. In what Giorgio Agamben calls the age of "total management," we seem no longer recognizably either human or animal, lost in the movement toward a techno-existence.[9]

It is time to grant *Homo erectus*, using the term for present purposes, the humanness and abilities which are the species" due—notably ecological flexibility and premier generalist status in the world.

The ultimate origin of the hominid family is that of the first bipedal apes, roughly 7.5 million years ago, not forgetting the contrast between the quite hierarchical nature of extant great apes and egalitarian hunter-gatherers. Ape-like in many or most respects were the Australopithecines in the original hominid birthplace, East Africa, until about three million years ago. This is the very approximate date for the beginning of the first human species, *Homo habilis*, or "handy man." And close to two million years ago *Homo erectus* appears, "much more human in appearance, brain size, stature and culture," judges Donald Merlin, adding that "With this species, a major threshold had been crossed in human evolution."[10]

Stable social structures and home bases have indicated to many that for *Homo erectus*, sharing and cooperation—as with contemporary foraging societies—were key parts of an optimum survival strategy.[11] *Homo erectus* lasted close to two million years, all the way into the Neanderthal period about 200,000 years ago, during which time half of Earth's mammal families became extinct. The persistence through time of *Homo erectus* is possibly the characteristic that stands out the most as we contemplate the potential brevity of *Homo sapiens*. Niles Eldridge reminds us that "That is, after all, the mark of success." Erectus was remarkably successful at persevering, which calls to mind the familiar adage, "If it ain't broke, don't fix it."[12] In balance with the world, *Homo erectus*" extreme durability of over 1.8 million years offers an extreme contrast with the continuously innovating and unstable *Homo sapiens* species.

To Paul S.C. Tacon it seems likely that "human ancestors have been behaviorally modern much longer than has generally been accepted," including *Homo erectus*.[13] There is clear evidence, for example, of very early stone tool use to butcher large mammals.[14] There is now, by the way, considerable weight in the literature to the effect that early *Homo* was not only an opportunistic scavenger of carcasses, but also a skilled hunter.[15] *Homo erectus*, well adapted for life on the African savannah, tall and immensely strong, traveling far, with large brains, rich diets, cooking hearths, pair-bonding bands, simple and efficient technology.

It is possible to see the hallmark of human evolution in terms of a release from proximity, as if estrangement from sensual interface with the natural world, rather than intimacy with it, were a desired goal. As if the loss of community and place were just an inevitable given. But it is not only that "both human social structure and human intellectual capabilities appeared quite early," as Belfer-Cohen and Goren-Inbar have it.[16] "Primal versions of fidelity and truth, not simply sex and brute strength, had become key forces" in *Homo erectus* society.[17] The face-to-face bonds of early Paleolithic society provided immeasurably more connection than those of face-in-the-crowd mass society. Their world as experienced by any of its members must have been so much more multidimensional and in-depth than our own social existence. Here in itself are credible grounds for Leslie White's conclusion that "Hunting and gathering was unquestionably the most satisfying social environment man has ever lived in."[18]

More specifically, various physical and experiential shifts mark the arrival and maturation of *Homo erectus*. It was the first human species to possess a nearly hairless, non-ape-like skin and the first to have a projecting bony nose. Because erectus was a meat-eater, the species lacked the pot-bellied shape housing the bulky intestines required to digest a plant tissue diet. From the Australopithecines to *Homo erectus* the size of the brain doubled; and while an Australopithecine male was typically about twice the size of the female, with erectus the difference narrowed greatly, to about what it is today.[19] Overall size doubled, and for the first time humans had an extended dependency period in infancy and an adolescent growth spurt.[20] From the fossilized east Kenya remains of so-called "Turkana boy" (1.6 mya) and earlier specimens it is clear that erectus was tall and lean, with arms and legs proportioned like ours. A body geared for endurance walking and running, like the famous Kenyan long-distance athletes of today.[21]

Anatomical shifts suggest increased longevity; increased size alone is an indicator of longer life, by the way. Hammer and Foler report that "longevity estimates are without exception larger" than previously thought,[22] while Swisher et al. judge that the "average *Homo erectus* probably lived six years longer than the average Australopithecine—that is, 50 years as against 44."[23] H. Helmut finds that a "major extension of life potential occurred with and after *Homo erectus*" based on "new calculations of Hominid maximum lifespan potentials," with erectus upper limits of 70 to 75 years.[24]

The species was the first to use fire, and lived in huts as well as caves.[25] Group size increased to about 100 on average, well beyond that of non-human primates or *Homo habilis*.[26] 1.8-million-year-old faunal remains obtained from different areas indicate a wide range of erectus activity, specifically that food was already being transported long distances to be shared at home bases.[27] Complex foraging and ranging behavior happened over greater and more diverse areas, greatly surpassing any earlier hominid species.

In fact, the emergence of *Homo erectus* coincides with its moving out across the world, which in itself is a difference from any other primates. This dispersal and its challenges constitute another marker of remarkable sapient development. Arrival in Java is verified as of 1.8 mya, in Dimansi in the Caucasus near the Caspian Sea from 1.8 to 1.96 mya, and in China around 1.9 mya. Huang Wanpo et al. push this further, concluding that "new evidence suggests that hominids entered Asia before 2 mya."[28]

There is so very much of the human panorama, of course, that most likely will remain unknown to us. But the capability of our distant ancestors, though discerned through fragmentary, disconnected evidence rather than a seamless narrative, is revealing and provocative.

About 850,000 years ago, *Homo erectus* was able to manage repeated sea crossings to the Indonesian island of Flores, 20 kilometers at the minimum. Stone tools that date from that period could not otherwise have been there.[29] This finding was almost unbelievable in light of the previous consensus that only *Homo sapiens* could have practiced such navigation. As Robert Bednarik noted, "Lower Paleolithic seafarers were technologically and cognitively far more advanced than archaeologists had ever thought possible."[30] Nila Alperson-Afil and her colleagues have found evidence in Israel of the organization of living spaces for different activities. Although this behavior was long thought to have been exclusively the province of modern humans, this encampment is 790,000 years old.[31] Sophisticated wooden implements have been found in Germany, in use about 400,000 years ago. It is very rare that wood is preserved as long, but the hunting spears of Schoningen provide "a completely new insight into the developmental stage and culture of early humans."[32] Beautifully carved, the long spears were made of specially selected hard cores of larch and have a perfect balance and proportion.[33] These examples barely scratch the surface of what must have been numerous techniques—outside the relatively common surviving stone tools—involving shell, bone, bamboo and other structural plant materials, cordage, skins, wrapping, and other ancient means to desired ends.

Richard Leakey wrote: "When I hold a *Homo erectus* cranium in my hand and look at it full face, I get a strong feeling of being in the presence of something distinctly human. It is the first point in human history at which a real humanness impresses itself so forcefully."[34] A being, perhaps, from the beginning of hunter-gatherer consciousness, impressing Leakey as a person. *Origins Reconsidered* goes on to find in erectus the real start of "the burgeoning of compassion, morality, and conscious awareness."[35]

An instructive instance is the remains of a woman who lived 1.7 mya, known by the museum registration number assigned to her, 1808. She had suffered from vitaminosis A, a "completely immobilizing" condition caused by ingesting too much carnivore liver or honey; yet she survived for some months after its onset. "The implication stared me in the face," wrote Walker and Shipman, "*someone else took care of her,*" or she "wouldn't have lasted two days in the African bush."[36] Their conclusion: "This was the appearance of a truly extraordinary social bond."[37] There are certainly other cases as well, involving toothlessness, spinal cord conditions, etc., that give evidence of mutual aid and support from this time period.[38]

"Looking at the group structure of Homo erectus," according to George Frankl, "we can see that it was neither patriarchal nor matriarchal and we will be justified in calling it primal community."[39] Sarah Blaffer Hrdy finds that early sharing was spontaneous and automatic, and that both males and females started out "with an innate capacity for empathy for others and for nurture" which provided, for instance, a sense of emotional security in children back in the Pleistocene.[40]

The earliest exodus from the east African birthplace of humanity happened a lot earlier than once thought, and the mastery of fire probably accompanied that exodus, also far earlier than was thought. Boaz and Ciochon refer to Kenyan evidence of fire use "dated to an astonishingly early 1.7 million years ago."[41] But it now appears that fire was a crucial component of movement out of Africa, enabling settlement in colder climes and at higher altitudes. Uncooked food required massive, thick teeth; smaller teeth and thinner tooth enamel argue for cooked food, a very early evolutionary trend that continues to this day.[42] Kingdon finds that "firing foods, or cooking, was a 'tool' that neutralized bacteria and toxins, released nutrients, and allowed a vast expansion in the food base by making indigestible material edible."[43] He also argues that fire was a likely success factor in excursions within and outside Africa, which speaks to "the possibility that it began to be used before two mya."[44] In addition to warmth and the means to thaw, cook and smoke food, fire also deterred predators and almost certainly promoted social life as a site of food sharing and familial-type relationships, including care of the young.

These feats show a depth of intelligence "noticeably higher than those usually ascribed" to those who lived so long ago.[45] The emerging record indicates that Homo erectus exhibited analogical reasoning, though Kate Robson Brown argues that minds in the Lower Paleolithic possessed a "cognitive capacity for which no current analogue exists."[46]

We know that brain size surged as Homo habilis gave way to erectus around two mya.[47] Some fairly recent theorizing posits cooked food as the chief factor in the increase.[48] But in any case the brain's shape may be as important as its size. Cerebral asymmetry also dates from this general period, as preferential handedness shows up.

"The largest Homo erectus brains were about 1250 ml...and modern brains average about 1200–1500 ml. in volume,"[49] thus matching our own in cranial volume. Neanderthal brain size, 150,000 years ago, by the way, was greater than ours on average; that is, there has been an overall decline in brain volume during the past 150,000 years.[50] There are also large variations at any given period; e.g. the noted author and playwright Ivan Turgenev's brain size was 2012 ml., while the perhaps equally gifted novelist and dramatist Anatole France's was only 1040 ml. in size.[51]

In the evolution of intelligence, apparently not all parts of the brain evolved equally, nor are all parts equally important.[52] As the erectus brain grew apace, there was little change in technics; whereas today, as brain size has actually been shrinking, technological change is immense and accelerating. It is often said that we only use about 10 percent of our brains; perhaps we use ever less overall, as our estrangement from the world and each other deepens.

Intelligence means the ability to handle knowledge as a whole; this is what humans excelled at in prehistory. It is we who are cognitively undeveloped.

And what can be grasped by examining stone tools, those most enduring of artifacts? Stones can indeed speak and reveal much, directly and indirectly, about those who fashioned them into solutions on this earth.

Of course, non-human animals also use tools. Crows, for example, use elevation as a tool, dropping nuts from suitable heights to crack them open; chimpanzees use sticks to force termites out of a log, etc. But they don't make tools; according to Cameron and Groves, "there is no convincing evidence to date that species other than *Homo* were involved in the manufacture of stone tools.[53]

The discovery of stone tool use from 3.4 million years ago is a huge finding,[54]

A very early lithic technology mode is called Oldowan, from the Olduvai Gorge area of east Africa. This mode is associated with *Homo habilis*, the earliest human species. Oldowan toolmakers used some tools to produce others, which no non-human primate has done. Archaeologists report ever-earlier dates for evidence of human capacities in this realm. Semaw et al. found that "The sophisticated control and raw material selection...strongly suggests that stone tool use may have begun prior to 2.6 mya but not earlier than 2.9 mya."[55] Barham and Mitchell point to research pushing the time of earliest tool manufacture even a bit further back.[56] They also conclude that such human practice at 2.6 mya shows "an already well-developed understanding of the mechanics of flaking" or knapping.[57]

As Ignacio de la Torre noted, "The early tool makers are [now] seen as having recognized the principles of conchoidal fracture and having had the knowledge and technical skills required...."[58] Concerning this same time frame, Sheila Mishra concluded, "The surprising thing about the Oldowan stone tool industry is its sophistication."[59] deHeinzelin et al. referred to the "surprisingly advanced character of...earliest Oldowan technology."[60] On evidence, *Homo habilis* was an intelligent, experienced, and technically accomplished tool maker.

Oldowan tools give way to the Acheulean styles as *Homo erectus* appears, with cranial development very much like ours. What immediately comes to mind, with the new double-edge or biface Acheulean style is the iconic hand axe: a generally teardrop-shaped tool with congruent symmetry in three dimensions. Among many other devices including picks and cleavers, the hand axe stands out for what developed into its stunning craftsmanship and beauty, and a blade that often surpasses the sharpness of surgical steel. The very sight of such a creation erases any doubt as to its maker's aptitude.

Associated Acheulean practices strengthen this impression. Two million years ago, ancient humans in what is now Kanjeera, Kenya carried selected stone raw materials more than 13 kilometers to the site where they were worked.[61] A bit later, in the early Acheulean, this distance increased to 20 kilometers.[62] But it is also clear that while they ranged over greater distances in their decision-making, activities "occurred in close spatial proximity and as responses to immediate needs."[63] This speaks to a direct, context-specific immediacy, perhaps the original example of James Woodburn's immediate return/delayed return contrast, in which the former social orientation is non-estranged, compared to the latter.

Although there is so much less surviving evidence, a great range of other non-stone lifeworld materials existed. Microscopic fibers detected on hand axes testify to likely woodworking. Bone tools have come down to us, and both early human species could well have made implements from shell, bamboo, etc., and leather bags, carrying skins, snares, and so many other perishable things.

The Acheulean style or level remained the norm for well over a million and a half years, all the way down to the next—and last—Paleolithic tradition, called Levallois, corresponding roughly to the appearance of Neanderthal humans about 250,000 years ago. The unchanging Acheulean has baffled the fields of archaeology and anthropology, especially because it's clear that limited intellectual capacity is *not* the explanation for this tremendously long period of stasis. A basic approach, demanding but elegant, neither died out or was changed during thousands of generations. Why cast this as a conundrum, why frame it in terms of our own cultural mania for ceaseless innovation? Evidently there simply was no felt need in all that time to craft anything more complex. If *Homo erectus* humans were disinclined toward complex society, why would they express themselves through complex technics, inasmuch as the two are inseparable? Their whole mode of being remained non-specialized, skilled as a whole. They crafted their tools and they crafted their face-to-face band society, the one obviously reflecting the other. As Loren Eiseley summed it up, they were "using the sum total of [their] environment almost as a single tool,"[64]—and in enduring balance with that environment.

ENDNOTES

1   *The ability to reason preceded symbolic culture by millions of years. Society was evidently not dependent on symbolic systems of thought, for as Paul Jordan observes, "symbolism of every sort is conspicuously lacking in the archaeological record until the arrival of the modern form of humanity."[65] It is unclear when language originated, but every other such aspect (e.g. cave art) is very recent.*

    A symbol is that which stands for something else, represents something else; it re-presents reality. Nonetheless, the term is used very loosely, which tends to obscure the significance of life outside the symbolic dimension. Henry de Lumley, for example, in discussing prehistory, refers to symbolic thought as an essential facet of human cognition, as a necessity for the emergence of consciousness, as synonymous with meaning or understanding.[66] Each of these assertions is baseless.

    Upper Paleolithic beads are a relatively recent case in point regarding the misuse of the term symbolic. In fine ahistoric fashion, d'Enrico assures us that "beads have many different functions in human society, all eminently symbolic,"[67] referring specifically to some that are 75,000 years old. Robert Bednarik makes a similarly sweeping assessment of prehistoric beads: "Their symbolic significance appears generically self-evident."[68] Klein and Edgar have in mind beads found in Europe ca. 30,000 years ago; they "required extraordinary time and effort, which underscores the likelihood that they had symbolic meaning.[69] But there are countless activities done for their own sake, for satisfactions directly derived, and that do not represent something else. The fact of beads in no way necessarily establishes a symbolic component.

    The use of ochre by Homo neanderthalensis in the Upper Paleolithic is an even more commonly cited practice that purportedly indicates a symbolic dimension. Here we are approaching the actual arrival of symbolic culture, relatively recently, but the much-

touted presence of ochre, especially in burial practices, is less than wholly persuasive. As evidence of symbolic or ritualistic ideas, its red color suggests blood or death, and thus has been found on human remains. But it is also known that ochre has anti-odor qualities, so its use may simply indicate "an hygienic disposal of corpses so as not to attract scavenging carnivores."[70] Burial itself, by the way, connotes respect for the dead and does not automatically include a symbolic connection. Evidence of ochre in settings other than graves has even less to do with symbolism or representation. Its anti-hemorrhage, antiseptic qualities are known to indigenous people today and probably to our forebears, along with its hide-curing properties and as a component in tool-hafting adhesives.[71]

Thomas Wynn could not detect the symbolic in the crafting of hand axes, with their grace and beauty. They "did not require grammar-like rules and did not require symbolic instruction."[72] Observation and practice, not symbols, account for proficiency. Darwin argued both in The Descent of Man and The Expression of the Emotions that it was quite possible to form concepts without words. "The earliest unequivocal evidence for the use of symbols occurs very late," according to Shipman and Walker.[73]

"The word prohibits the senses…. The speaking tongue kills the tasting tongue," warns Michel Serres.[74] But symbols began to structure social life. The more complex the representational systems became, the more distancing from reality was involved, and the more complex and stratified society slowly became.

Ultimately we arrived at our present state of radical insufficiency, so removed from the essentials of existence. The feeling of being part of everything, including the cycle of birth and death, has been overcome by a preoccupation with control or mastery over everything.

Death is denied by the lonely modern individual engaged in a life without connection, without meaning. The loss of a sense of a full life makes life unbearable and death shameful, something to be hidden. Adorno referred to "the expropriation even of his dying, [which] destroys even the appearance of life's meaning as a coherent whole, that seals the loss of humane, autonomous subjectivity."[75]

Philippe Ariès wrote of the invisibility of modern death, as indicative of the loss of communal solidarity and the increasing control of experts over social and personal life.[76] Once managed openly as a part of vivid, direct life, death becomes invisible and silenced. As we live less completely, death becomes more of a terror. In his old age, contemplating an aged crow, Loren Eiseley gave us a healthy counter-perspective: "Neither of us had much further to go, and the harsh simplicity of it was somehow appropriate and gratifying."[77]

For thousands of centuries human life was virtually unchanged, in the vast time before overpopulation, drudge work, wars, the objectification of women, political authority. But of course there are those who lament this extended "failure" to innovate and progress. George Dimock looks at The Odyssey to decry the absence of forward movement. He focuses on the self-satisfied, non-domesticated Cyclops, who "put hand to no planting or plowing." Dimock argues that this paradisical state is actually a negative condition, in that it "deprived them of the stimulus to develop human institutions." Pain is needed for self-development, according to Dimock. Technology in particular "assists the birth of the individual…by separating him from the natural world."[78] Domestication/civilization in a nutshell, in its repressive essence.

We see the falsity of such a formulation much more clearly now, as the toll of "development" mounts in every sphere of life. Grahame Clark, in fact, reversed the dominant notion many decades ago, noting, "I venture to think that Paleolithic man has more meaning than the Greeks."[79] That timeless, history-less past and what followed might be seen in this light: "History exists only in a persisting society which needs history to persist."[80]

With very early Homo we may be encountering a human animal "without any modern parallels."[81] However that may be—and we will never know with full clarity—that make-up, that orientation to our mother Earth exerts a definite pull. Darwin writes of the Fuegian Jemmy Burton, who spent many years in England only to rapidly return to native ways upon a return voyage to South America.[82] What dismayed Darwin should encourage us. The tie was not broken and the lure of non-regimentation remained, as it was also felt by European colonists who "went native," attracted by indigenous life-ways.

Glenn C. Conroy opens his Reconstructing Human Origins with this: "To all creatures wild and free I dedicate this book. The success of human evolution has not been kind to you."[83]

We are among those creatures. We have forgotten how we once lived, how we were meant to live. With the connection to the living world all but gone in this techno-world. Our species wars against itself; what touches our hearts now is sadness and disquiet. And yet the abundance that was persists, a beacon to guide us back toward a vivid, healed, being-present state.

1   D.W. Cameron, "Early Hominid Speciation at the Plio/Pleistocene Transition," HOMO 54/1 (2003), p. 1.

2   Zinzhi Wu and Frank E. Poirier, Human Evolution in China (New York: Oxford University Press, 1995), p. 113.

3   Cited in Robert A. Wenke, Patterns in Prehistory (New York: Oxford University Press, 1999), p. 165.

4   Sibel Baruti Kusimba, African Foragers (Walnut Creek, CA: AltaMira Press, 2003), p. 117, for example.

5   "The Oldest Homo sapiens: Fossils Push Human Emergence Back to 195,000 Years Ago," Science Daily, February 28, 2005.

6   W. Henry Gilbert in Gilbert and Bershane Asfa, eds., Homo erectus: Pleistocene Evidence from the Middle Awash, Ethiopia (Berkeley: University of California Press, 2008), p. 424.

7   Colin Tudge with Josh Young, The Link: Uncovering our Earliest Ancestors (New York: Little, Brown, 2009), pp 198, 199.

8   C. Nadia Seremetakis, The Senses Still (Boulder: Westview Press, 1994), p. 724.

9   Giorgio Agamben, The Open: Man and Animal (Stanford: Stanford University Press, 2004), p. 77.

10   Donald Merlin, Origins of the Modern Mind (Cambridge, MA: Harvard University Press, 1991), p. 112.

11   Tim Megarry, Society in Prehistory (New York: New York University Press, 1995), p. 222, for instance.

12   Both quotes: Niles Eldridge, Dominion (New York: Henry Holt, 1995), p. 75.

13   Paul S.C. Taçon, "Identifying Ancient Religious Thought and Iconography," in Colin Renfrew and Iain Morley, eds., Becoming Human (New York: Cambridge University Press, 2009), p. 70.

14   Heinzelin et al., "Environment and Behavior of 2.5 Million-Year-Old Bouri Hominids," Science 284 (23 April 1999), p. 625.

15   Manuel Dominguez-Rodrigo, "Hunting and Scavenging by Early Humans: The State of the Debate," *Journal of World Prehistory* 16:1 (March 2002), for example.

16   Anna Balfer-Cohen and Naana Goren-Inbar, "Cognition and Communication in the Levantine Lower Paleolithic," *World Archaeology* 26:2 (1994), p. 153. Also, "*Homo erectus* seems to represent a kind of turning point for information donation among hominids," Barbara J. King, *The Information Continuum* (Santa Fe, SAR Press, 1994), p. 109.

17   Chip Walter, *Thumbs, Toes and Tears* (New York: Walker and Company, 2006), p. 121.

18   Leslie White, *The Evolution of Culture* (New York: Grove Press, 1959), p. 107.

19   R.W. Wrangham et al., "The Raw and the Stolen: Cooking and the Ecology of Human Origins," *Current Anthropology* 40:3 (December 1999), p. 574.

20   Carl C. Swisher III, Garniss H. Curtis, Roger Lewin, *Java Man* (New York: Scribner, 2000), p. 132. Also J.F. O'Connell et al., "Grandmothering and the Evolution of *Homo erectus*," in Jack M. Broughton and Michael D. Cannon, *Evolutionary Ecology and Archaeology* (Salt Lake City: University of Utah Press, 2010).

21   Rick Potts, *Humanity's Descent* (New York: William Morrow, 1996), p. 125. *Homo erectus*, it should be added, is also commonly referred to as *Homo ergaster* in African contexts.

22   M.L.A. Hammer and R.A. Foler, "Longevity and Life History in Hominid Evolution," *Journal of Human Evolution* 11:1 (1996), p. 64.

23   Swisher et al., *op.cit.*, p. 159.

24   H. Helmut, "The Maximum Lifespan Potential of Hominidae—A Re-evaluation," *HOMO* 50/3 (1999), p. 64.

25   Dean Falk, *Braindance* (Gainesville: University of Florida Press, 2004), p. 172.

26   Peter Carruthers and Andrew Chamberlain, *Evolution and the Human Mind* (New York: Cambridge University Press, 2000), p. 253.

27   D.W. Phillipson, *African Archaeology* (Cambridge, U.K.: Cambridge University Press, 2005), p. 50.

28   Huang et al., "Early *Homo* and Associated Artifacts from Asia," *Nature* 378 (1995), pp 275–278. Also, Ian Tattersall and Jeffrey H. Schwartz, *Extinct Humans* (New York: Westview Press, 2000), p. 160.

29   Robert G. Bednarik, "Replicating the First Known Sea Travel by Humans: the Lower Pleistocene Crossing of the Lombok Strait," *Journal of Human Evolution* 16:3 (2001), p. 229.

30   Robert G. Bednarik, "Seafaring in the Pleistocene," *Cambridge Archaeological Journal* 13:1 (2003), p. 57.

31   John Noble Wilford, "Excavation Sites Show Distinct Living Areas Early in Stone Age," *Science* 18 (December 2009).

32   Thieme Hartmut, "Lower Paleolithic Hunting Spears from Germany," *Nature* 385 (1999), p. 810.

33   Bo Gräslund, *Early Humans and their World* (New York: Routledge, 2005), pp 112-113.

34   Richard Leakey and Roger Lewin, *Origins Reconsidered: In Search of What Makes us Human* (New York: Doubleday, 1992), p. 55.

35   *Ibid.*, p. 67.

36   Alan Walker and Pat Shipman, *The Wisdom of the Bones* (New York: Alfred A. Knopf, 1996), pp 165–166.

37   *Ibid.*, p. 167.

38   Donald C. Johanson and Kate Wong, *Lucy's Legacy* (New York: Harmony Books, 2009), pp 206–207.

39   George Frankl, *The Social History of the Unconscious* (London: Open Gate Press, 2003), p. 76.

40   Sarah Blaffer Hrdy, *Mothers and Others* (Cambridge, MA: Belknap Press, 2009), pp 12, 290.

41   Noel T. Boaz and Russell L. Ciochon, *Dragon Bone Hill: An Ice-Age Saga of Homo erectus* (New York: Oxford University Press, 2004), p. 104.

42   Peter S. Ungar, ed., *Evolution of the Human Diet* (New York: Oxford University Press, 2007), pp 60, 352.

43   Jonathan Kingdon, *Lowly Origin* (Princeton: Princeton University Press, 2003), p. 273.

44   *Ibid.*

45   Belfer-Cohen and Goren-Inbar, *op.cit.*, p. 146.

46   Kate Robson Brown, "An Alternative Approach to Cognition in the Lower Paleolithic: The Modular View," *Cambridge Archaeological Journal* 3:2 (1993), p. 231.

47   Phillip V. Tobias, "The Craniocerebral Interface in Early Hominids," in Robert S. Corruccini and Russell L. Ciochon, eds., *Integrative Paths to the Past* (Englewood Cliffs, NJ: Prentice Hall, 1994), p. 193, for example.

48   "Did Cooked Tubers Spur the Evolution of Big Brains?," *Science* 283 (March 26, 1999), p. 2004. Also R. Rowlett, "Did the Use of Fire for Cooking Lead to a Diet Change that Resulted in the Expansion of Brain Size in *Homo erectus*...?," *Science* 283 (1999), p. 2005.

49   Christopher Stringer and Clive Gamble, *In Search of the Neanderthals* (New York: Thames and Hudson, 1993), p. 82.

50   Stephen Oppenheimer, *The Real Eve* (New York: Carroll & Graf, 2003), p. 11.

51   Boaz and Ciochon (2004), *op.cit.*, p. 124.

52   Robert Foley, *Humans before Humanity* (Cambridge, MA: Blackwell, 1995), p. 165.

53   David W. Cameron and Colin P. Groves, *Bones, Stones and Molecules* (New York: Academic Press, 2004), p. 282.

54   Shannon McPherron et.al., "Evidence for stone-tool-assisted consumption of animal tissues before 3.39 million years ago in Didika, Ethiopia," *Nature*, August 12, 2010.

55   Semaw et al., "2.6 Million-year-old Stone Tools and Associated Bones from OGS-6 and OGS-7, Gona, Afar, Ethiopia," *Journal of Human Evolution* 45 (2003), p. 176.

56   Lawrence Barham and Peter Mitchell, *The First Africans* (New York: Cambridge University Press, 2008), p. 82.

57   *Ibid.*, p. 157.

58   Ignacio de la Torre, "Evaluating the Technological Skills of Pliocene Hominids," *Current Anthropology* 45:4 (August-October 2004), p. 439.

59   Sheila Mishra, "The Lower Paleolithic: A Review of Recent Findings," *Man and Environment* xxxiii (1)-2008, p. 16.

60   de Heinzelin et al., "Environment and Behavior of 2.5 Million-Year-Old Bouri Hominids," *Science* 284 (April 23, 1999), p. 629. Also de la Torre et al., "The Oldowan Industry of Peninj and its Bearing on the Reconstruction of the Technological Skills of Lower Pleistocene Hominids," *Journal of Human Evolution* 44 (2003), pp 203–224.

61   Shanta Barley, "Earliest Evidence of Humans Thriving on the Savannah," *New Scientist* 18:07 (October 21, 2009).

62   Michael P. Noll and Michael D. Petraglia, "Acheulean Bifaces and Early Human Behavior Patterns in East Africa and South India," in Marie Soressi and Harold L. Dibble, eds., *Multiple Approaches to the Studio of Bifacial Technologies* (Philadelphia: University of Pennsylvania Museum of Archaeology and Anthropology, 2003), p. 3.

63   *Ibid.*, p. 47.

64   Loren Eiseley, *The Invisible Pyramid* (New York: Scribner, 1970), p. 58.

65   Paul Jordan, *Neanderthal* (Thrupp, UK: Sutton, 1999), p. 152.

66   Henry de Lumley, "The Emergence of Symbolic Thought," in Renfrew and Morley, *op.cit.*, p. 10.

67   Francesco d'Enrico and Marian Vanhaeren, "Evolution or Revolution? New Evidence for the Origin of Symbolic Behavior in and Out of Africa," in Paul Mellars, ed., *Rethinking the Human Revolution* (Cambridge, U.K.: David Brown, 2007), p. 276.

68   Robert G. Bednarik, "Beads and Pendants of the Pleistocene," *Anthropos* 96 (2001), p. 545.

69   Richard G. Klein with Blake Edgar, *The Dawn of Human Culture* (New York: Wiley, 2002), p. 265.

70   Salley McBrearty and Alison Brooks, "The Revolution that Wasn't," *Journal of Human Evolution* 39:5 (2000), p. 519.

71   Bruno S, "The Multi-Use of Ochre in Prehistory," *Human Evolution* 23:3 (2008), pp 233–239.

72   Thomas Wynn, "Handaxe Enigmas," *World Archaeology* 27 (1995), p. 10.

73   Walker and Shipman, *op.cit.*, p. 283.

74   Michel Serres, *The Five Senses* (New York: Continuum, 2009), p.186. It could be that signaling theory in anthropology and disjunction in philosophy

may help provide alternatives to the symbolic's more or less exclusive claim on communication and knowledge. See Rebecca Bliege Bird and Eric Alden Smith, "Signalling Theory, Strategic Interaction, and Symbolic Capital," *Current Anthropology* 46:2 (April 2005); Adrian Haddock and Fiona Macpherson, eds., *Disjunctivism* (New York: Oxford University Press, 2009); Alex Bryne and Heather Logue, eds., *Disjunctivism* (Cambridge, MA: MIT Press, 2009).

75   G. Schweppenhaus, *Theodor W. Adorno* (Durham, NC: Duke University Press, 1009), p. 67.

76   Philippe Ariès (translated by Helen Weaver), *The Hour of Our Death* (New York: Alfred A. Knopf, 1981.

77   Loren Eiseley, *The Unexpected Universe* (New York: Harcourt, Brace & World, 1969), p. 191.

78   George E. Dimock, *The Unity of the Odyssey* (Amherst: University of Massachusetts Press, 1989), p. 10.

79   J.G.D. Clark, *Economic Prehistory: Papers on Archaeology by Grahame Clark* (New York: Cambridge University Press, 1989), p. 416.

80   Elias J. Bickerman, "Mesopotamia," in John A. Garraty and Peter Gay, eds., *The Columbia History of the World* (New York: Harper & Row, 1972), p. 49.

81   M.D. Petraglia et al., "A Case Study from India: Life and Mind in the Acheulean," in Clive Gamble and Martin Porr, eds., *The Hominid Individual in Context* (New York: Routledge, 2005), p. 217.

82   Charles Darwin, *Voyage of the Beagle* (New York: Penguin Books, 1989 [1839]. Introduction by Janet Browne and Michael Neve, p. 24.

83   Glenn C. Conroy, *Reconstructing Human Origins* (New York: W.W. Norton, 2005), frontispiece.

CHAPTER SEVEN

ORIGINS AND THE TRICKSTER

FOR A WHILE NOW the culture, more and more a technoculture, has gravely negated the realm of ends or goals. The erosion of hope for a better tomorrow, for some different destination than this projected one, has also banned the topic of origins. To rule out ends is to take away the legitimacy of seeking beginnings. That there was, is, and always will be only this broken condition is the cardinal thesis of the still dominant postmodern cultural ethos.

Theory awaits a massive qualitative infusion from somewhere. Would it be surprising to find that what originates and what has been experienced along our journey from our sources can be of value to us now? The need to think about and pursue disalienated ends may be linked to understanding the origins of our current state.

Nietzsche probably did more to dismiss the importance of starting points than any other modern figure. In *Daybreak* he claimed that "the more insight we possess into origin the less significant does the origin appear."[1] This charge of irrelevance is erroneous.

Something in us resists giving up our beginnings, even as modernity pushes the sense that we are well past all of that. "Postmodernity" is the conscious suppression of any awareness of origins, any lingering hopes for originary thinking.

Origin is source, that from which something else derives. The forgetting and denial of origin is a phenomenon of some importance, an historical development in itself.

All myths have as their subject the origin of something. And are we ever without myth? The anarchy myth is, at base, a story of original innocence corrupted by institutions. In a similar vein, Schelling asserted that "everything that surrounds us points back to a past of incredible grandeur."[2] In *Myth and Reality*, Mircea Eliade wrote of the hope for a rebirth that is part of returning to origins. That return is much less a question of repair than of re-creation, in his view.[3]

But in an age of no meaning, one does not try to restore "original" meaning. We seem to be officially barred from the idea that origins research and origins stories tell how the world changed, was made richer or poorer.

Marx, Nietzsche and Heidegger each disclosed a primal state destroyed by the progressive domination of capital, Christian morality, or technology. Marx projected class struggle and production onto all previous history and confused the liberation of productive forces with the liberation of humans. His origin was a lack: we initially failed at satisfying our basic needs. Nietzsche looked at the violent and bloody origins of Christian morality and found them unjustifiable. Heidegger counseled us to step back into origins to better see how technological nihilism has put an end to metaphysics.

But thought has turned away from this theme. "We have grown increasingly suspicious of accounts of origins over the past hundred years," according to James Hans.[4] The same is true of much radical social theory. In terms of French insurrectionary politics, for example, Tiqqun's "Bloom" figure, existing only in the present, expresses "no lament over the loss of authenticity or autonomy."[5] Given that we are perpetually impoverished in this here-and-now, such an orientation might appear strange. The main explanation as to why many do not find it strange is the failure of long-range predictions based on theory, e.g. Marxism. The destructive outcomes of Marxism in practice had already been perversely implicit in Hegel's view that from an original primal unity would emerge a higher, perfected state of the world. Needless to say, we witnessed nothing of the sort.

Something went profoundly wrong, and not just in theory. Adorno's insight is deeply relevant today: "More in line with the catastrophe that impends is the supposition of an irrational catastrophe in the beginning."[6] In the beginning, that is, of domestication and civilization, at their origination. But as Hilary Lawson has it, "...we are lost. Lost in a world that has no map."[7]

When confidence succumbs to a sense of failure, a map is no longer sought. Then we have not only lost our way; we have lost our sense of the immanence and immediacy of origins. And the toll of this loss mounts. The suppression or denial of originary thinking drives up levels of anxiety and fearfulness. "The pressures are unbearable," says the German sociologist Ulrich Beck.[8] It becomes harder and harder to blithely agree with Kant that paradise is an origin it is better to forget, a utopia lost once and for all.

There must be some primordial notion that directs us on some level to know the loss, to miss deeply a reunion denied. To miss "the meaningful times for whose return the early Lukacs yearned..."[9] And to move to a situation, in Kevin Tucker's marvelous phrase, when "ancestral bodies begin to remember."[10]

Before/outside the dimension of calendars, domestication, monotheism, writing, etc., the boundaries of past, present, and future were more permeable, as were the boundaries between humans and other animals. Some of this perseveres among indigenous people today, carried along mainly by countless creation stories in various parts of the world. These stories, told in a more originary than representational manner, make for a past-as-present that abides. Creation as a privileged moment in which origin discloses essence.

The cosmologies may speak of events prior to the creation of humans, when animals and gods were impossible to distinguish. Further on, perhaps, the creation of human beings who managed the world in the gods" interests, revealing along the way much about changes in society. The adaptive identities of contemporary Native America often find strength in the authentic pasts that stay alive in such sources as stories of beginnings, as well as those in current indigenous literature. Louis Owens, among many others, expresses connection with "eternal and immutable" values and insights in resisting the fragmentation of the present.[11]

The origin can also open up primary paradigms that cast light on our plight today, on negative underpinnings. Stories of emergence so very often repeat a tale of order out of primordial chaos, wherein formless disorder (e.g. water and nothing else) is overcome by structure, a.k.a. civilization. A basic Babylonian myth posits Marduk's victory over Tiamat, establishing Marduk's royal authority. The Rig Veda from Vedic India features the god Indra who masters Vitra, primordial chaos. Vitra is very much like the Egyptian figures Apep or Apophis: darkness, lack of order.

Andaman Islanders, hunter-gatherers east of India, practice no cult, no ritual sacrifice or prayer of thanks.[12] But the Vedic Indians sacrificed, their ritual marked off by a furrow of cultivation to fence out the forces of chaos. A natural order versus the maintenance of civilized, political order. Always the origin before the official one.

The Canaanite Ba'al subdued the unruly cosmic waters, Yahweh of the Israelites likewise, most graphically by parting the Red Sea and enabling the flight from Egypt. Power over nature and the movement to domesticated monotheism. The creation story is over and history begins. Banished: the time of no days and no years.

A cosmic egg is central to emergence stories in Africa, Polynesia, and Japan, to name a few sites. It is an archetypal symbol of agriculture and fertility, announcing the arrival of the nascent regime. Water symbolism is present not only as prehuman flux but also as destruction: flood stories are found in many cultures, both as a promise of a new order and a threat to those who would resist it. The earth-diver is another common motif, a figure who dives deep into the water to bring up the first, founding bits of the Earth. Charles Long associated "the dualism in the earth-diver myths with the tension between hunting-fishing and agricultural orientations" in North America.[13]

In the central Diné/Navajo emergence story, First Man undertakes the subduing and organizing of nature with a sacred Red-White Stone. But this involves a question: "Why is the sacred stone which brings about the desired upward movement also that which violently disturbs the people and makes them afraid?"[14] Meanwhile, the "upward movement" goes on and growth, not balance, proceeds. "...and growth is most assuredly going on because the eleventh crop is being planted."[15] Patriarchy and domestication seem to develop in tandem, but again, not without misgivings or other, resistant paths. "As time went on the men's agriculture increased," along with more ritual, "while the women played and were promiscuous with the various lower forms of life."[16] "Promiscuous" with Coyote, the trickster, in particular. Southwest Indian narratives, including Navajo ones, reveal the movement of hunter shamans away from a hunter-gatherer ethos to greater emphasis on ceremonial knowledge. At the same time egalitarian human flux recedes in value.[17]

In the basic Navajo story there are many beginnings and as many endings, thus yet keeping alive the possibility of the egalitarian condition. The early gods lived there as divine tricksters, unafraid of "chaos." When the cosmos was being ordered into fixity, we see who confronted such an approach: "Then Coyote came in and said, 'What is going on?" And snatched the bag of stars and spilled them all over the sky."[18]

As Coyote, or in other guises, the trickster is the oldest figure in Native American stories, indeed in all mythologies. Scandinavia's Wotan embodies trickster sensibility; there is Anansi the Spider in West Africa; Polynesia has its tricksters. How about Renard the Fox of medieval French legend, and Shakespeare's Caliban, protesting against civilization?

Trickster tales reach back from a time of a world that once was whole, but was already in fragments when the first attempts to record these stories took place. Trickster stories are not meant to edify, but to account for and participate in the origin of the universe. And Coyote, for example, has to do with local origins, and so leads the people to explore their heritage and their environments.

"The trickster," according to Mathias Guenther, "is a virtually universal figure in world mythology, especially that of hunter-gatherers, on whose mythological landscape he holds center stage."[19] Coyote is a wanderer, one who does not quite belong—especially in domesticated society. No one quite belongs in civilization, so the trickster's appeal has outlasted hunter-gatherer life, an unusual focus of interest—apparently never more so than today. A relative of the shaman, "the Trickster would return to make the happy world that once was."[20]

The trickster's elemental, amoral energy does not recognize boundaries. Speaking of which, it is not so easy to get a fix on this character, who fairly often displays contradictory elements. And in the literature there is not always a formal distinction between trickster and non-trickster narratives; the Ewe people, for example, do not divide their stories in that way. Coyote is certainly too lively and restless to be contained within academic systems.

Ture is a Zande trickster of Africa. Azande parents warn their children about this depraved being. He flouts every convention and is indomitable, a hero who helps his people—and yet his uninhibited acts can be monstrous.[21] Another African trickster is the Yoruba rascal known as Ajàpá, a tortoise. In stories mainly told by women, Ajàpá is averse to work, lazy and carefree. Though far from flawless, he is an aid to the people; in the "Bounteous Ladle" tale, for instance, he acts on behalf of starving creatures.[22] Wild and a creature of his appetites as he often is, the trickster may act from a pure joy of trickery.

A trickster may seem to be animal, human, animal-human, even a shaman's invaluable assistant. Generally disrupting and subverting social and cultural norms, but often with compassion and humor, illustrating the fact that laughter can open doors and allow us to see reality differently. As Michael Jackson concluded, "All trickster tales seem to imply that immersion in the given, established values and conventions of the social order must be offset by free play, experimentation and detachment."[23]

Sto:lo Coast Salish scholar Jo-Ann Archibald (Q'um Q'um XIIEM) goes further, referring to the "weak and fragmented" condition of many indigenous communities and how trickster stories help communities survive despite the odds.[24]

Colardelle-Diarrassouba, commenting on the Hare cycle of stories of the Ewe in Togo, tells us that it is primarily about the preservation of ancestral traditions.[25] Tomson Highway of the Cree Nation states that without the Trickster, "the core of Indian culture would be gone forever," adding that the role of the Trickster "is to teach us about the nature and the meaning of existence on the planet earth."[26]

Coyote can move from mythic into modern times. The Comanches of the southern plains tell how he tricked white soldiers and preachers.[27] Coyote of the Nez Perce people may depose a chief if he is acting inappropriately.[28] Wishram Chinook people of the Columbia River give us this quote: "Coyote said: Salmon is a chief, Eagle is a chief, and people will be chiefs. I am Coyote, I am no chief."[29] But in Barre Toelken's judgment, Coyote is "the exponent of all possibilities."[30]

Many American Indians now live in cities, and coyotes, Canis latrans— also known for adaptive skills—live there also. Both sets of city-dwellers have striking talents as survivors, against great odds. Like the Azande trickster Spider (Ture in the Zande language), a creature that makes a web out of itself, trickster Coyote and animal coyote are clever, tenacious, and elusive. Both can live interstitially—on the margins and across borders— escaping the negative structures of society to survive and carry on.

The trickster, as Barbara Babcock-Abrahams reminds us, "keeps the possibility of transcending the social restrictions we regularly encounter."[31] He does so hunter-style: every hunter is necessarily a trickster in order to be successful. Paul Radin wrote of the Winnebagos" trickster, "With the worlds of nature he is still in close contact."[32] A century and a half ago, Daniel Brinton referred to the advice of the Tonkaways, a "wild people" in Texas: "Do as the wolves do...never cultivate the soil."[33] Robert Pelton felt it "likely that hunters have imagined their tricksters differently from agriculturalists."[34]

If the trickster was "the chief mythological figure of the Paleolithic world," in Joseph Campbell's phrase,[35] he is also part of the transition to the more controlled role of cultural hero. Even the primal vitality of this sometimes obscene funster feels the force of repression, as hunter-gatherer life gave way to settled, agricultural societies. The role of the trickster diminishes the more strongly a people has been influenced by a domesticated way of life.[36] William Bright points out that in California and the Great Basin, where most indigenous people were hunters and gatherers until the mid-nineteenth century, Coyote is most often the "prototypical mythic trickster." In the more sedentary and largely agricultural indigenous Southwest, he is generally the loser or bungler.[37]

And yet Trickster persists, and has a wide appeal. In some incarnations he ends up domesticated, like us. "He" is overwhelmingly the correct pronoun, but there are some females (e.g. among the Hopi and Tiwa).[38]

A defiantly domesticated spirit remains compelling. This defiance continues to haunt an increasingly tamed and unhappy world. It may be that the incidence of trickster tales has a direct relationship to the degree of social oppressiveness.

Trickster may flaunt ideal ceremonial behaviors, ridiculing whatever is regarded with the greatest reverence or respect. Wadjunkago, for instance, of the Winnebagos.[39] Wadjunkago also savagely satirized the customs of war, that staple of domestication.[40]

Going against all that is forbidden, trickster certainly does not always win. In a comic inversion of the official story, he deconstructs social limits. As Nanabozho of the Ojibway tradition, he is alternately the savior of his people, and a buffoon and sexual aggressor.[41] Some tales have nothing to do with breaking taboos or bringing disorder, it should be added.

The late Micmac writer Patricia Clarke Smith cautioned that non-Native attempts to grasp the meaning of Coyote are fraught with pitfalls.[42] Non-Native Barre Toelken spent 30 years studying Navajo Coyote stories and conceded an appropriate humility and sense of limits. Most especially, he realized that the stories may be used for healing ceremonies and are not to be compromised.[43]

This tiny survey does not begin to approach the magnitude and depth of its subject. Distantly, I may be part of the Zerza tribe of Kurds, as I was told on a visit to Turkey. But I have no living connection at all to this people. I offer the words of this essay in acknowledgement of my place as a non-Native outsider, in hopes of possible, if slight use-value. Anarcho-primitivist in orientation, I respect and am deeply inspired by the indigenous dimension, past and present.

Postmodernism, in particular and in its more general cultural sense, has pitted itself against the idea of creation stories and grounded Trickster realities. The voice of cynicism, isolation, and technological ungroundedness, postmodernism insists on the "effacement of historical origins and endings."[44] Accepting the fragmented and depthless reality of mass society, postmodernism is the turn away from traditions, away from origins, to the weightless zone of surface and word play.

Jacques Derrida, postmodern deconstructionist par excellence, stressed that there can be no stable meaning at all, because its sense is endlessly being deferred ("différance"). Deconstruction is a prime aspect of what Stefan Morawski has called the resultant "universal theory of the impossibility of theory." A debilitating approach reflecting a debilitated cultural condition, that of the victorious pressure of modern civilization.[45]

Contra "the possibility to mean that the trickster celebrates," in Anne Doneihi's phrase,[46] postmodernism denies both its possibility and its possible connection to an independent reality. "There is nothing outside the text," as Derrida famously proclaimed, to which he later appended, there is no "inside" either.[47] Inside the symbolic, that is, there can only be a play of an infinity of "meanings," with no real contact with anything else. This is the case, was always the case, and always will be the case, it proclaims.

Any actual origins must, by definition, be denied; for they are obviously extralinguistic. The myth of some lost Native land of thought must be abandoned. Even the original—and persevering—expression of any such thought is discarded. Oral tradition? Derrida's absurd privileging of writing over speech is the answer to that deeply meaningful source. To see the "world" as so many marks on paper or a screen, marks whose meanings can only be arbitrarily constituted, is to refuse active, living process.

The consequences of reducing everything to the linguistic are, of course, profound. Paul de Man avers that "Ethics has nothing to do with the will (thwarted or free) of a subject, nor a fortiori with a relationship between subjects."[48] Language itself, "defining" everything, refers after all only to itself. Therefore to speak of ethics among people who really exist makes no "sense." The impossibility of a determined discursive position is necessarily the end of responsibility. Perfect for a corrupt, declining social order from which community has evaporated.

Postmodernism clearly feeds a shrunken sense of human agency, one without origins or goals. It bespeaks a fatalistic pessimism and is the mode of the digital age, in thrall to the functioning of massive technological systems. It is the dominant outlook, too severely limited to be capable of rational critique of the present, ominous conditions of society and the biosphere.

"Postmodernism is what you have when the modernization process is complete and nature is gone for good," summarized Frederic Jameson.[49] Another chilling facet, reminding us that, as David Wood put it, "the value of nature today is inseparable from mourning." Wood added that this "is not mourning for a lost purity, a privileged identity, but rather for a lost wealth of differential possibility."[50]

The possibility that postmodernism defines itself against. But it seems to me that the doors to these riches—so disrespected by some—are locked from the inside. To go forward, Adorno tells us that "hope is not a memory held fast, but the return of what has been forgotten."[51]

"Postindian consciousness is a rush of shadows in the distance, and the trace of natural reason to a bench of stones; the human silence of shadows, and animate shadows over presence. The shadow is that sense of intransitive motion to the referent; the silence in memories. Shadows are neither the absence of entities nor the burden of conceptual references. The shadows are the prenarrative silence that inherits the words; shadows are the motions that mean the silence, but not the presence or absence of entities. The sounds of words, not the criteria of shadows and natural reason, are limited in human consciousness and the distance of discourse."[52]

Which Parisian postmodernist wrote the above, you may ask? None other than Anishinaabe Gerald Vizenor, among the most gifted and provocative Native American writers of recent decades. This opaque passage does not do adequate justice to the range of Vizenor's generally playful, original and stimulating stories, novels, essays, and poetry,[53] but it does illustrate why he has his detractors among both indigenous and non-indigenous commentators.

Vizenor's frequent references to post-structuralist/postmodern theorists such as Derrida and Roland Barthes, along with such unreadable passages as the one quoted above, help to identify him as a writer who is uninterested in the clear prose of Native stories. In fact, for him, according to Robert Berner, "traditional tribal narratives are only the inevitably tragic remnants of dying cultures."[54]

This is not to say that he is indifferent to the plight of Native people. Survival and hope are key themes of his trickster fiction and poems, such as "Anishinaabe Grandmothers," and very often his main characters are Anishinaabe. But as a postmodernist, in the view of Osage critic Robert Warrior, Vizenor's insistence on "the conclusions and praxes of French theory" is at the expense of indigenous needs.[55] Niigonwedom James Sinclair refers to the common designations of Vizenor as a cultural relativist engaged in "the process of undermining, subverting, and exploding almost all parts of Native identity."[56]

On the other hand, Deborah Madsen applauds his "deconstructive hermeneutic discourse of survivance [as] a powerful strategy for subverting monologic U.S. colonial structures of oppression."[57] Some academics defend Vizenor precisely as postmodern; other figures tend to see such archly Eurocentric and obscurantist theory as itself colonizing, or, at a minimum, far from liberatory. At the 1998 "Translating Native Cultures" conference at Yale, Santee/Yankton Sioux writer Elizabeth Cook-Lynn tore into academic "postindian" ideas as confused and ridiculous.[58]

Vizenor's first and best-known novel, *Bearheart*, displays virtuoso comedic gifts, among other strengths. It mocks the repressive sociologists of the word at the Bioavaricious Word Hospital, who demand clarity (that enemy of the postmodern), in a chapter called "Word Wars in the Word Wards."[59] More generally, and often in a trickster vein, he asserts that words heal by refusing to take themselves seriously, and that postmodern writing is not the place to look for meaning or truth.

When asked for his definition of postmodernity, Vizenor answered pithily, "The notion that words are wild, of course."[60] The problem, of course, is that words are not wild, despite their unequalled worship by postmodernists. For Vizenor the language game itself is the ultimate trickster.

For this gifted storyteller, the free play of words undermines fixed meanings and "terminal creeds." The latter Vizenorian term refers to any foundational orientation, which postmodernism categorically rejects (a foundational stratagem in itself.) In this vein, Vizenor castigates Scott

Momaday as wanting to hold on to a past Indian golden age.[61] This is a racialist mistake, he avers. Native people are "postindian" now, with the city, not the reservation as the dominant lifeworld. In *Braveheart*, for example, Belladonna Darwin-Winter Catcher dies because she clings to "the perfections of the past" rather than "surviving in the present."[62]

To begin with the working refusal of fixed meanings is, to some, a refusal of any grounding from which to address indigenous social and political concerns. Craig Womack wonders how any political movement of significance can exist without stable grounds.[63] Jennifer Nez Denetdale, in her Navajo meditation "Remembering Our Grandmothers," feels that "ancestral memory and the form it takes as oral tradition provides one of the most powerful resources that Indigenous peoples have for asserting Indigenous status."[64]

The overall postmodern techno-consumerist ethos cuts us off from origins, from goals, and also from the self. The decentered, fragmented subject has somehow been enthroned as both a reality and even as an ideal. And yet, do we not have need of a stable, committed sense of life?

The intuition that human existence should not be as painful as most people find it lies at the heart of many perennial stories. Again and again, and seemingly everywhere, tales are told to explain why things are not as they ought to be. And there is always the option (a forced option, really) of accommodation to the general decline deeply felt by people of all backgrounds. Todd May pointed out the acceptance of the loss of community, the surrender involved in redefining it, in "The Community's Absence in Lyotard, Nancy, and Lacoue-Labarthe."[65] Marianna Torgovnick reminds us of the beacon of unity and connectedness that can be seen in primitive cultures, a light that has not been so extinguished as some would hope.[66]

A fundamental connection is certainly that of each person with nature. Native activist Janet McCloud: "Your heart is always beating and your breath is always moving in and out, isn't it? The laws of nature are with you wherever you are.... Your body is nature. You have a river, a sun, and moon inside, too. Everything that's out there is also in here."[67]

The connection to beginnings is not separate from the connection to the regularity of the natural world, in the face of the Machine's relentless project to sunder both. With its postmodern accomplice, the technosphere counsels all to submit. It is no coincidence that arch-postmodernist Donna

Haraway's cyborg figure is designed explicitly to cut off interest in origins.[68] A bitter irony is the name of CyberLife's biological simulation engine: Origin.

If we are to grasp our ominous condition, insights into how we got here are required. A grasp of the whole could hardly be more needed. While not in any way denying their particularity, indigenous voices and traditions should be heard, for survival itself.

We must not succumb to blind obedience, being swept along by forces that have always arrayed themselves against Original people, and much else of value. The effort goes on and, as Benjamin soberly put it, "Only a redeemed mankind receives the fullness of its past."[69] I'll cast my lot with this line from Celan: "There will be a return, a great one, far beyond the borders they draw for us."[70]

ENDNOTES

1   Friedrich Nietzsche, *Daybreak*, translated by R.J. Hollingdale (New York: Cambridge University Press, 1982), Thesis 44, p. 46.

2   F.W.J. von Schelling, *The Abyss of Freedom/Ages of the World* (Ann Arbor: University of Michigan Press, 1997 [1813]), p. 121.

3   Mircea Eliade, *Myth and Reality* (New York: Harper & Row, 1963), p. 30.

4   James S. Hans, *The Origin of the Gods* (Albany: State University of New York Press, 1991), p. 1.

5   Branden W. Joseph, "Dark Energy," in *ArtForum*, February 2011, p. 197.

6   Theodor Adorno, *Negative Dialectics* (New York: Continuum, 2007), p. 323.

7   Hilary Lawson, *Closure: A Story of Everything* (New York: Routledge, 2001), p. ix.

8   Quoted in David Simpson, *Situatedness, or Why We Keep Saying Where We're Coming From* (Durham: Duke University Press, 2002), p. 233.

9   Adorno, *Negative Dialectics*, p. 191.

10   Kevin Tucker, "When the Lights Go Out," on *The Agrarian Curse* [CD] (Milwaukee: FC Records, 2008).

11   Louis Owens, *Mixedblood Messages: Literature, Film, Family, Place* (Norman: University of Oklahoma Press, 1998), pp 25–26.

12   Mircea Eliade, *The Sacred and the Profane* (New York: Harper & Row, 1961), p. 123.

13   Charles Long, *Alpha: The Myths of Creation* (Chico, CA: Scholars Press, 1963), p. 192.

14   Sheila Moon, *A Magic Dwells* (Middletown, CT: Wesleyan University Press, 1970), p. 67.

15   *Ibid.*, p. 140.

16   *Emergence Myth According to the Hanelthnayhe or Upward-Reaching Rite*, recorded by Berard Haile, O.F.M. (Santa Fe: Museum of Navajo Ceremonial Art, 1949), p. 129.

17   Karl W. Luckert, *The Navajo Hunter Tradition* (Tucson: The University of Arizona Press, 1975), p. 188.

18   Moon, *op.cit*, p. 161. Also J. Frank Dobie, Mody C. Boatwright and Harry H. Ransom, eds., *Coyote Wisdom* (Dallas: Southern Methodist University Press, 1965), p. 72.

19   Mathias Guenther, "The Trickster," in Bron Taylor et al., eds., *Encyclopedia of Religion and Nature*, vol. II (New York: Thoennes Continuum, 2005), p. 1663.

20   Weston La Barre, *The Ghost Dance: Origins of Religion* (New York: Dell Publishing, 1972), p. 216.

21   E.E. Evans-Pritchard, *The Zande Trickster* (Oxford: The Clarendon Press, 1967), pp 32, 28.

22   Oyekan Owomoyela, *Yoruba Trickster Tales* (Lincoln: University of Nebraska Press, 1997), p. x111.

23   Michael Jackson, *Allegories of the Wilderness: Ethics and Ambiguity in Kuranko Narratives* (Bloomington: Indiana University Press, 1982), p. 296.

24   Jo-ann Archibald (Q'UM Q'UM XIIEM), *Indigenous Storywork: Educating the Heart, Mind, Body, and Spirit* (Vancouver: University of British Columbia Press, 2008), p. 129.

25   Zinta Konrad, *Ewe Comic Heroes: Trickster Tales in Togo* (New York: Garland Publishing, 1994), p. 19.

26   Cited in Archibald, *op.cit.*, p. 7.

27   William Bright, *A Coyote Reader* (Berkeley: University of California Press, 1993), p. 19.

28   Deward E. Walker, Jr., *Blood of the Monster: the Nez Perce Coyote Cycle* (Worland, WY: High Plains Publishing, 1994), p. 224.

29   Dell Hymes, *Now I Know Only So Far* (Lincoln: University of Nebraska Press, 2003), p. 279.

30   Cited in Bright, *op.cit.*, p. 21.

31   Barbara Babcock-Abrahams, "A Tolerated Margin of Mess: A Trickster and his Tales Reconsidered," in *Journal of the Folklore Institute* 11 (1974), p. 147.

32   Paul Radin, *The Trickster* (Westport, CT: Greenwood Press, 1969), p. 133.

33   Daniel G. Brinton, *Myths of the New World* (New York: Leypoldt & Holt, 1868), p. 231.

34   Robert D. Pelton, *The Trickster in West Africa* (Berkeley: University of California Press, 1980), p. 271.

35   Cited in David Leeming and Jake Page, *The Mythology of Native North*

America (Norman: University of Oklahoma Press, 1998), pp 46, 48.

36   Marc Linscott Rickett, "The North American Trickster," History of Religions 5 (1965), P. 328.

37   Bright, op.cit., p. 367.

38   Ellen Datlow and Terri Windling, The Coyote Road: Trickster Tales (New York: Viking, 2007), pp 11–12.

39   Babcock-Abrahams, op.cit., p. 178.

40   Radin, op.cit., p. 154.

41   John A. Grim, The Shaman: Patterns of Siberian and Ojibway Healing (Norman: University of Oklahoma Press, 1983), p. 85.

42   Patricia Clark Smith, "Coyote Ortiz: Canis Latrans in the poetry of Simon Ortiz," in Studies in American Indian Literature, Paula Gunn Allen, ed. (New York: Modern Language Association of America, 1983), p. 194.

43   Barre Toelken, "Life and Death in Navajo Coyote Tales," in Recovering the Word, Brian Swann and Arnold Krupat, eds. (Berkeley: University of California Press, 1987), pp 388–401.

44   Christopher Nash, The Unravelling of the Postmodern Mind (Edinburgh: Edinburgh University Press, 2001), p. 124.

45   Stefan Morawski, "My Troubles with Postmodernism," in The Philosophical Forum XXVII no. 1 (Fall 1995), p. 78.

46   Anne Doueihi, "Inhabiting the Space Between Discourse and Theory in Trickster Narratives," in William J. Hynes and William B. Doty, eds., Mythical Trickster Figures (Tuscaloosa: University of Alabama Press, 1993), p. 201.

47   Cited in David Wood, The Step Back: Ethics and Politics after Deconstruction (Albany: State University of New York Press, 2005), p. 223.

48   Paul de Man, Allegories of Reading (New Haven: Yale University Press, 1979), p. 206.

49   Frederic Jameson, Postmodernism, Or the Cultural Logic of Late Capitalism (London: Verso, 1993), p. ix.

50   Wood, op.cit., p. 185.

51   Theodor Adorno, "On the Final Scene of Faust," in Notes to Literature (New York: Columbia University Press, 1991), vol. 1, p. 120.

52   Gerald Vizenor, "Shadow Survivance," Manifest Manners: Postindian Warriors of Survivance (Hanover, NH: University Press of New England, 1994), p. 64.

53   One of my favorites is "Manifest Manners: The Long Gaze of Christopher Columbus," in American Indian Persistence and Resurgence, Karl Kroeber, ed. (Durham: Duke University Press, 1994), pp 224–236.

54   Robert L. Berner, Defining American Indian Literature (Lewiston, NY: The Edwin Mellen Press, 1999), p. 54.

55   Cited in "A Sovereignty of Transmotion," by Niigonwedom James Sinclair, in North American Indian Writing, Storytelling and Critique, Henry et al., eds. (East Lansing: Michigan State University Press, 2006), p. 132.

56   *Ibid.*, p. 129.

57   Deborah L. Madsen, ed., *Native Authenticity: Transnational Perspectives on Native American Literary Studies* (Albany: State University of New York Press, 2010), p. 14. Madsen goes on to stress Vizenor's emphasis on irony, failing to see the irony of her book's title. Authenticity is a concept thoroughly decried by postmodernism as an illusion. Baudrillard, Deleuze and Guattari, and other such theorists, with whom Vizenor has consistently linked his approach, base their fundamental orientation on this very point. See Arnold Krupat, *The Turn to the Native* (Lincoln: University of Nebraska Press, 1996), p. 67.

58   Elizabeth Cook-Lynn, "American Indian Studies: An Overview. Keynote address at the Native Studies Conference, Yale University, February 5, 1998," in *Wicazo Sa Review* 14:2 (Autumn 1999), pp 14–24.

59   Gerald Vizenor, *Bearheart: The Heirship Chronicles* (Minneapolis: University of Minnesota Press, 1990). See Elizabeth Blair, "Text as Trickster: Postmodern Language Games in Gerald Vizenor's *Bearheart*," *MELUS* 20, No. 4 (Winter 1995), p. 88.

60   Gerald Vizenor and A. Robert Lee, *Postindian Conversations* (Lincoln: University of Nebraska Press, 1999), p.21.

61   Chadwick Allen, *Indigenous Identity in American Indian and Maori Literature and Activist Texts* (Durham: Duke University Press, 2002), p. 191.

62   Blair, *op.cit.*, p. 79.

63   Henry et al., *op.cit.*, pp 227, 229.

64   Jennifer Nez Denetdale, "Remembering our Grandmothers: Navajo Women and the Power of Oral Tradition," in Julian E. Kunnie and Nomalungelo I. Goduka, eds., *Indigenous Peoples' Wisdom and Power* (Burlington, VT: Ashgate, 2006), p. 82. In a 1999 interview, Vizenor lauded U.S. constitutional democracy as having best served the interests of Native Americans. Astounding, no irony here! Hartwig Isernhagen, *Momaday, Vizenor, Armstrong: Conversations on American Indian Writing* (Norman: University of Oklahoma Press, 1999), p. 94.

65   Todd May, "The Community's Absence in Lyotard, Nancy, and Lacone-Labarthe," in *Philosophy Today* 37 (Fall 1993), especially p. 280.

66   Marianna Torgovnick, *Gone Primitive* (Chicago: University of Chicago Press, 1990) and *Primitive Passions* (New York: Alfred A. Knopf, 1997)

67   Janet McCloud, "On the Trail," in Jonathan White, *Talking on the Water* (San Francisco: Sierra Club Books, 1994), p. 253.

68   Jane Bennett, *The Enchantment of Modern Life* (Princeton: Princeton University Press, 2001), p. 177.

69   Walter Benjamin, "Theses on the Philosophy of History," in *Illuminations* (New York: Harcourt, Brace & World, 1968), thesis III, p. 256.

70   Paul Celan, "A Boat full of Brain," in *Last Poems*, translated by Katherine Washburn and Margret Buillemin (San Francisco: North Point Press, 1986), p. 187.

CHAPTER EIGHT

COMPLEXITY

THE DOMESTICATING CONTROL LOGIC of civilization is the connective drive that joins origins to the present. A slightly different, if intimately related, factor or dimension of this connection is complexity.

Mass society is inherently complex. The inseparable accompaniment of modernity is complexity, and its levels increase constantly in every society within a globalized context. In our insecure, violent world, the social and technological mediations of complexity dominate our lives at the expense of community. All relationships feel the pressure of impersonality, a hallmark of complexifying reality. In so many ways, present reality demonstrates that the dynamic of complexity is failing, not paying off. For example, complexity equals more than three hundred clinically identifiable psychiatric disorders, when once we lived in peace with and in our bodies.

At the Feral Visions gathering in Arizona a few summers ago, we gathered at dusk to experience the sunsets: so vastly more magnificent and real than any computer or TV screen, and not "complicated" at all. Each one gloriously unique, its "complexity" fully present, altogether unlike social or technological complexity. It is the latter I address here, which is the opposite of diversity, richness, and the unique. Every fire we gaze into, like the sunsets and sunrises, returns us to ourselves and connects us to each other. Complexity led us out of ourselves, into overheated dwellings, overeating kitchens, loads of stuff for storage units,[1] every buffer from healthy lived existence. Why does it have uniformity and standardization as its results, along with the faux intimacy of (anti-) "social networks"?

As distinct from "complexity" in nature, with its creative, myriad unfoldings, complex society is homogenous, the fruit of manufactured extension, the deadly obvious path of the built world. As IBM enjoins, "Let's Build a Smarter Planet," epitaph for the real one.

Spengler referred to "the world-embracing spatial energy of modern technics," a close parallel to complexity itself. He saw the dehumanization and its concluding, deathly closure;[2] the destruction of our perceptual, spiritual, and environmental habitats. This is the totalizing environment of complexity, which now is overtaking its masters in terms of the world economy as well as the global techno-grid.

There are many still who counsel that we cannot disassemble the enormous, interwoven web: "The task we face now is not to reject or turn away from complexity but to learn to live with it creatively."[3] Meanwhile some of these same complicitous voices admit that one of humanity's oldest dreams is to reduce complexity to simplicity, and that the more complex the world becomes, the stronger the longing for simplicity.[4]

What is the real strength of social complexity anyway, compared to animate nature? "Computing capacity" may be a slightly unfortunate choice of words, but Greg Bear provides a healthy perspective: "The computing capacity of even bacterial DNA was enormous, compared to man-made electronics."[5]

We forget that "things in themselves lack nothing, just as Africa did not lack whites before their arrival."[6] We forget that while complexity makes some tasks easier, its overall effect is to increase work and make life more complicated and deprived. The postmodern mantra, "It's all too complex," is avoidance of the starkly obvious facts of complexity. The remark should be meant humbly, directed at the non-made world—its multi-dimensionality and flowing life.

Meanwhile, a reconstitution of our very being is underway, and this is currently on display in most striking ways. J.H. van den Berg observed that "the measure of (repressed) unconsciousness of the individual is equal to the degree of derangement of the community."[7] Bernard Stiegler takes this further with his discussion of the "decomposition of the social" in this hyper-industrial epoch in which the "imminent possibility of the total atomization of the we[8] has emerged. Stiegler's meditation focuses on Richard Durn, who committed a massacre shooting in France in 2002. Psychically obliterated by complexity, Durn's incapacity to be heard or even to speak led to the "derangement" prophesied in general terms by van den Berg 30 years earlier. Michel Serres gives us a summary judgment and warning: "We are masters of the earth, and we are constructing a world that is almost universally miserable and that is becoming the objective, founding given of our future."[9]

The other "founding given" was that which obtained for so long outside the sickness of complex systems, before the systematic distancing from the world as such, in opposition to the lethal hubris of the notion that nature must be "perfected" (Marx, et al.) I refer, of course, to the companionship and anti-inequality ethos of band societies, their deep sense of sharing internally and sharing with a living environment.[10]

A primary question is: how was this world lost? How does the consent of the dominated to their domination develop? The answer may very well lie in gradually increasing complexity, from our earliest beginnings, in a primary way; with the nascent conquest of the unbuilt life-space and the associated objectification that it promoted.

Art, for example, is widely considered an important monitor of social complexity. Margaret Conkey found Paleolithic art to be an attempted resolution of the stress arising from new complexity on the eve of domesticated society.[11] Art as a form of social control makes sense in the context of a need for reinforced social solidarity. Complexity apparently introduces strains at basic levels, early on in the progression of the symbolic. Jacques Lacan shed light on the connection with this succinct conclusion: "The symbolic world is the world of the machine."[12]

The formalized discipline of ritual rehearses the move to repetitive, standardized production, the road to mechanization. Guy Swanson found that in due course the degree of abstraction and elevation of a society's deities matches the complexity of that society's social structure.[13] Each level leads to further complexity, further removes from uniqueness. Each part of the machine orientation is never an item complete in itself, but bears a quality of abstraction that gives it meaning only as a part of production logic. This abstraction is as necessary for commodity equivalence and exchange as it is for further heights of social coordination and integration.

Archaeologist Joseph Tainter observed that as complexity increases, a society spends more resources on its maintenance, to the point of ever-diminishing returns.[14] The size of this self-preservation expenditure is very likely the single best index of social complexity. Thus it is easy to discern such societies" highest value. "Complexity of organization becomes more important than content," according to linguist Edward Sapir.[15] At the same time the content of the human condition fragments, the fabric of social life is disrupted and torn. Political "solutions" that do not address complexity are irrelevant; the only kind of socialist "alternative" that has ever emerged in complex societies is centralized state socialism.

Complexity's central component is the division of labor, that which takes away the wholeness and integrity of an individual's life. Production processes require, under the sign of efficiency, an always more elaborate specialization. Only when tools, and the rest of life, are direct and autonomous can complexity be disposed of. Life must literally be in one's own hands, crafted and wielded outside control systems, in opposition to the impositions that complexity enforces across the board. Deleuze and Guattari referred to the "primordial unity of desire and production."[16] A superior anti-complexity formulation is embodied in the traditional lifeways of the Yupik people of Alaska, wherein there is no separation between daily activity and spirituality. Archaeologist C. Melvin Aikens reversed the proposition that agriculture was a fundamental precondition for the growth of sociopolitical complexity, arguing that complexity created the conditions leading to domestication.[17] Whether complexity is a cause or an effect, I believe it is useful to focus on complexity per se.

Regarding the study of formal systems, such as those in physics, H.A. Simon concluded that complexity always leads to hierarchical structuring.[18] We tend to look at it in general as manifest destiny or obviously fated, but it isn't clear why complexity or development takes place at all. Henry Quastler has argued that adaptation, for example, may not be the last word in evolution, since it is unable to explain the complexification of living beings.[19] The observable reality is that such a tendency exists, and that, according to Ervin Laszlo, "once a new hierarchical level has emerged, systems on the new level tend to become progressively more complex."[20] We also know that complexity of one type tends to consort with other types of complexity, in the direction of convergence of systems.

The managers and ideologues of social complexity have long dreamed of foundational certainty for their project of governing diversity and multiplicity. Kurt Gödel's *Incompleteness Theorem* (1931) proved, however, that no formal system can be both complete and consistent. He demonstrated that even elementary arithmetic is too complex to be totalized or completed on both of those grounds at once. In the universe at large there are no closed systems, thus the struggle for cognitive control over nature and society is an enterprise of ever escalating demands with no possibility of a final victory.

But the overall regime of domestication strives toward maximum scope and power. These days such a judgment could hardly be missed. Simpler societies and systems are absorbed by more complex ones, usually not without a fight. The more complex setup has a more elaborate legal structure, but also tends toward disorder and instability.

We should keep in mind the fact that the human intellect's capacity for complexity management (instrumental reason) is limited. Nature is vastly more "complex" than the human brain. Similarly, physical things have not only more properties than they will ever overtly manifest, but more than they can ever possibly manifest.[21]

Complexity theory and chaos theory do not deny this, but neither do they reject the goal of mastery. They retain a distanced stance from which to make reality, however variegated, obey. Instead of the humility and freedom of immersion in the world, such theoretics in fact mirror the alienated norms of today's "network culture." The touted "interactivity" is, in both spheres, that of machines more than of free agents.

Thanks to complexity, we have never been so plugged in to the world— or are we integrated into a global complex? The term "plugged in" gives it all away, in more ways than one. We are supposedly more "in touch." Minus texture and context (and rarely with much content) how are we "touching" the world? Plugged in is the more apt term, and that reality also creates a different "world" to connect to. Our contact is ever more mediated and superficial, corresponding to an ever more complexified world.

20 years ago I didn't have a phone, though I had the use of one in the office of the housing coop where I lived. I could be reached rather easily; I had, for example, a pretty widespread correspondence. The communications I had were generally more in depth and consequential than on the Internet. What is handy and instantaneous is the flip side of a toxic culture that redefines "friends" and "community," and mocks the "social" part of social networks. The epidemic of the great turn-off of autism and the steady rise of rampage shootings are only two of the more graphic signs of the terrible inner vacancy of complex "society."

Who doesn't feel more centered or grounded, the less wired one is? Note the unintended irony expressed by Jean-François Lyotard: "...the world is not evolving toward greater clarity and simplicity, but rather toward a new degree of complexity in which the individual may feel very lost but in which he can in fact become more free."[22]

To be more adrift, lost, isolated is evidently the path toward freedom for some. It is more valid to see complexity as a disease or trauma, and there will be no healing until the ravages, the wounding are ended. As for freedom, mounting complexity brings ever greater control and individual insignificance. A central motif of Sartre's *Critique of Dialectical Reason* is that social institutions meant to advance freedom or liberation by overcoming the inertia of domination ossify and themselves join the weight of oppression. The lack of freedom is a function of complexity itself; advocates of democratization or self-management miss this point completely.

The disease of complexity dis-ables us in so many ways. Our techno-fried brains are becoming "rewired," according to many studies and projections. Of course, the term is but another symptom of the rapid shift that's underway. Understanding drowns in a widening sea of information bytes, basic aptitudes are replaced by dependency on complex systems. And yet I'd say that Edward O. Wilson strikes a true note: "The brain appears to have kept its old capacities, its channeled quickness. We stay alert and alive in the vanished forests of the world."[23]

A useful and healthy point, but not enough. Approaching the slaughterhouse, some creatures smell blood and bellow. That's not enough either, but we could start there.

—*2009*

ENDNOTES

1   See Daniel Miller, *The Comfort of Things* (Malden, MA: Polity, 2008). Sad, postmodern work on commodities as "helpmates," etc.

2   Oswald Spengler, *The Decline of the West I* (New York, Alfred A. Knopf, 1926), p. 81.

3   Mark C. Taylor, *The Moment of Complexity: Emerging Network Culture* (Chicago: The University of Chicago Press, 2001), p. 4.

4   *Ibid.*, pp. 137, 138.

5   Greg Bear, *Blood Music* (New York: Arbor House, 1985), p. 22.

6   Bruno Latour, *Irreductions* (Cambridge, MA: Harvard University Press, 1988), p. 193.

7   J.H. van den Berg, *Divided Existence and Complex Society* (Pittsburgh: Duquesne University Press, 1974), p. 173.

8   Bernard Stiegler, *Acting Out*, trans. David Barison, Daniel Ross, and Patrick Crogan (Stanford: Stanford University Press, 2009), p. 82.

9   Michel Serres with Bruno Latour, *Conversations on Science, Culture, and Time* (Ann Arbor: The University of Michigan Press, 1995), p. 177.

10   A good overview is Peter M. Gardner, "Foragers" Pursuit of Individual Autonomy," *Current Anthropology* 32:5 (December 1991), pp. 543–572.

11   Margaret W. Conkey, "Art and Social Geography," in Carmel Schrire, ed., *Past and Present in Hunter Gatherer Studies* (Orlando: Academic Press, 1984), p. 264.

12   Jacques Lacan, *Ego in Freud's Theory and in the Technique of Psychoanalysis, 1954–55*, trans. Sylvana Tomaselli (New York: Cambridge University Press, 1988), p. 47.

13   Guy Swanson, *The Birth of the Gods* (Ann Arbor: The University of Michigan Press, 1960), pp. 82–86.

14   Joseph Tainter, *The Collapse of Complex Societies* (New York: Cambridge University Press, 1988), p. 92.

15   Edward Sapir, *The Collected Works of Edward Sapir III*, eds. Regna Darnell and Judith T. Irvine (New York: Mouton de Gruyter, 1999), p. 30.

16   Ann Fienup-Riordan, *Yuunaqpiallerput: The Way We Genuinely Live* (Seattle: University of Washington Press, 2007), e.g. p. 24.

17   C. Melvin Aikens, "The Last 10,000 Years in Japan and Eastern North America: Parallels in Environment, Economic Adaptation, Growth of Social Complexity, and the Adoption of Agriculture," *Senri Ethnological Studies* 9 (1981), especially p. 262.

18   H.A. Simon, "The Architecture of Complexity," *Proceedings of the American Philosophical Society* 106, pp. 467–482.

19   Heinz von Foerster, Margaret Mead, and Hans Lukas Tenber, eds., *Cybernetics: Circular Causal and Feedback Mechanisms in Biological and Social Systems [Transactions of the Ninth Conference]* (New York: Josiah Macy, Jr. Foundation, 1955), especially pp. 173, 178–179.

20   Ervin Laszlo, *The Grand Synthesis* (Boston: Shambhala, 1987), p. 25.

21   Nicolas Rescher, *Complexity: A Philosophical Overview* (New Brunswick, NJ: Transaction Publishers, 1998), p. 38.

22   Quoted in Scott Sullivan, "A Maze of Lost Illusions," *Newsweek*, April 22, 1985, p. 80.

23   Edward O. Wilson, *Biophilia* (Cambridge, MA: Harvard University Press, 1984), p. 101.

CHAPTER NINE

REVOLT AND HERESY IN THE LATE MIDDLE AGES

AS THE FOURTEENTH CENTURY PROCEEDED, Europe entered
a time of proliferating challenges to authority across the board. We tend to
think of the Middle Ages as a time when most people were pious and accepting of their lot, but the many active crises of the late medieval period
strongly belie this image. Most striking were the frequency and violence
of uprisings, mostly by peasants. Even more potent were upheavals that
combined the demands of the materially oppressed with the radically millenarian views of heretical movements.

Increasingly during this period, every disturbance was seized upon
as an opportunity for wider rebellion. Because of the central authority
wielded by the Church, it is not stretching matters a lot to infer that all that
all subversive social and political ideas were necessarily also theological
heresies. Growing intrusiveness by the State (e.g. heavy taxation and other
assaults on local autonomy), plus the oppressive weight of the Church
in daily life, provided a situation of unavoidable collision with radical
movements. The power of both Church and State was on the line with
mounting urgency.

Feudalism as a system, identical with society itself, was under
attack, even as ecclesiastical strength declined. Revolts and radical heresies

managed to persevere in the allegedly closed society of the late Middle Ages, because in fact it was no longer so effectively closed. There was an inner hollowness to ruling power that was exposed time and time again. Concerning the Church's actual power, Raoul Vaneigem went so far as to assert that the Middle Ages were no more Christian than the late Eastern Bloc was communist. As the chasm widened between rich and poor, civil authority resorted to very harsh punishments. Sound familiar? For late modernity as well, no part of the integrated whole is completely integrated... or pacified.

The three great peasant risings of the fourteenth century involved the "blue nails" of maritime Flanders (1323–1328), the French *jacquerie* (1358), and the massive English revolt of 1381. In 1378, day laborers raised a major urban challenge in Florence. And scores of other insurrections took place, shaking the reigning structures, often borne forward by apocalyptic desires. Either explicitly or just below the surface, grew chiliastic expectations of a return to the innocence, freedom and immediacy of society prior to exchange and private property. Many were inspired by some version of a lost anarcho-communal Golden Age.

Of course, specific grievances triggered upheavals according to time and place. Privations as a result of the Hundred Years War with England had much to do with fourteenth century outbursts in France, for example. More generally, a deep and growing restlessness was noted, an anxiety in various countries related to a decisive shift in time consciousness.

In the early medieval period, there were only three "hours" based on the daily round of the monastery. But the modern 24-hour day made its arrival: clocks were common after 1300, and standardized, homogeneous time was in general use beginning around 1330 in Germany and 1370 in England. This change had a tremendous effect. Heretofore, time took its meaning from the substance of life; precise clock time measured life as an external, abstract presence. A much more ordered, disciplined work life was a principal result, and a source of deep dissatisfaction. Like money, and private property itself, the clock helped those in authority enforce a significantly more quantified and regulated existence. It is no surprise that those who pursued perfected control were given to hymns of praise to dominant clock time—much as today's techno-world boosters laud the Machine.

We should also note that resistance could always be found making itself known against official mores and culture. In fact, an extensive sector of outsiders, present throughout the medieval period, swelled in size by the fourteenth century. They included the 11th and 12th century "forest people," and the thirteenth-century renegade Helmrecht, who rebelled against peasant life. The Goliards were anti-clerical wanderers who begged and sang their way from town to town, suspected of heresy and subversion. François Villon belonged to this tradition, and to the heritage of refractory Parisian students before and since. The famed poet was also a law-breaker and vagabond, and narrowly escaped the hangman's noose.

The Feast of Fools was a widespread, long-running ensemble of various kinds of performances, unmercifully mocking the Church and its authorities. Making its first appearance in 12th century France, the Feast included, characteristically, the Witches" Sabbath or Black Mass, ridiculing both clergy and liturgy in very pointed nocturnal celebrations. The texts that Carl Orff set to music in his *Carmina Burana* belong to this tradition; these Goliard lyrics are a decidedly non-Christian musical ode to drinking, sensual love, and the vagaries of fortune.

Violent antagonisms were on the rise in the 1200s, with the number of conflicts more and more manifest, especially in the second half of the century. The people of Piacenza and Florence revolted in 1250 because of the high cost of food and the activity of speculators. Disturbances took place in Parma in 1255, Bologna in 1256, Milan in 1258, Siena in 1262, and again in Florence in 1266. To the north, an agitation in favor of equal rights for the poor broke out in the region of Liège in 1250, leading to violence there in 1254. Flemish textile workers also revolted in Ypres, Bruges, and Douai in 1280. Before the century was out, the merchant-industrialists of Flanders were reduced to seeking French aid to suppress the workers. This move led to defeat for King Philip and the French army, for it precipitated a powerful alliance between textile laborers and artisans. At Coutrai in 1302, the united urban proletariat wiped out Philip's forces.

Also in Flanders, the first large-scale medieval revolt raged from 1323 to 1328; it was the most prolonged and intense of the many peasant revolts of the fourteenth century. Peasants waged what amounted to a war of extermination against landlords, capitalists and clergy; they were often joined by textile workers, who took up arms once again. The watchword of this rising was "war against the rich and the priests." Another civil war in 1348–49 ended when the French army massacred weavers in Bruges, Ghent, and Ypres; but the weavers rose again in 1359 and held out against all opposition for two years. Assassinations of magistrates and desecration of churches were among the features of such open warfare. And one could compile a very long list of eruptions in several countries, such as those of Calais in 1298 and Saint Malo and Genoa in 1306, when the mutinies of sailors against shipowners spread to involve many others. The tally only multiplied as the fourteenth century progressed.

Both heresies and millennial outbursts long pre-dated the last two centuries of the Middle Ages. But earlier heresies, such as the Cathars and Bogomils, had been predominantly dualistic and neo-Manichean: Gnostic, repressive and anti-nature in character. Typical of a newer anti-Church outlook was the Free Spirit, a heretical movement that emerged in the early fourteenth century, honoring freedom, sensuality, and pantheistic belief in individual divinity as a natural state. Free Spirit adherents were influenced by mystics such as Joachim of Fiore and Meister Eckhart, and by the joy and innocence of Francis of Assisi. The Beguines and Beghards (partner organizations of women and men) were even closer to the Free Spirit, with their basis of simplicity and poverty.

The issue of poverty is noteworthy and curiously modern. Upholding poverty as a cardinal virtue sufficed for the Church to continually suspect the Beghards and Beguines of heresy, and quite often to persecute them. Then as now, the command to shop was implicit and its refusal was seen as a source of subversion.

In 1311, Pope Clement V, disturbed by the success of the movement of the Free Spirit, denounced its "abominable kind of life, which they call freedom of the spirit, which means the freedom to do anything they like." In Paris Margaret of Porète, author of The Mirror of Simple Souls, was burned at the stake in the same year. She was a Beguine who proposed that the world might be rehabilitated to its state before the Fall by "giving nature what it demands." It was in fact the major role of women that heightened the Church's active persecution of such voices, and the Free Spirit insistence on unlicensed sexuality is understood to have been related to a strong presence of women in similar groupings.

The anti-authoritarian and erotic millenarianism of the Free Spirit partook of an even wider wave of apocalyptic desire for the restoration of a lost Golden Age. Its sense of primal sinlessness and natural liberty bespoke its partisans" project of total emancipation in the present. They were opposed to private property, not in order to replace it with a world of communist cooperative labor, but with freedom from toil. Adherents fought for this general social myth; a bloody battle in 1307 near Milan in which some 400 Free Spirit brethren were killed was not the first waged by such radical heretics. Visionary religious utopianism was beginning to form a backdrop for social struggles across Europe.

One of the best-known fourteenth-century revolts was the 1357-58 outburst of peasant energy in northern France known as the Jacquerie, for the common peasant name Jacques. Jacques has denoted a poor, rebellious peasant—and a Jacquerie a peasant uprising— ever since. Including rural artisans and craftsmen, and typical of the widespread willingness to rise up against oppression, the Jacquerie was inspired by heretical sects of several countries. "Let's let anything go and all be masters" was one of its rallying cries. An alliance formed between peasants and the people of Paris, which was especially alarming to those within the power structure. The threat was so grave that although England was then at war with France, help was rushed across the Channel to suppress this great explosion.

Florence in 1378 witnessed the "Tumult of the Ciompi," following other significant disturbances such as those in Siena in 1368 and 1371. The Ciompi (wool carders) failed to make common cause with the peasantry, but their revolt succeeded for a few months. These purely urban rebels liberated prisoners and armed themselves, but succumbed to internal divisions and to the illusion that governance would work to their advantage.

What happened in Florence was the opening round of a four-year tempest that raged across a large part of Europe until early 1382. In 1380, for example, Parisians known as *maillotins* (from the hammers and mallets they carried) attacked government buildings, burning records, killing tax collectors, and opening the jails. Similar risings took place in Rouen and other French cities and in Flanders, also precipitated by tax increases. From the Tuchin movement throughout southern France (Tuchins were "outlaws"—as designated by their enemies), to revolts in the German city of Lübeck and Novgorod in Russia, the decade opened with a rising tempo of serious contestations in Europe.

Perhaps the largest and best known was the Peasants" Revolt of spring and summer 1381 in large parts of England. Its heartlands were Kent and Essex, where imposed labor (the corvée) had actually been less onerous than in other counties; the revolt is associated with figures such as Wat Tyler and John Ball. City workers joined peasants to quickly capture and occupy London. Possibly 30,000 took part in the general and well-planned rising. Anti-clerical in spirit, the revolt nonetheless included members of the impoverished and radicalized lower clergy, known as Lollards. For a time it looked as though the monarchy would be swept away on a torrent of anger. But with the capital completely in their hands, the leaders foolishly trusted the king, who promised to act on their demands. This proved fatal, and the revolt was lost within months of its inception.

But during the spring and summer something marvelous had been pursued with great vigor. Lollard preacher John Ball gave voice to a typical sentiment: "Good folk, things cannot go well in England nor ever shall until all things are in common and there is neither villein nor noble, but all of us are of one condition." The equality of all and the original absence of social classes fired the insurgent consciousness, the goal of a primal state where no one is above another. Norman Cohn connected it to the "mystical anarchism of the Free Spirit." Of course it is more than mystical when put into practice.

This was not the end of peasant resistance in England. Between 1381 and 1405 there would be five regional revolts, especially in Kent, Cheshire, and Yorkshire. In France the vineyard workers of Auxerre gave the authorities disquieting memories of the Jacquerie and the Maillotins with the disturbances they led there in 1393. Rebellion in Catalonia brought the burning of harvests and landlords" dwellings in 1410; riots erupted in Paris in 1413 and 1418. A monk at St. Denis spoke to the nature and extent of the late fourteenth century upheavals and their aftermath: "Nearly all the people of France had rebelled and were agitated with great fury and, according to general rumor, they were excited by messengers from the Flemish, who were themselves worked upon by the plague of a similar rebellion, stimulated by the example of the English."

The radical wave near the end of the Middle Ages reached its apogee with the great Taborite insurrection of Bohemia, the longest-lasting and most militant example of millenarianism in action. What began as a University of Prague reform program associated with Jan Hus succumbed to an immensely strong primal, Paradise-now undertow. Its passion spread like wildfire, similar to the contagious interplay described by the monk of St. Denis. Tabor was an actual society between 1420 and the mid-1430s, a movement that repeatedly destroyed large forces intent on destroying it. Women fought side-by-side with men—extraordinary for any age, much less the medieval epoch.

The most radical Taborite elements included the Pickhards (a version of "Beghard") and especially the Adamites, fighting for a return to the world before the Fall from grace—zealots who went naked at all times. Part of their philosophy prescribed that "in this time no king shall reign nor any lord rule on earth, there shall be no serfdom, all dues and taxes shall cease, nor shall any man force another to do anything, because all shall be equal, brothers and sisters."

Based on handicrafts, the key strongholds of Tabor were invincible for almost 15 years. On August 14, 1431, the people's army met a vast pan-European army of knights and others at the battle of Tauss. These legions of feudal authority were decimated and routed there by the Taborites and their highly disciplined guerrilla tactics, but they finally succeeded in 1434 at Lipian, in Bohemia.

For some decades resistance flowered and overcame Church and State in open battle, repeatedly if not definitively. Equipped with some version of the visionary, we too may embody resistance to the domesticated world.

—2008

SELECTED BIBLIOGRAPHY

Michael Barkun, *Disaster and the Millennium* (New Haven: Yale University Press, 1974)

Max Beer, *Social Struggles in the Middle Ages* (London: Leonard Parsons, 1924)

Norman Cohn, *The Pursuit of the Millennium* (Fairlawn, NJ: Essential Books, 1957)

Alfred W. Crosby, *The Measure of Reality: Quantification and Western Society, 1250–1600* (Cambridge: Cambridge University Press, 1997)

Guy Fourquin, *The Anatomy of Popular Rebellion in the Middle Ages* (Amsterdam: North-Holland Publishing Co., 1978)

John Jolliffe, editor and translator, *Froissart's Chronicles* [Jean Froissart, 1337–1410] (London: Harville Press, 1967)

Michael Jones, editor, *The New Cambridge Medieval History, Volume VI c. 1300–c. 1415* (Cambridge, Cambridge University Press, 1995)

John Howard Lawson, *The Hidden Heritage* (New York: Citadel Press, 1950)

Gordon Leff, *Heresy in the Later Middle Ages* (Manchester: Manchester University Press, 1967)

Robert E. Lerner, *The Heresy of the Free Spirit in the Later Middle Ages* (Berkeley: University of California Press, 1972)

REVOLT AND HERESY IN THE LATE MIDDLE AGES

Michel Mollat, *The Poor in the Middle Ages* (New Haven: Yale University Press, 1986)

Michel Mollat and Philippe Wolfe, *The Popular Revolutions of the Late Middle Ages* (London: George Allen & Unwin Ltd., 1973)

Herman Pleij, *Dreaming of Cockaigne: Medieval Fantasies of the Perfect Life* (New York: Columbia University Press, 2001)

Michael J. St. Clair, *Millenarian Movements in Historical Context* (New York: Garland Publishing, 1992)

Raoul Vaneigem, *The Movement of the Free Spirit* (New York: Zone Books, 1994)

Daniel Waley, *Later Medieval Europe* (London: Longmans, 1964)

CHAPTER TEN

DENYING THE UNAVOIDABLE

HOW HAVE WE WINNOWED DOWN the heavens and the earth, the great blaze of existence, to machine systems and subjugation? Staring at electronic screens during more and more of our lives; shrinking, not expanding our contact with the realness of life, shriveling the soul. Why not be always interrupted by Twitter and iPhone? There's nothing much left here.

The spirit bleeds from wounds we try not to know about. The greatest secrets are those spread out before us, and the actual is what could grow at our feet. "No culture ever achieved the degree of asceticism that our so-called consumer society, our banquet, imposes on us today, wrote Michel Serres.[1] Thomas Merton concluded, "There is no misery to compare with that which exists where technology has been a total success."[2]

We see it all happening, through the window of a tear, in a time of confusion and displacement, fears and anxieties, ever more total crises. Kierkegaard found in melancholy the opening to understanding modern life. The all-consuming technoculture, approaching the erasure of the biological-digital demarcation, provides no meaning except that it means we are losing our sense of reality. The subject withers and the very idea of nature is rewritten in order to discard what survives. "The individual who lives in the technical milieu knows very well that there is nothing spiritual anywhere," according to Jacques Ellul.[3]

Will they find the black box of our drowned lives and wonder why? Or will we discover that "we are all walking a tightrope that is stretched taut, about two inches off the ground," as Jeff Benjamin has it, and heed his advice to step off?[4]

But technology, civilization's incarnation, is also the organizing principle of our lives: the always advancing, never retreating division of labor, moving away from tools and toward systems. And as "radically neutral," in Carl Schmitt's term, technology has always gotten away with everything. Technology still hopes to maintain a faith that it can solve the problems it created in the first place. While we experience a deepening ruin everywhere, IBM proclaims, insanely, "Let's Build a Smarter Planet."

The dynamic project of technology is the defining and most characteristic mark of modernity. Technology has no goal or value outside itself but is, despite its basic nihilism, the bottom line of our history. Its progressive victory over both nature and history, endorsed by both Left and Right, towers over other developments. We have traded loss of contact with the earth and each other for the pursuit of total control.

During the two million years before civilization, tools were a dependably stable solution to life's needs. Domestication, the control dynamic of civilization, launched the never-ending *progression* of technology. Before domestication, we lived in a continuum of present moments. Now we inhabit a "present" that looks away from or denies the present. And denies the real past and the now unmistakable future. Globalization reigns, the full "actualization of technology, its concrete universal."[5] The global culture that abhors and flattens the world.

Jerry Mander summed it up: "The web of interactions among the machines becomes more complex and more invisible, while the total effect is more powerful and pervasive. We become ever more enclosed and ever less aware of that fact. Our environment is so much a product of our invention that it becomes a single worldwide machine."[6]

The place of understanding, however, is a strangely limited terrain. Internet culture in general is the intended master narrative for our lives, and some see a framework of salvation there. Virtual Life programmer Steve Grand, for example, finds in software the restoration of the spiritual domain.[7] Or the very similar loopy claims of Ignacio L. Gotz: namely, that community life is "emerging in cyberspace" and that 'Through the power of computation, the universal spirit of divine creativity" is being extended.[8]

By Buckminster Fuller's bizarre logic, it is technology's record of failure that compels us to complete and perfect the technological project—and thereby aim at utopia.[9] Speaking of which, Frederic Jameson turned so often to the subject of utopia only to offer, in his *Valences of the Dialectic* (2010), a tepid progressive stance in explicit league with the liberals to strengthen both technology and the state. In a typically Marxist move, Mike Davis concludes his *City of Quartz* (1990) bemoaning the loss of Los Angeles steel plants. Gaia visionary James Lovelock has turned to nuclear power as the planet's last hope. Wendell Berry stresses the idea that the ecological crisis is about character, is not a political or social crisis. Deep Ecology adherents are likewise oblivious to the realities of such key factors as industrialism and technological rationality; some are fine with genetic engineering.

But the across-the-board failure of well-known "critical" voices, slightly sampled above, is much less interesting to me than that of a different category of thinkers. I mean those who have contributed important, in-depth critiques, only to take it all back with concluding comments that contradict or mock the critiques themselves. This is an almost universal phenomenon, which of course reinforces the prevailing denial of reality instead of challenging it. We are free to learn from the insightful content and ignore the so-often bizarrely inconsistent, cop-out endings, needless to say, but we need to do the whole job and not surrender to the Machine in our conclusions.

Martin Heidegger is a prime example of profound understanding and obvious failure to remain true to it. He saw that all has become grist for technology's totalizing mill, its mere "standing reserve," as he famously put it. The enormity of this global movement transforms everything, signifying definitive environmental destruction, the triumph of mass industrial culture, and the end of philosophy. The imposition of technology and its passion for control closes thought off from other ways of thinking.

The inescapably necessary response to this reality, one would logically expect, must lie in resisting it, so as to bring its ghastly reign to an end. But Heidegger counsels nothing of the kind, opting instead for a non-sequitur passivity in which simply understanding the techno-imperialism is key.[10] Changing one's perspective in the absence of consequences of course changes nothing, despite Heidegger's claim that it could provide a "free relationship" to technology.

The fact that almost no one remarks on such an abject surrender or betrayal of all that precedes it must be attributable to the universality of this pattern. Friedrich Georg Juenger's *The Failure of Technology* emphatically underlines, in a much more down-to-earth style, Heidegger's dire picture of the march of technology. Its progress, he writes, "is a self-impelled and irreversible process, which, left to itself, must end in a completely regimented and mechanized society that lives in a state of exhaustion, both of natural and human reserves."[11] He goes on to warn that "Nothing is further from my mind than the romantic rejection of technology."[12]

Enlarging the focus somewhat, we encounter valuable analyses of domestication and civilization, which produce the transition from tools to systems of technology. Paul Shepard provided one of the very most trenchant explications of the fateful move away from healthy, free and egalitarian hunter-gatherer life to its opposite: domesticated existence. He also noted that this shift to what he called the "barnyard" leads directly to present-day technologies like genetic engineering and nanotechnology; such outcomes are implicitly announced in the move to domesticate. In *The Tender Carnivore* and similar works, Shepard upheld the virtues of our hunter-gatherer ancestors: "we remain creatures of the older time...and in this lies our hope for tomorrow."[13] But he hastened to add, "I do not mean by backtracking through the barnyard." True to the observed pattern, he takes back the very heart of what he had given us. Absurdly, he concludes that we have to go forward with domestication in order to bring the "heart of the hunter-gatherer" to fruition.[14]

Daniel Quinn's *Ishmael* was a 1990s sensation, featuring a Socratic dialogue with a gorilla who seeks to save the world. The popular novel portrays hunter-gatherers and agriculturalists as Leavers and Takers, the latter as the non-sustainable civilizers whose project is the problem, not the solution. But—of course—we should not leave civilization or destroy its technological basis; we should just look at it differently.

Sherry Turkle, author and scholar at M.I.T., focuses on both psychology and high-tech culture. The latter is "where people and machines are in a new relation to each other [and] indeed can be mistaken for each other."[15] On October 17, 2007 I attended a public lecture by Turkle at the University of Oregon. Her main point, a very moving one, was the terrible effect that the pervasive online ethos has on the young, with special reference to her teenage daughter. Turkle spoke of how an all-absorbing Internet culture undermines and deforms the cognitive and emotional makeup of kids. The rapt audience heard how her daughter cannot, in important respects, grasp the difference between machines and living beings. At the very end of her talk she said, with something of a smile, "Oh well, that's modern life." (I think those were her exact words, or very close.) First with a question, I said, in so many words, "Surely you cannot just leave it at that, after your very devastating account of what technology is doing." Her reaction was a complete non-response, as if my point was not worth a reply. One or two others raised a similar point, based, I think, on the disconnect between her remarks and the utter surrender of her finale. How is the human spirit expected to live with such moral and intellectual bankruptcy?

Liquid Love: On the Frailty of Human Bonds by Zygmunt Bauman is an account rather like the gist of Turkle's talk. I felt the sadness of the book's description of rampant desociation, how we are always somewhere else, how in the electronic network world "getting in touch is no obstacle to staying apart."[16] And yet, "it would be foolish and irresponsible to blame electronic gadgets for the slow yet consistent recession of personal, direct, face-to-face, multi-faceted and multipurpose, continuous proximity."[17] So close to irony and yet so far. Tom Darby, quoted above, has displayed a deep understanding of how negative the all-pervasive techno-juggernaut is. Lacking the courage of his apparent convictions, however, he closes the door to transformation: "We do know this: at least for this age, and for the life of the West, technology is here to stay...."[18] It is here to stay insofar as we permit it to stay.

Jared Diamond is probably the best-known diagnostician of civilizations. In sum, they all fail, because of domestication, a.k.a. agriculture. 99.6 percent of human history was free of domestication, but its arrival about 10,000 years ago constituted "the worst mistake in the history of the human race."[19] Moving away from this insight, Diamond's *Collapse* is a grave disappointment. Having demonstrated the reason for civilization's downfall, in the last third of the book Diamond makes the ridiculous general assertion, based on nothing, that somehow things will all turn out fine. It isn't that there weren't weaknesses in Diamond's argument prior to *Collapse*, but in that work he looks to some completely unspecified "long-term" thinking to solve the problem of civilization. Embarrassing, in the way of Al Gore's *An Inconvenient Truth* film, when once again, the conclusion flies in the face of all that preceded it. The enormity of the eco-crisis, forcefully presented, followed by the change-your-lightbulbs "solution." Ridiculous, even to many liberals.

David Abram is a leading environmental philosopher, and his *The Spell of the Sensuous* is a key text. He posits the sensuous world as a victim of the alphabetic, technologically mediated world and its voracious progress in reducing our senses. Lyrical and poignant, Abram's book uncovers the insidious march of technology, the terrible damage it wreaks in severing our connection to our earth. Only to take it all back by proposing "a multiplicity of technologically sophisticated" cultural approaches as the solution to the unerringly destructive techno-trajectory he describes so persuasively.[20] Is such a jarring reversal the price of getting published?

Andy Fisher's *Radical Ecopsychology* stresses technology's disdain for life, and its relentless immiseration of the natural world. With, you guessed it, this proviso: "I want to be very clear that such counterpractice [which in daily life may somehow counter 'the pattern of technology'] does not involve getting rid of technology...."[21] Small wonder that Abram wrote the foreword to Fisher's book.

There is a constant stream of lesser books that follow this almost invariant pattern. Pressing, ecocidal reality is no bar to the familiar litany of useful contents and denial conclusions. In *The Most Powerful Idea in the World* (2010), a workmanlike history of industrial technology, William Rosen admits that global overheating is a function of aggregate industrialism. Every measure of industrialization is, step by step, the measure of the greenhouse gas effect that is warming the planet. But the answer is more technology, not less; no way to put the genie back in the bottle. All technology and its expansion of course rely on a concomitant expansion of that without which it would not exist—industrialism. Without mining, smelting, warehouses, assembly lines, there is no technology. Shiny, clean green technology exists nowhere in reality.

There is something totalitarian about this pattern, the hammering against a still-prevailing denial, only to end in conformity, again and again.

Giorgio Agamben has commented on the massive, historic loss of direct experience and imagination that techno-modernity has wrought.[22] Loneliness, the sense of dependency and de-skilling, the simple boredom and emptiness of a world of devices where the only "diversity" is flattened and machine-like. If there ever was a "technological sublime" or somehow a sense of transcendence, technology's failure to deliver—despite the fever pitch of marketing new lures—could scarcely be more manifest. The sad present, however, in its impoverished state, has only more and more of this desert on offer, connecting nowhere to nowhere.

The reform of technology's world? When has it ever happened? Specialization and domestication never go backward.

But we can have "social network" "friends" as we have fewer actual friends, visit them less often, tend as never before to live alone. In our homelessness we can have a "home page." Community reduced to what erases and mocks it. The medium itself encourages bad style, bad manners, and a fast-food version of content. Online and feeling worse, weaker afterward, like watching TV. Japan has perhaps the most superficial, mega-consumerist technotopia and what Henry Hitchings referred to as "the creepy infantilism that percolates through most of [its] popular culture."[23]

Once we felt alive, in the natural world, part of a larger whole. In an individualistic (mass) society such as the U.S., the individual is quite anonymous. Strangely enough, such a condition does not exist in indigenous, "group"-oriented societies, where the individual is never anonymous.

A feeling of meaninglessness began to arise as the Industrial Revolution began. We've come all the way to the age of Virtual Reality, megachurches, and life coaches, a measure of how deep the disembodiment and disempowerment have become. The self and its community are emptied of substance and therefore meaning, a global phenomenon. In India, the Bhagavad Gita and yoga sutras are, commonly, annotated texts for heightened production and consumption.

Civilization is this draining servitude to a Machine that is now completely global. Aztecs feared that the universe would come to a stop if they did not sacrifice pulsing hearts to feed their own pulsing social dynamics. As the current, unitary civilization desecrates and destroys the very support systems that make life possible, it is easy to see the dependence of all parts on the whole, and their functional equivalence. In Don DeLillo's novel *Underworld*, the character Matt wonders, "How can you tell the difference between orange juice and agent orange if the same massive system connects them?"[24]

But as Native American philosopher Linda Hogan reminds us, "The world is there in its entirety, not in segments."[25] When we connect with nature, it happens directly and specifically. Not ideologically, but in practice, bodily, in a way that can draw on practices that do not massify or erase connection with the earth. Elizabeth Marshall Thomas offers wonderful observations on the digging stick, which remains in use in some places. She points out its availability, versatility ("It can balance a load, extend your reach, or become a lever," a tool to knock nuts from a tree or discourage a predator. It weighs less, is easier to carry, and costs nothing" in contrast to a shovel. The digging stick also requires less energy and preserves contact with what is being dug.[26]

A shovel requires shoes, which brings us to Christopher McDougall's *Born to Run* (2010). This entertaining work reveals that the more technologically advanced runners" shoes are, the more chronic are injuries of the foot, leg, hip, etc. McDougall contrasts the health of barefoot long-distance runners in mountainous Mexico, the peaceful, horticultural Tarahumara; perhaps the best in the world, for whom running a hundred miles is a commonplace. Again, the unmediated is best.

Seemingly inexorable and limitless, does the ever-expanding techno-ethos really offer more freedom or individuality, and less work? The opposite is the case, a social existence that is limited, generic, and hollow, with an almost total dependence on experts, and a lived environment as thin and non-diverse as that of most of the biosphere. We approach our merger with machines, possibly the greatest technological watershed in human history. Modernity's goal of total mastery turns out instead to be more and more industrial disasters. The control logic of techno-Progress comes to mean that the Machine is out of control. Who is left who believes in redemption through technology, despite the fact that we are still held hostage to it?

Meanwhile we are losing what were thought to be basic human aptitudes. GPS devices supplant map-reading skills and even a sense of direction. There is a "baby-cry" app for iPhones that translates a baby's cries into one of five emotional states, including hunger and fatigue.[27] We walked on this Earth for millions of years knowing where we were, and knowing the meaning of an infant's cry. Without machines, how astounding! Heidegger saw the current era as "no longer able to experience its own destitution," a most apt observation.[28]

Some manage to speak of harmony, the wish for a "balance" with technology. The need, for example, for technology to be more people-oriented and/or respectful of nature. As if it is so already but just needs to be more so. Gandhi, by the way, who stressed such traits as simplicity and self-reliance, on occasion said that industry is fine so long as it respects these traits. But of course the point is that it does not respect them. One might as well say that cancer is OK so long as it respects the body, behaves harmoniously, in a "balanced" way. Another version of this wishful thinking is seeing the technoculture as acceptable insofar as we don't worship it. But it makes no difference whether we "worship" it or not; its power and effects move forward all the same.

The fall-back, bottom-line attitude is, bluntly, acceptance—because of the inevitability of ever-evolving technology. We've come too far along the road, the argument goes, to consider a qualitatively different destination. Michael Pollan expressed this idea quite simply: "The doors to Eden have closed."[29]

Behind the denial and the threadbare delusions, something of "Eden" has persisted. Colin Turnbull told us that "All Mbuti talk, shout, whisper, and sing to the forest...addressing it as mother or father or both, referring to its goodness and ability to 'cure" or 'make good.'"[30] Turnbull judged "that in terms of conscious dedication to human relationships that are both affective and effective, the primitive is ahead of us all the way."[31] Consider the Bajans of Southeast Asia, whose connection to the earth includes the ability to find a particular patch of ocean on overcast nights, out of sight of land.[32]

Marx got it wrong when he reversed himself and decided that we can't do without division of labor after all. Deleuze and Guattari got it wrong when they counseled that we should "do away with foundations, nullify endings and beginnings."[33] Vattimo and Rorty didn't even try, with their postmodern "weak thought" that eschews confrontation with the extremity of our time, in favor of a very mild reformist hope.[34] Noam Chomsky concurs. Variations on the theme of the monumental failure of the Left.

The physical, psychic and moral avoidance builds up, accompanied by the rest of the devastation. We need, in Marie-Florine Bruneau's prescription, "a radicality that consists in an unrelenting resistance to and an undoing of procedures of reification."[35] Without such an effort with real consequences, the "inescapable" outcome is just that. We must breach the doors of the barrenness and heal the rupture between realms of being. "We are all part of Mother Earth. We cannot break away from that. We are going to have to understand this so we can look at each other," according to Hopi spokesperson Thomas Banyacya.[36]

We long to be exiles no longer, and the pressure is ready to boil out from under the lid. It's later than that for an order that plainly has no answers. So when something is falling, give it a kick, goes some good advice. We can step off the two-inch-high tightrope, and exult in a world no longer controlled or directed. Mendelssohn's *Elijah* gives a call: "O come everyone that thirsteth, O come to the waters."

—*September 2010*

ENDNOTES

1   Michel Serres, *The Five Senses*, translated by Margaret Sankey and Peter Cowley (New York: Continuum International Publishing Group, 2008), p. 234.

2   Thomas Merton, *Dancing in the Water of Life* (New York: Harper Collins, 1995), p. 240.

3   Jacques Ellul, *The Technological Society* (New York: Vintage, 1964), pp 142–143.

4   Jeff Benjamin, personal communication, February 28, 2010.

5   Tom Darby, *Sojourns in the New World: Reflections on Technology* (Ottawa: Carleton University Press, 1986), p. 58.

6   Jerry Mander, *In the Absence of the Sacred* (San Francisco: Sierra Club Books, 1991), p. 32.

7   Steve Grand, *Creation: Life and How to Make It* (Cambridge, MA: Harvard University Press, 2000), p. 4.

8   Ignacio L. Gotz, *Technology and the Spirit* (Westport, CT: Praeger, 2001), pp. 235, 239.

9   Buckminster Fuller, *Utopia or Oblivion* (New York: Overlook Press, 1972).

10   The key text is "The Question Concerning Technology" and a quite adequate discussion is Richard Rojcewicz, *The Gods and Technology* (Albany: State University of New York Press, 2006).

11   Friedrich Georg Juenger, *The Failure of Technology* (Hinsdale, IL: Henry Regnery Company, 1949), p. viii.

12   *Ibid.*, p. 144.

13   Paul Shepard, *The Tender Carnivore and the Sacred Game* (New York: Charles Scribner's Sons, 1973), p. 36.

14   *Ibid.*, p. 259.

15   Sherry Turkle, *Life on the Screen* (New York: Simon & Schuster, 1995), p. 17.

16   Zygmunt Bauman, *Liquid Love: On the Frailty of Human Bonds* (Cambridge, UK: Polity Press, 2003), p. 62.

17   *Ibid.*, p. 64.

18   Tom Darby, "On Spiritual Crisis, Globalization, and Planetary Rule," in Peter Augustine Lawler and Dale McConkey, *Faith, Reason and Political Life Today* (Lanham, MD: Lexington Books, 2000), p. 60.

19   Jared Diamond, "The Worst Mistake in the History of the Human Race," *Discover*, May 1987.

20   David Abram, *The Spell of the Sensuous* (New York: Vintage Books, 1996), p. 272. His *Becoming Animal* (2010) is a rehash of *Spell*, with the same refusal to take on what continues to destroy that which he purports to value.

21   Andy Fisher, *Radical Ecopsychology* (Albany: State University of New York Press, 2002), p. 161.

22   Giorgio Agamben, *Infancy and History*, translated by Liz Heron (New York: Verso, 2005), e.g. pp. 27, 29.

23   Henry Hitchings, "Making Dates," review of a Shuichi Yoshida novel in the *Times Literary Supplement*, August 20 & 27, 2010.

24   Don DeLillo, *Underworld* (London: Picador, 1998), p. 465.

25   Kathleen Dean Moore et al., eds., *How It Is* (Tucson: University of Arizona Press, 2007). Foreword, p. xi.

26   Elizabeth Marshall Thomas, *The Old Way* (New York: Picador, 2006), p. 12.

27   A product of Barcelona's Biloop Technologic, S.L. Ki Mae Heusser et al., ABC News, November 6, 2009.

28   Martin Heidegger, *Poetry, Language, Thought* (New York: Harper & Row, 1971), p. 93.

29   Quoted in John Opie, *Virtual America* (Lincoln: University of Nebraska Press, 2008), p. 204.

30   Colin Turnbull, *The Human Cycle* (New York: Simon & Schuster, 1983), p. 30.

31   *Ibid.*, p. 21.

32   James Hamilton-Paterson, *Seven-Tenths* (London: Europa, 2009), p. 311.

33   Gilles Deleuze, *A Thousand Plateaus: Capitalism and Schizophrenia* (Minneapolis: University of Minnesota Press, 1987), p. 25. This is the rhizome concept.

34   Richard Rorty and Gianni Vattimo, *The Future of Religion* (New York: Columbia University Press, 2004).

35   Marie-Florine Bruneau, *Women Mystics Confront the Modern World* (Albany: State University of New York Press, 1998), p. 6.

36   David Suzuki and Peter Knudson, eds., *Wisdom of the Elders* (New York: Bantam Books, 1992), p. 242.

DENYING THE UNAVOIDABLE

PART THREE

THE WAY WE ARE NOW

CHAPTER ELEVEN

memory.loss

MEMORY, according to Henri Bergson, occupies the space between mind and body. Poet W.S. Merwin called it "what we forget with." Contrarily, one of Freud's strongest convictions was that the past once experienced is indestructible.

Today modernity carries all along at a dizzying pace, away from what was once lived. The current cultural preoccupation with memory, for example as a focus of contemporary historiography[1], testifies to a generalized and very uneasy sense of loss.[2] A sense that so much has lost its meaning in modern life. In the high-tech mass culture lifespace "memory itself is perceived to be in a state of insecurity or even disintegration."[3] The self seems episodic, cut off from a continuity with what has come before. Memory seems adrift, atrophying, suggesting a dystopian nightmare of a future without memory.[4]

It is the search for grounds for actively living, as distinct from passively hoping to survive a darkening world, that establishes memory as a cognitive issue. Memory is a link to what is instinctual, non-instrumental. Charles Scott referred to its "escape from systems and formulations."[5] And consider the paradox involved in the injunction to remember. Characteristically, memories emerge as spontaneous evocations, in a non-domesticated way, outside of our command.

In the case of traumatic memory, the work of mourning is required, and not only where individual pain is concerned. Critical memory may be a necessary part of insight and healing, where personal and collective memory meet. We remember what the reigning culture expects us to remember, but this social process can be altered.

Memory is multifaceted. Why are so many memoirs of childhood written late in life? How is that a person exposed to a life-threatening situation may experience a panoramic memory in which her whole life passes before her in an instant? Why has memory changed so drastically in our own time? As John Kotre sees it, "The context of autobiographical memory [now] is vastly different from what it was [in 1900] and light years away from what it was for almost all of human existence."[6]

Yet what is more uniquely personal than memories that come back to us—a priceless flavor that calls to us, awakening our senses and our emotions. Theodor Adorno revealed, "I simply wanted to return to where I had my childhood, ultimately from the feeling that what we achieve in life is little more than the attempt to realize our childhood while transforming it."[7] Early experiences ground us in time and place; little wonder we seem to cling to them, seek them, as life tears us away from this grounding. "Where is here tonight? Where am I? Where are you?" wondered Kerouac in *Vanity of Duluoz*, a memoir of his youth.[8]

From another perspective, memory is just one more social instrument that legitimates a mad, malignant society. But the Greek word for memory, *anamnesis*, signifies a return, retaking, or recovering of what has been experienced. And the lure of what we sense as innocent and spontaneous is a pleasurable motive. Like dreams, memories are not delivered or bound by time. Time cannot touch them.

We know that social memory is fractured by history, but flashes of our very early background may remain in personal memory. All life on Earth is threatened now, no less our own lives; a new kind of recollection is called for, a re-collecting of experience that has been largely buried, and is now urgently needed. "Remembrance of the past may give rise to dangerous insights, and the established society seems to be apprehensive of the subversive contents of memory," observed Herbert Marcuse.[9] We must recover some kind of deep memory to operate against the structural amnesia engineered and constantly reproduced by civilization. Memory's best potential is the promise of a lifeline to the 99 percent of human existence outside of the machine of domestication which is civilization. What is not altogether dead may be reawakened and reanimated, if we can free ourselves from the order of time.

There is bodily memory, an intimate of the corporeal intentionality that ties us to our Mother Earth in the first place—an active immanence of the lived past in our physical selves. In mental life nothing which has once been formed can perish, Freud concluded. This principle applies most deeply to the kind of memory that inheres in us from the depth of so many millennia prior to our enslavement. For Walter Benjamin, a key aspect of Proust's thought is "a not-yet-conscious knowledge of what has been." He went on to describe how the novelist's project is turned toward the future: an "imminent awakening is poised, like the wooden horse of the Greeks, in the Troy of dreams."[10] Lewis Carroll also happened upon this latent opportunity. " 'I'm sure [my memory] only works one way," Alice remarked. 'I can't remember things before they happen." 'It's a poor sort of memory that only works backwards," the Queen remarked."[11]

Memory is bodily, alive. But memories—like so much else in our lives today—are becoming unmoored. The very notion of memory may be approaching its end. As the conscious apprehension of past experience, it is compromised as unique, direct experience loses itself in the welter of an ever more troubled life-sphere. This is not an overnight development. In his essay "The Storyteller," written in 1936, Walter Benjamin judged that "experience has fallen in value."[12] Adorno saw that "the specter of man without memory...is more than an aspect of decline...it is necessarily linked with the principles of progress in bourgeois society."[13] The withering of experience has only become more dominant in the techno-world. Beset by "information sickness," a mounting data overload cut off from any living basis, we now must struggle *for* experience as much as we sometimes struggle *with* it. Memory tends to evaporate in this denuded context.

Everything we experience only vicariously, instead of personally, erodes the wellsprings of our autonomous depth and memory. The trajectory is not one of increasing forgetfulness but of increasing non-memory: we have less and less to forget. Maurice Halbwach's comment that "History starts only when tradition ends"[14] traces this movement back to the clash between history and the lived past. In this sense, (written) history is pitted directly against memory, displacing its importance as social memory.

History's emergence coincides, roughly speaking, with the domination of tools by systems of technology, as civilization arose. "What is peculiar to a history of memory is the history of the modes of its transmission," as Paul Ricoeur put it[15], bringing the two dimensions into focus.

Technical means of extending voluntary recall are prosthetic, and diminish the uniqueness of the passing moment. Technical means come in various forms. Plato argued that literacy did not promote remembering, but undermined it; both writing and printing can be seen as technologies that render original memory redundant. Technology subordinates life to its measure, objectifying experience as technological transmission. In studies about remembering displayed objects, Gary Lupyan found that verbal labels actually impair memory—a recent example of how symbolic modes get between us and—the world.[16]

It's obvious that technology is central to the rampant, global eco-crisis. Just as evident is the high-tech loss of thought, feeling, and memory. "How much memory do you have?" of course has only one meaning now, a reminder of the collapsing distinction between human and machine.

A sense of the past in any sense at all is a casualty of postmodern technoculture. Lost, like so many dimensions, places, senses, as memory is continually transmuted into a "series of pure and unrelated presents,"[17] presents robbed of presentness, immediacy, and texture. Langdon Winner summed it up perfectly: technology "is a license to forget."[18]

Memory is a selective, not a unitary phenomenon. Forager/hunter-gatherer societies, with no institutional authority, have had no need to memorialize those who preceded them. However, we need to draw on what Merleau-Ponty called "the world's vast Memory."[19]

"In the last decades the relationship between history and memory, history and oblivion, has been scrutinized with unprecedented intensity," as Carlo Ginzburg noted.[20] Part of the oblivion, in an ever more technological lifespace, is the pressure against memory that comes from the collapse of the distinction between machine and human, and the growing reification of human relations. This leads in turn to the extinguishing of specific individual experience.

In the mid-'90s I tried to explore memory[21], and even before the next decade is out, it's clear how much more invasive the pressures on memory have become. Insomnia affects millions, as stress and anxiety exact an increasing toll. (Stress produces cortisol, a hormone that corrodes memory, to cite one particular.)

By deepening our recollection of two million years of human life before civilization, can we begin to make a bridge to that reality, so different from our nightmare existence now?

ENDNOTES

1   Jeffrey Blustein, *The Moral Demands of Memory* (New York: Cambridge University Press, 2008), p. 176.

2   Geoffrey Cubitt, *History and Memory* (Manchester: Manchester University Press, 2007), p. 244.

3   *Ibid.*, p. 61.

4   Andreas Huyssen, *Twilight Memories* (New York: Routledge, 1995), p. 7.

5   Charles E. Scott, *The Time of Memory* (Albany: State University of New York Press, 1999), p. 9.

6   John Katre, *White Gloves: How We Create Ourselves through Memory* (New York: Free Press, 1995), p. 9.

7   Theodor W. Adorno, "Auf Die Frage: Warum sind Sie zurückgekerht" (1962 radio address), in *Gesammelte Schriften* (Frankfurt am Main: Suhrkamp, 1986), p. 395.

8   Jack Kerouac, *Vanity of Duluoz* (New York: Penguin Books, 1994), p. 205.

9   Herbert Marcuse, *One-Dimensional Man* (Boston: Beacon Press, 1964), p. 48.

10 Walter Benjamin, *The Arcades Project* (Cambridge, MA: The Belknap Press of Harvard University Press, 1999), p. 883.

11 Lewis Carroll, *Alice's Adventures in Wonderland and Through the Looking Glass* (New York: Penguin Books, 1998), p. 172.

12 Walter Benjamin, "The Storyteller," in *Illuminations* (New York: Harcourt, Brace & World, 1968), pp 83–84.

13 Theodor Adorno, quoted in Herbert Marcuse, *op.cit.*, p. 99.

14 Quoted in Paul Ricoeur, *Memory, History, Forgetting* (Chicago: The University of Chicago Press, 2004), p. 398.

15 *Ibid.*, p. 386.

16 Christine Kenneally, "When Language Can Hold the Answer," *New York Times*, April 22, 2008, p. D3.

17 David Harvey, *The Condition of Postmodernity* (Cambridge, MA: Blackwell, 1990), p. 301.

18 Langdon Winner, *Autonomous Technology* (Cambridge, MA: The MIT Press, 1977), p. 315.

19 Maurice Merleau-Ponty, *Phenomenology of Perception* (New York: Humanities Press, 1962), p. 70.

20 Carlo Ginzburg, "History and/or Memory," in Robert S. Westman and David Biale, eds., *Thinking Impossibilities* (Toronto: University of Toronto Press, 2008), p. 173.

21 John Zerzan, "In Memoriam," in *Running on Emptiness* (Los Angeles: Feral House, 2002); the essay was first published in 1994.

CHAPTER TWELVE

SILENCE

SILENCE USED TO BE, to varying degrees, a means of isolation. Now it is the absence of silence that works to render today's world empty and isolating. Its reserves have been invaded and depleted. The Machine marches globally forward and silence is the dwindling place where noise has not yet penetrated.

Civilization is a conspiracy of noise, designed to cover up the uncomfortable silences. The silence-honoring Wittgenstein understood the loss of our relationship with it. The unsilent present is a time of evaporating attention spans, erosion of critical thinking, and a lessened capacity for deeply felt experiences. Silence, like darkness, is hard to come by; but mind and spirit need its sustenance.

Certainly there are many and varied sides to silence. There are imposed or voluntary silences of fear, grief, conformity, complicity (e.g. the AIDS-awareness "Silence=Death" formulation), which are often interrelated states. And nature has been progressively silenced, as documented in Rachel Carson's prophetic *Silent Spring*. Nature cannot be definitively silenced, however, which perhaps goes a long way in explaining why some feel it must be destroyed. "There has been a silencing of nature, including our own nature," concluded Heidegger,[1] and we need to let this silence, as silence, speak. It still does so often, after all, speak louder than words.

There will be no liberation of humans without the resurrection of the natural world, and silence is very pertinent to this assertion. The great silence of the universe engenders a silent awe, which the Roman Lucretius meditated upon in the first century BCE: "First of all, contemplate the clear, pure color of the sky, and all it contains within it: the stars wandering everywhere, the moon, the sun and its light with its incomparable brilliance. If all these objects appeared to mortals today for the first time, if they appeared to their eyes suddenly and unexpectedly, what could one cite that would be more marvelous than this totality, and whose existence man's imagination would less have dared to conceive?"[2]

Down to earth, nature is filled with silences. The alternation of the seasons is the rhythm of silence; at night silence descends over the planet, though much less so now. The parts of nature resemble great reserves of silence. Max Picard's description is almost a poem: "The forest is like a great reservoir of silence out of which the silence trickles in a thin, slow stream and fills the air with its brightness. The mountain, the lake, the fields, the sky—they all seem to be waiting for a sign to empty their silence onto the things of noise in the cities of men."[3]

Silence is "not the mere absence of something else."[4] In fact, our longings turn toward that dimension, its associations and implications. Behind the appeals for silence lies the wish for a perceptual and cultural new beginning.

Zen teaches that "silence never varies...."[5] But our focus may be improved if we turn away from the universalizing placelessness of late modernity. Silence is no doubt culturally specific, and is thus experienced variously. Nevertheless, as Picard argues, it can confront us with the "original beginnings of all things,"[6] and presents objects to us directly and immediately. Silence is primary, summoning presence to itself; so it's a connection to the realm of origin.

In the industrially-based technosphere, the Machine has almost succeeded in banishing quietude. A natural history of silence is needed for this endangered species. Modernity deafens. The noise, like technology, must never retreat—and never does.

For Picard, nothing has changed human character so much as the loss of silence.[7] Thoreau called silence "our inviolable asylum," an indispensable refuge that must be defended.[8] Silence is necessary against the mounting sound. It's feared by manipulative mass culture, from which it remains apart, a means of resistance precisely because it does not belong to this world. Many things can still be heard against the background of silence; thus a way is opened, a way for autonomy and imagining.

"Sense opens up in silence," wrote Jean-Luc Nancy.[9] It is to be approached and experienced bodily, inseparably from the world, in the silent core of the self. It can highlight our embodiment, a qualitative step

179

away from the hallmark machines that work so resolutely to disembody us. Silence can be a great aid in unblocking ourselves from the prevailing, addictive information sickness at loose in society.[10] It offers us the place to be present to ourselves, to come to grips with who we are. Present to the real depth of the world in an increasingly thin, flattened technoscape.

The record of philosophy vis-à-vis silence is generally dismal, as good a gauge as any to its overall failure. Socrates judged silence to be a realm of nonsense, while Aristotle claimed that being silent caused flatulence.[11] At the same time, however, Raoul Mortley could see a "growing dissatisfaction with the use of words," "an enormous increase in the language of silence" in classical Greece.[12]

Much later, Pascal was terrified by the "silence of the universe,"[13] and Hegel clearly felt that what could not be spoken was simply the untrue, that silence was a deficiency to be overcome. Schopenhauer and Nietzsche both emphasized the prerequisite value of solitude, diverging from anti-silence Hegel, among others.

Deservedly well known is a commentary on Odysseus and the Sirens (from Homer's *Odyssey*) by Horkheimer and Adorno. They depict the Sirens" effort to sidetrack Odysseus from his journey as that of Eros trying to stay the forces of repressive civilization. Kafka felt that silence would have been a more irresistible means than singing.[14]

"Phenomenology begins in silence," according to Herbert Spiegelberg.[15] To put phenomena or objects somehow first, before ideational constructions, was its founding notion. Or as Heidegger had it, there is a thinking deeper and more rigorous than the conceptual, and part of this involves a primordial link between silence and understanding.[16] Postmodernism, and Derrida in particular, deny the widespread awareness of the inadequacy of language, asserting that gaps of silence in discourse, for example, are barriers to meaning and power. In fact, Derrida strongly castigates "the violence of primitive and prelogical silence," denouncing silence as a nihilist enemy of thought.[17] Such strenuous antipathy demonstrates Derrida's deafness to presence and grace, and the threat silence poses to someone for whom the symbolic is everything. Wittgenstein understood that something pervades everything sayable, something which is itself unsayable. This is the sense of his well-known last line of the *Tractatus Logico-Philosophicus*: "Of that which one cannot speak, one should remain silent."[18]

Can silence be considered, approached, without reification, in the

SILENCE

here and now? I think it can be an open, strengthening way of knowing, a generative condition. Silence can also be a dimension of fear, grief—even of madness and suicide. In fact, it is quite difficult to reify silence, to freeze it into any one non-living thing. At times the reality we interrogate is mute; an index of the depth of the still present silence? Wonder may be the question that best gives answers, silently and deeply.

"Silence is so accurate," said Mark Rothko,[19] a line that has intrigued me for years. Too often we disrupt silence, only to voice some detail that misses an overall sense of what we are part of, and how many ways there are to destroy it. In the Antarctica winter of 1933, Richard Byrd recorded: "Took my daily walk at 4PM... I paused to listen to the silence...the day was dying, the night being born—but with great peace. Here were imponderable processes and forces of the cosmos, harmonious and soundless."[20] How much is revealed in silence through the depths and mysteries of living nature. Annie Dillard also provides a fine response to the din: "At a certain point you say to the woods, to the sea, to the mountains, to the world, Now I am ready. Now I will stop and be wholly attentive. You empty yourself and wait, listening."[21]

It is not only the natural world that is accessible via silence. Cioran indicated the secrets in the silence of things, deciding that "All objects have a language which we can decipher only in total silence."[22] David Michael Levin's The Body's Recollection of Being counsels us to "learn to think through the body...we should listen in silence to our bodily felt experience."[23] And in the interpersonal sphere, silence is a result of empathy and being understood, without words much more profoundly than otherwise.

Native Americans seem to have always placed great value on silence and direct experience, and in indigenous cultures in general, silence denotes respect and self-effacement. It is at the core of the Vision Quest, the solitary period of fasting and closeness to the earth to discover one's life path and purpose. Inuit Norman Hallendy assigns more insight to the silent state of awareness called inuinaqtuk than to dreaming.[24] Native healers very often stress silence as an aid to serenity and hope, while stillness is required for success in the hunt. These needs for attentiveness and quiet may well have been key sources of indigenous appreciation of silence.

Silence reaches back to presence and original community, before the symbolic compromised both silence and presence. It predates what Levinas called "the unity of representation,"[25] that always works to silence

181

the silence and replace it with the homelessness of symbolic structures. The Latin root for silence, *silēre*, to say nothing, is related to *sinere*, to allow to be in a place. We are drawn to those places where language falls most often, and most crucially, silent. The later Heidegger appreciated the realm of silence, as did Hölderlin, one of Heidegger's important reference points, especially in his *Late Hymns*.[26] The insatiable longing that Hölderlin expressed so powerfully related not only to an original, silent wholeness, but also to his growing comprehension that language must always admit its origin in loss.

A century and a half later, Samuel Beckett made use of silence as an alternative to language. In *Krapp's Last Tape* and elsewhere, the idea that all language is an excess of language is strongly on offer. Beckett complains that "in the forest of symbols" there is never quiet, and longs to break through the veil of language to silence.[27] Northrup Frye found the purpose of Beckett's work "to lie in nothing other than the restoration of silence."[28]

Our most embodied, alive-to-this-earth selves realize best the limits of language and indeed, the failure of the project of representation. In this state it is easiest to understand the exhaustion of language, and the fact that we are always a word's length from immediacy. Kafka commented on this in "In the Penal Colony," where the printing press doubled as an instrument of torture. For Thoreau, "as the truest society approaches always nearer to solitude, so the most excellent speech finally falls into silence."[29] Conversely, mass society banishes the chance of autonomy, just as it forecloses on silence.

Hölderlin imagined that language draws us into time, but it is silence that holds out against it. Time increases in silence; it appears not to flow, but to abide. Various temporalities seem close to losing their barriers; past, present, future less divided.

But silence is a variable fabric, not a uniformity or an abstraction. Its quality is never far from its context, just as it is the field of the non-mediated. Unlike time, which has for so long been a measure of estrangement, silence cannot be spatialized or converted into a medium of exchange. This is why it can be a refuge from time's incessancy. Gurnemanz, near the opening of Wagner's *Parsifal*, sings "Here time becomes space." Silence avoids this primary dynamic of domination.

So here we are, with the Machine engulfing us in its various assaults on silence and so much else, intruding deeply. The note North Americans spontaneously hum or sing is B- natural, which is the corresponding tone of our 60 cycles per second alternating current electricity. (In Europe, G-sharp is "naturally" sung, matching that continent's 50 cycles per second AC electricity.) In the globalizing, homogenizing Noise Zone we may soon be further harmonized. Pico Ayer refers to "my growing sense of a world that's singing the same song in a hundred accents all at once."[30]

We need a refusal of the roar of standardization, its information-noise and harried, surface "communication" modes. A No to the unrelenting, colonizing penetrability of non-silence, pushing into every non-place. The rising racket measures, by decibel upticks and its polluting reach, the degrading mass world—Don DeLillo's White Noise.

Silence is a rebuke to all this, and a zone for reconstituting ourselves. It gathers in nature, and can help us gather ourselves for the battles that will end debasement. Silence as a powerful tool of resistance, the unheard note that might precede insurrection. It was, for example, what slave masters feared most.[31] In various Asian spiritual traditions, the muni, vowed to silence, is the person of greatest capacity and independence—the one who does not need a master for enlightenment.[32]

The deepest passions are nurtured in silent ways and depths. How else is respect for the dead most signally expressed, intense love best transmitted, our profoundest thoughts and visions experienced, the unspoiled world most directly savored? In this grief-stricken world, according to Max Horkheimer, we "become more innocent" through grief.[33] And perhaps more open to silence—as comfort, ally, and stronghold.

—December 2007

ENDNOTES

1   Martin Heidegger, *What is a Thing?* (Chicago, Henry Regnery Company, 1967), p. 288.

2   Quoted in Pierre Hadot, *The Veil of Isis*, translated by Michael Chan (Cambridge, MA: Bellknap Press, 2000), pp 212–213.

3   Max Picard, *The World of Silence* (Chicago: Henry Regnery Company, 1952), p. 139.

4   Bernard P. Dauenhauer, *Silence: the Phenomenon and Its Ontological Significance* (Bloomington: Indiana University Press, 1980), p. vii.

5   Chang Chung-Yuan, *Original Teachings of Ch'an Buddhism* (New York: Vintage, 1971), p. 12.

6   Picard, *op.cit.*, p. 22.

7   *Ibid.*, p. 221.

8   Henry David Thoreau, "A Week on the Concord and Merrimack Rivers," in *The Works of Thoreau*, edited by Henry Seidel Canby (Boston: Houghton Mifflin, 1946), p. 241.

9   Jean-Luc Nancy, *Listening*, translated by Charlotte Mandell (New York: Fordham University Press, 2007), p. 26.

10 I first encountered this term in Ted Mooney's novel, *Easy Travel to Other Planets* (New York: Farrar Straus & Giroux, 1981).

11 Aristotle, *Works of Aristotle*, translated by S. Forster, Vol. VII, *Problemata* (Oxford: Clarendon Press, 1927), p. 896, lines 20–26.

12 Raoul Mortley, *From Word to Silence I* (Bonn: Hanstein, 1986), p. 110.

13 Blaise Pascal, *Pensées*, edited by Phillipe Seller (Paris: Bordas, 1991), p. 256.

14 Franz Kafka, Parables, cited in George Steiner, *Language and Silence* (New York: Atheneum, 1967), p. 54.

15 Herbert Spiegelberg, *The Phenomenological Movement*, Vol. Two (The Hague: Martinus Nijhoff, 1969), p. 693.

16 Martin Heidegger, "Letter on Humanism," *Basic Writings* (San Francisco: Harper San Francisco, 1992), p. 258.

17 Jacques Derrida, *Writing and Difference*, translated by Alan Bass (Chicago: University of Chicago Press, 1978), p. 130.

18 Ludwig Wittgenstein, *Tractatus Logico-Philosophicus* (London: Routledge, 1974), p. 89.

19 Quoted in James E.B. Breslin, *Rothko: A Biography* (Chicago: University of Chicago Press, 1993), p. 387.

20 Quoted in Hannah Merker, *Listening* (New York: HarperCollins, 1994), p. 127.

21 Annie Dillard, *Teaching a Stone to Talk* (New York: HarperPerennial, 1982), pp 89–90.

22 E.M. Cioran, *Tears and Saints*, translated by Ilinca Zarifopol-Johnson

(Chicago: University of Chicago Press, 1995), p. 53.

23   David Michael Levin, *The Body's Recollection of Being* (Boston: Routledge, 1985), pp 60–61.

24   Norman Hallendy, *Inuksuit: Silent Messengers of the Arctic* (Toronto: Douglas & McIntyre, 2000), pp 84–85.

25   Emmanuel Levinas, *Proper Names*, translated by Michael B. Smith (Stanford, CA: Stanford University Press, 1996), p. 4.

26   Emery Edward George, *Hölderlin's "Ars Poetica": A Part-Rigorous Analysis of Information Structure in the Late Hymns* (The Hague: Mouton, 1973), pp 308, 363, 367.

27   Samuel Beckett, "German letter" dated 9 July 1937, in C.J. Ackerley and S.E. Gontorski, *The Grove Companion to Samuel Beckett* (New York: Grove Press, 2004), p. 221.

28   Northrup Frye, "The Nightmare Life in Death," in J.D. O'Hara, editor, *Twentieth-Century Interpretations of Malloy, Malone Dies, and The Unnamable* (Englewood Cliffs, NJ: Prentice-Hall, 1970), p. 34.

29   Thoreau, *op.cit.*, p. 241.

30   Pico Ayer, *The Global Soul* (New York: Knopf, 2000), p. 271.

31   Mark M. Smith, *Listening to Nineteenth-Century America* (Chapel Hill: The University of North Carolina Press), p. 68.
See also Thomas Merton, *The Strange Islands* (New York: New Directions, 1957); specifically, this passage from "The Tower of Babel: A Morality":
Leader: Who is He?
Captain: His name is Silence.
Leader: Useless! Throw him out! Let silence be crucified!

32   Alex Wayman, "Two traditions of India—truth and silence," *Philosophy East and West* 24 (October 1974), pp 389–403.

33   Max Horkheimer, *Dawn and Decline: Notes 1926–1931 and 1950–1969* (New York: Seabury Press, 1978), p. 140.

CHAPTER THIRTEEN

LOVE

THE VERTIGO of techno-modernity is an invasive sense of nothingness. This certainly also registers on the level of what is directly felt, not just thought. Already in 1984 Frederic Jameson referred to a "waning of affect" in postmodern society, an emotional shriveling or retreat. There is a thinness or flatness making its way into this most vital terrain of being human.

Our affective state is the very texture and timbre of our lives. Nothing is more immediate to us than our own feelings. This is constitutive, gives us the "feel" we have of the world, is what actually connects us to reality. Emotions are cultural artifacts, more so than ideas.

In this vein Lucien Febvre (1938, 1941) called for a history of the sensibilities, and Anne Vincent-Buffault (1986) contributed *Histoire des larmes* (*History of Tears*). Are our passions not at the core of our existence?

Every culture has its own emotional climate, every political struggle is an affective one. The fight against the drive of civilization is of course included. Things are felt before they are thought or believed, and so hegemony—or its undoing—has its foundation here. Adam Smith's first book, *The Theory of Moral Sentiments* (1759), saw in emotions the thread that weaves together the fabric of society. None of this is a remarkable finding, but we often act as though the field of affect is of no real relevance.

Reason and reflection are somewhat refined expressions of the passions themselves. Antonio Damasio, in fact, provides the notion that "consciousness begins as a feeling, a special kind of feeling to be sure, but a feeling nonetheless...a feeling of knowing" (1999, p. 312). His suggestion reknits the mind-body split so essential to life in mass society.

So many debilitating splits: humans from nature, work from play, among others. We are also being moved away from physical sensations, from direct experience. Feelings are embodied, but what is happening to the context of that embodiment? Isolation grows apace and social bonds keep weakening. Friends are exchanged for online network "friends," and the one-person household is an ever-larger percentage of all homes. Where is home? The subject is dispersed and the social, according to Baudrillard, really no longer exists.

We feel all this, even if the depthlessness of the dominant culture does work, as Jameson suggests, to deform and superficialize our emotional core in its image. This core is its own embodiment, perhaps the strongest redoubt of resistance. Otherwise, in a bitter irony, we wouldn't be in so much dis-ease. We wouldn't be so viscerally aware of the heart-brokenness of this modern void. We wouldn't be so anxious and in so much pain.

The Affective Turn (2007) reflects by its title current awareness of the centrality of emotion as culture. Introduced by communist Michael Hardt, it is, however, much more an example of the dominant paradigm than a helpful corrective. The leftist commitment to industrialized Progress is a key part of the onslaught against inner nature. Problem, not solution.

We embody a continuous history of love and suffering, bearing witness to what has moved us. Love, as Kierkegaard stressed, is the ground of all significance in life as we know it. We have loves and cares before we learn to formulate anything in language. As Martin Amis put it (*The Times*, 6/11/06), "Love turns out to be the only part of us that is solid, as the world turns upside down and the screen goes black."

But the failure of the event of love in contemporary societies is as obvious as it is painful, as recounted variously in the novels of Michel Houllebecq, for example. Anarcho-novelist Tom Robbins has emphasized the question, "How do you make love stay?" We may well agree with Ecclesiastes (6:16) that "A faithful friend is the medicine of life," but where are the friends? The marked decline in friendship in the U.S. in recent decades is well-documented (e.g. McPherson, Smith-Lovin and Brashears, *American Sociological Review*, June 2006).

And it is precisely here that radical theory fails, or fails even to show up. Why is it "desire" (or more alienated still, "seduction," with Baudrillard) that is the focus, not love? As bell hooks reported, "When I talked of love with my generation, I found it made everyone scared" (*All About Love*, p. xix). Yet there's such a need for it in this desert of the spirit, our culture of mounting lovelessness.

The opposite of love isn't hate, by the way, but indifference, hallmark of postmodern cynicism and hipness. So far, all has knelt before productionist existence in the draining technoculture. But we need to summon the depth of relationship against the dominant depthlessness, wherein so very much is shifting and disposable. A key feature is love of the unrealized potential of affective actuality, both in ourselves and in others.

There are of course potential dead ends and snares in the way. For example, the sexist assumptions that so often compromise romantic love in a patriarchal, male-defined culture. Or the frequently world-denying aspects of religious love, its tendency to retreat from authentic individuality in favor of a devouring identification that negates rather than accepts otherness.

If emotion is a behavior, love is certainly also an action as well as a basic mental process. It is a key to emotional growth and strength that should lead us into greater communion with the world. Love redeems and gives meaning, emphasizing grace and the gift. The gift as the opposite of a merciless present, as the right life.

Luce Irigaray expresses this ably: "The gift has no goal. No for. And no object. The gift—is given. Before any division into donor and recipient. Before any separate identities of giver and receiver. Even before the gift."

To speak of what may be given can be a reminder of what has been taken away. In the 1950s Laurens van der Post encountered people who could carry all that they owned in one hand. He referred to "that wonderful Bushman laugh which rises sheer from the stomach, a laugh you never hear among civilized people" (*The Lost World of the Kalahari*, p. 244). What a feat, the erasure of such joy at being alive on the earth. Freud's psychoanalytic goal was to change neurotic misery into "normal" unhappiness; Lacan's was that the analyst learn to be as wretched as everyone else.

It is striking (e.g. Ronald Miller, *Facing Human Suffering*, 2004) how extremely rare is the mention of terms like suffering, anguish, sorrow in the literature of psychology. Such things are clearly of no real theoretical concern, merely symptoms to be classified under "less emotional" descriptions. Simone Weil went to the factories to understand suffering. The factories are still there, but the immiseration is arguably more generalized now in a more placeless, synthetic society. Elaine Scarry (*The Body in Pain*, 1985) saw torture as "a miniaturization of the world, of civilization" (p. 38). Post-traumatic stress disorder, originally diagnosed as stemming from combat trauma, is now very widely applied as a diagnosis; another commentary on the state of society which contains more everyday blows, even everyday atrocities. Chellis Glendinning's observation (1994) applies: personal trauma commonly reflects the trauma of civilization itself.

It is a commonplace that mental/emotional illness is the nation's leading health problem. And as Melinda Davis has observed (*The New Culture of Desire*, 2002, p. 66), "Anxiety is the black plague—and the common cold—of our days." A helpful exercise, as I see it, is to put all of politics in terms of health, i.e. what in social life is healthy or unhealthy? Isn't this, after all, the bottom line?

The overall picture is indeed well-known. Anxiety and stress undermine the immune system; as many as 50 percent who have an anxiety condition also suffer from major depression. The surge in anxiety occurs against the backdrop of a rise in depression across all industrialized countries (e.g. Pettit and Joiner, *Chronic Depression*, 2006). Interestingly, R.C. Solomon (*The Passions*, 1993, pp 62–63) sees depression as a "way of wrenching ourselves from the established values of our world." Along these lines the poet W.S. Merwin wrote, "And yet his grief is a great guide through this world. Even, perhaps, the surest of guides. As long as guides are needed." (in *Breathing On Your Own*, 2001, p. 192).

At the beginning of May 2008, several reports surfaced about the high incidence of chronic physical pain: almost 30 percent of the U.S. population is so afflicted. To go along with all the rest of it, from increasing numbers of random, rampage shootings to serious obesity now causing diabetes and heart disease in children; kids on behavior-modification drugs from infancy; mushrooming rates of asthma, autism, and allergies; parents killing their children; millions hooked on Viagra; tens of millions dependent on pharmaceuticals for sleep, etc. etc. The whole picture is increasingly pathological and frightening.

It is little wonder that we find tons of self-help books sold, an intense preoccupation with psychological well-being, and an endless pageant of emotional suffering on television and the Internet. Notice the rather rapid transit of the succession of four best-selling magazines: *Life, People, Us,* and *Self*. The narrowing of perspective in an already individualistic society is obvious.

Christopher Lasch's *Culture of Narcissism* (1979) cited "a sense of inner emptiness, boundless repressed rage" in America (p. 74). Writing in 2008, Patricia Pearson concluded that we now inhabit "a state far colder than narcissism" (*A Brief History of Anxiety*, p. 127).

An always accommodating postmodern sensibility proclaims the end of a core self, in favor of a multiplicity of shifting roles to be played. As social ties wither, is there a core anything left? Dispersed, with the human touch as systematically disappearing as contact with nature, we fear being alone with ourselves. A diffused, distracted mode of life represses memories of suffering and longs for a caress.

What is Progress, a.k.a. Modernity? "It is the high residues of hazardous and potentially lethal chemicals inside your fat cells. It is you sitting inside and turning on the television or computer on a beautiful day. It is you shopping when you are depressed. It is the feeling you get that something is missing." (Kevin Tucker, "What is the Totality?") It is perhaps odd that Descartes, progenitor of modern alienation, identified wonder as the first of his six primitive passions in *The Passions of the Soul* (1649). Where is our capacity for genuine wonder in disenchanted society?

I can tell you that I am moved by the crickets" persevering song, their strong life-voice as summer shuts down in the Pacific Northwest. It is always a special joy to hear the geese migrating high above, their honking sounding to me like dogs softly barking way up there. There is no consciousness separate from an experienced object. What happens when all that is experienced is masses, commodities, images?

The waning of affect, as Jameson put it, as everything else that's alive wanes too. Can we really live meaningless (technified, non-enchanted, indirect) lives? What is vivid and immediate does not exist on a screen. How spiritually impoverished and lacking in vitality is this emotional culture. And what is on the horizon, if not still worse?

We know in what direction health lies. Freud wrote to Wilhelm Fliess, "Happiness is the deferred fulfillment of a prehistoric wish. That is why wealth brings so little happiness" (January 16, 1898). Simplicity contains everything and in simplicity all is present. Albert Camus (*Lyrical and Critical Essays*, p. 172) hit this note well: "I grew up with the sea and poverty for me was sumptuous; then I lost the sea and found all luxuries gray and poverty unbearable."

—2008

CHAPTER FOURTEEN

HAPPINESS

IS HAPPINESS REALLY POSSIBLE in a time of ruin? Can we somehow flourish, have complete lives? Is joy any longer compatible with the life of today?

A deep sense of well-being has become an endangered species. How often does one hear "It is good to be here"? (Matthew 17:4, Luke 9:5, Luke 9:33) or Wordsworth's reference to "the pleasure which there is in life itself"[1]? Much of the prevailing condition and the dilemma it poses is expressed by Adorno's observation: "A wrong life cannot be lived rightly."[2]

In this age happiness, if not obsolete, is a test, an opportunity. "To be happy is to be able to become aware of oneself without being frightened."[3] We seem to be desperate for happiness, as bookshelves, counseling rooms, and talk shows promote endless recipes for contentment. But the well-worn, feel-good bromides from the likes of Oprah, Eckhart Tolle, and the Dalai Lama seem to work about as well as a Happy Meal, happy hour, or Coke's invitation to "Pour Happiness!"

Gone is the shallow optimism of yesteryear, such as it was. The mandatory gospel of happiness is in tatters. As Hélène Cixous put it, we are "born to the difficulty in taking pleasure from absence."[4] We sense only "a little light/in great darkness," to quote Pound, who borrowed from Dante.[5]

How do we explore this? What is *expected* re: happiness? In light of all that stands in its way or erodes it, is happiness mainly a fortuitous accident?[6]

Very often, to be sure, happiness is approached in terms of what it *isn't*. Walter Kerr's *The Decline of Pleasure* opens with this: "I am going to start out by assuming that you are approximately as unhappy as I am."[7] "We are a society of notoriously unhappy people," according to Erich Fromm.[8]

But we are not supposed to go around admitting this bottom-line truth about ourselves and society. Various contemporary theorists, by the way, have steadily chipped away at the very notion of the self, redefining it as nothing more than an intersection of shifting discourses. When the self is all but erased, "happiness" can no longer even be a valid topic.

But our yearning for well-being is not so easily written off. Elisabeth Roudinesco provides a plausible judgment: "The more individuals are promised happiness and the ideal of security, the more their unhappiness persists, the steeper the risk profile grows, and the more the victims of unkept promises revolt against those who have betrayed them."[9]

In this precarious world happiness and fear are oddly joined. People are afraid. "They are afraid," Adorno claimed, that "they would lose everything, because the only happiness they know even in thought, is to be able to hold on to something."[10] This condition contrasts qualitatively with what is known of so many non-domesticated people: their lack of fear, their trust in the world they inhabit.

The Himalayan nation of Bhutan attracted much notice in the middle of the first decade of this century for its Gross National Happiness concept: the decision to measure the quality of its society not by industrial output (Gross National Product), but in terms of its citizens" happiness. Apparently, however, Bhutan quickly lost the somewhat isolated character of its culture, which had spurred the GNH idea in the first place. Inundated by pop culture, celebrity consciousness, consumer fads, and the rest of a globalized modernity, the emphasis on happiness as a national value has faded.

Mass society restricts "happiness" to the spheres of consumption and distraction to a great degree. Yet happiness remains an experience of fullness, rather than seriously misguided efforts to fill emptiness. Many studies show that happiness levels fall with increasing accumulation of wealth.[11] In removing ourselves from nature, we become insensible to its wholeness and approach it as another passive object to be consumed.

Is there a truth of happiness, on whose basis happiness can be judged? Happiness is as encompassing as it is immediate. It has many facets and manifestations. It is elemental, potent; like health, happiness is contagious and breeds hope in others. Happiness has to do with one's whole reaction to life, and for that reason alone, it is personal as well as mysterious. The philosopher Wittgenstein had a harsh and pessimistic temperament and experienced his share of intense anguish. His seems the portrait of an

FUTURE PRIMITIVE REVISITED

unhappy man, and yet his biographer Norman Malcolm reports that his last words were, "Tell them I've had a wonderful life."[12] John Keats" brief life was overshadowed by illness, but he often claimed that things are gorgeous *because* they die. The sources of happiness lie in various spheres of our lives, but characteristically these are not so separate. Human life has never been lived in isolation, so we seek experiences that are more than just meaningful for ourselves alone. Vivasvan Soni's insight says a lot: "No part of life can be bracketed as irrelevant to happiness. All of life counts infinitely. There is no greater tragedy than unhappiness, and no greater responsibility for us than happiness."[13]

In my experience, the cornerstone of happiness is love. Here is the dimension where we find the greatest fulfillment. Frantz Fanon, better known for his work on other subjects, subscribed to a standard of "authentic love—wishing for others what one postulates for oneself."[14] There are other satisfactions, but do they match the satisfying and enriching quality of love relations? If a child has love and protection, there is the basis for happiness throughout life. If neither is provided, his or her prospects are very limited. If only one of them is to be given, I think that love outranks even protection or security in terms of the odds for happiness.

Some have dissented as to the centrality of love. Nietzsche and Sartre seem to have seen love as confining, closing off prerogatives. That bloodless master of cheap irony, E.M. Cioran, provides this little meditation: "I think of that emperor dear to my heart, Tiberius, of his acrimony and his ferocity.... I love him because his *neighbor* seemed to him inconceivable. I love him because he loved no one."[15]

What would a history of happiness look like? Once happiness was a central focus of thought in the West. Aristotle's *Nicomachean Ethics*, for example, is a major discourse on the subject. Epicurus spent his life facing the question of how to attain happiness, arousing the ire of our modern friend Cioran. The latter referred to Epicurus" writings as a "compost heap," citing him as indicative of the false path that occurs "when the problem of happiness supplants that of knowledge."[16]

Much later, the Cartesian account of emotions as so many sensations enters the picture, and Voltaire (1694-1778) was the last happy writer, according to Roland Barthes. The eigthteenth century saw a deluge of writing about happiness, mainly focused on private well-being. A thorough de-politicizing of what was meant by happiness was taking place, on the eve of mass society. Kant typified this trend, by bonding—even equating—duty-oriented morality with happiness.

The new century exhibited the Romantic emphasis on joy rather than happiness (Blake, Wordsworth, et al.), with joy's strong connotation of that which is fleeting. Transient indeed was the hymn to a hopeful future expressed in Beethoven's Ninth Symphony, in particular its final movement based on Schiller's "Ode to Joy." The work has justly been termed the last serious music expressing happiness/joy. As industrial life began to spread, it can be no coincidence that Hegel saw human history as the record of irredeemable misfortune.

Modern wage labor and political social contract theorizing (Rousseau, the U.S. Constitution, etc.) legitimated the pursuit of *private* happiness. In the public sphere, the question of general happiness was downplayed. Reward became the name of the game. For Hegel, property and personality were almost synonymous; Marx associated happiness with the satisfaction of interests alone.

Sentimentalism was an important facet of the nineteenth century cultural ethos: the underlying emotional tableau of lost community. A fragmented, anonymous society had all but abandoned the goal of widespread happiness. The early Victorian utilitarianism of John Stuart Mill, less crude than that of its founder Bentham at least, failed to recognize the impoverishment of the age. Mill was the last philosopher of social happiness.

Jean-François Lyotard placed "the withdrawal of the real" at the center of the experience of modernity.[17] We are losing the referents, the real things, felt contact with what is non-simulated. How could happiness not decline in the bargain? It has declined; the technoculture's ascent is the descent of happiness.[18] Today's dreary, isolating technological frenzy keeps sinking it further, with various pathological effects. But our quest remains what it was for Spinoza: the search for happiness, with the reality of our bodies in a real, bodily world.

In the 1890s Anton Chekhov visited Sakhalin Island, with its Gilyak hunter-gatherers. He observed that they had not yet come to grips with roads. "Often," he noted, "you will see them...making their way in single file through the marshes beside the road."[19] They were always somewhere, and were uninterested in being nowhere, on industrialism's roadway. They had not yet lost the singularity of the present, which technology exactly takes away. With our dwindling attention spans, foreshortening shallowness of thought, and thirst for diversions, how much are we actually in the world? The disembodied self becomes increasingly disengaged from reality, including emotional reality.

Anxiety has replaced happiness as the hallmark sensation, now that community is absent.[20] We no longer trust our instincts. Maintaining a vast distance from the rhythms of nature and primary experiences of the senses in their intimate concreteness, the leading "thinkers" so often consecrate or uphold this unhappy, disembodied state. Alain Badiou, for example, concurs with Kant that truth and overall health are "independent of animality and the whole world of sense."[21]

But what is abstract about happiness? Its states are complete at each moment—each embodied moment. "Each happiness comes for the first time," as Levinas realized.[22] Czeslaw Milosz described his happy childhood: "I lived without yesterday or tomorrow, in the eternal present. That is, precisely, the definition of happiness."[23] Postmodern irony and detachment, with their bedrock of embracing the techno-sphere, constitute one more means of wresting us from the present moment.

A most basic human longing is to belong, to experience union with something other than oneself. Bruno Bettelheim described a feeling, engendered in his case by great art, "of being in tune with the universe... [of] all needs satisfied. I felt as though I were in touch—in communication with man's past and connected with his future."[24] He associated this with Freud's "oceanic feeling," the sensation of "an indissoluble bond, of being one with the external world as a whole."[25]

I think it plausible to see this as vestigial—as a visceral, surviving link to a previous condition. There is a great deal of anthropological/ethnological literature describing indigenous peoples who live in oneness with the natural world and one another. Survival itself necessitated a borderlessness between inner and outer worlds. Our ultimate survival requires that we recover that oneness. At times we still feel a return to that unified state. Fairly often in psychological counseling, there is a search for a time in childhood when one was healthy and happy. Arguably, to apply the "ontogeny recapitulates phylogeny" thesis, each of us re-enacts the larger history of humanness. T.S. Eliot's designation of our return is "through the unknown remembered gate."[26]

Freud counterposed civilization and happiness because civilization [domestication, more precisely] is "based on compulsory labor and instinctual renunciation."[27] "Having to fight against the instincts is the formula for decadence; so long as life is ascending, happiness and instinct are one thing," observed Nietzsche.[28]

The internalization and universalization of this renunciation of freedom is what Freud called sublimation. As Norman O. Brown saw it, sublimation "presupposes and perpetuates the loss of life and cannot be the mode in which life itself is lived."[29] The very progress of civilization requires an even greater measure of renunciation, an even greater setting ourselves apart from our environment. And yet the "oceanic feeling" can still be powerfully felt, recalling that earlier state of being. How much fresher, more vivid and more valued life can feel after a serious illness; this many be the case upon our recovery from the sickness we call civilization.

But here we are now, so very far from any original wholeness or fullness. And "the horror," in Adorno's judgment, "is that for the first time we live in a world in which we can no longer imagine a better one."[30] At present the only happy context is the imagined one, or at least, the happiness achieved in expressing the truth about unhappiness. In Milosz" heartfelt words: "It would seem that all human beings should fall into each other's arms, crying out that they cannot live...."[31]

The aim of life is to live it strongly, to be fully awake. This aim collides with a new malaise of civilization, an End Times sense of everything, a "post"-you-name-it cultural landscape. A sense of helplessness promoted in no small part by the postmodern doctrine of ambiguity and ambivalence.

Happiness entails refusal of Foucault's "docile bodies" condition, insistence on being vivid rather than domesticated, determination to live as "barbarians" resisting the unfreedom and numbness of civilization. An instinct tells us that there is something different, however distant it may seem; we know we were born for something better. The reality of deep unhappiness is the reminder of that instinct, which lives and struggles to be heard. The story of happiness did not have to unfold as it did.

In our own lives we are so lucky to have a sense of being blessed, to have some gladness, a sense of worth. To have a certain astonishment at being here at all. For ourselves, meaning and happiness are always interwoven. Happiness is grounded in meaningfulness; a life of meaning is the meaning of life. "To happiness, the same applies as to truth: one does not have it, but is in it," in Adorno's pithy formulation.[32]

He also said, "Philosophy exists in order to redeem what you see in the look of an animal."[33] "To meet myself face to face," in Thoreau's words.[34] To realize ourselves in our distinctly human capacities within what is possible (i.e. not to blame ourselves for the limits imposed on us). And to find the strength to speak the unsaid. Unhappiness is not the result of understanding the real depth of our predicament; in fact, this understanding can be liberating, strengthening. It may lead to something that could hardly be more momentous: the quest for directness and immediacy in the real world. The project of confronting the very nature of our domesticated, civilized, technology-ridden unhappiness.

—2011

ENDNOTES

1   Quoted in John Cowper Powys, *The Art of Happiness* (New York: Simon and Schuster, 1935), p. 49.

2   Theodor Adorno, *Minima Moralia* (London: MLB, 1974), #18, p. 39.

3   Walter Benjamin, *One-Way Street and Other Writings* (London: NLB, 1979), p. 71.

4   Hélène Cixous, *First Days of the Year* (Minneapolis: University of Minnesota Press, 1998), p. 142.

5   Ezra Pound, *The Cantos of Ezra Pound* (New York: New Directions, 1972), #CXVI, p. 795.

6   Its etymology is of interest in this regard. From *hap* (Greek): chance, fortune, as in happen. Our English word luck comes, in fact, from the German for happiness, *Glück*.

7   Walter Kerr, *The Decline of Pleasure* (New York: Touchstone, 1962), p. 1.

8   Erich Fromm, *To Have or to Be?* (New York: Harper & Row, 1976), p. 5.

9   Elisabeth Roudinesco, *Philosophy in Turbulent Times: Canquilhem, Sartre, Foucault, Deleuze, Derrida* (New York: Columbia University Press, 2008), p. xii.

10   Theodor Adorno, *Negative Dialectics* (New York: The Seabury Press, 1973), p. 33.

11   Jeremy Rifkin, *The Empathic Civilization* (New York: Penguin, 2009), p. 498.

12   Norman Malcolm, *Ludwig Wittgenstein: A Memoir* (Oxford: Oxford University Press, 1958), p. 106.

13   Vivasvan Soni, *Mourning Happiness: Narrative and the Politics of Modernity* (Ithaca: Cornell University Press, 2010), p. 494.

14   Frantz Fanon, *Black Skin, White Masks*, translated by Charles Lam Markmann (New York: Grove Press, 1967), p. 41.

15   E.M. Cioran, *The Temptation to Exist* (New York: Quadrangle, 1968), p. 200.

16   *Ibid.*, pp 168–169.

17   Jean-François Lyotard, *The Postmodern Condition: a Report on Knowledge* (Minneapolis: University of Minnesota Press, 1984), p. 79.

18   Albert Borgmann, *Technology and the Character of Contemporary Life* (Chicago: University of Chicago Press, 1984), pp 124, 130.

19   Quoted and discussed in Timothy Taylor, *The Artificial Age* (New York: Palgrave MacMillan, 2010), p. 192.

20   Peter LaFrenière, *Adaptive Origins: Evolution and Human Development* (New York: Psychology Press, 2010), pp 288, 296–297. Also Patricia Pearson, *A Brief History of Anxiety...Yours and Mine* (New York: Bloomsbury, 2008).

21   Quoted in Peter Hallward, translator's introduction to Alain Badiou, *Ethics: an essay on the understanding of evil* (New York: Verso, 2001), p. xxi.

22   Emmanuel Levinas, *Totality and Infinity* (Pittsburgh: Duquesne University Press, 1998), p. 114.

23   Czeslaw Milosz, *Proud to be a Mammal: Essays on War, Faith and Memory* (New York: Penguin Classics, 2010), p. 80.

24   Bruno Bettelheim, *Freud's Vienna and Other Essays* (New York: Alfred A. Knopf, 1990), p. 115.

25   Sigmund Freud, *Civilization and its Discontents*, translated by James Strachey (New York: W.W. Norton, 1962), p. 12.

26   T.S. Eliot, "Little Gidding," in *Collected Poems 1909–1962* (New York: Harcourt, Brace & World, Inc., 1963), p. 208.

27   Sigmund Freud, *The Future of an Illusion*, translated by James Strachey (New York: W.W. Norton, 1961), p. 12.

28   Friedrich Nietzsche, *Unmodern Observations*, William Arrowsmith, ed. (New Haven: Yale University Press, 1990), p. xv.

29   Norman O. Brown, *Life Against Death: The Psychoanalytic Meaning of History* (New York: Vintage Books, 1959), p. 171.

30   Theodor Adorno and Max Horkheimer, "Dialogue," *NLR* September/October 2010, p. 61.

31   Czeslaw Milosz, *op.cit.*, p. 296.

32   Theodor Adorno, *Minima Moralia*, *op.cit.*, #72, p. 112.

33   Adorno and Horkheimer, "Dialogue," *op.cit.*, p. 51.

34   Henry David Thoreau, *Journal* (Toronto: Dover Publications, 1962), p. 51.

feralhouse.com